Practical social work

Published in conjunction with
the British Association of Social Workers
Series Editor: Jo Campling

BASW

Social work is at an important stage in its development. The profession is facing fresh challenges to work flexibly in fast-changing social and organisational environments. New requirements for training are also demanding a more critical and reflective, as well as more highly skilled, approach to practice.

The British Association of Social Workers has always been conscious of its role in setting guidelines for practice and in seeking to raise professional standards. The concept of the *Practical Social Work* series was conceived to fulfil a genuine professional need for a carefully planned, coherent series of texts that would stimulate and inform debate, thereby contributing to the development of practitioners' skills and professionalism.

Newly relaunched, the series continues to address the needs of all those who are looking to deepen and refresh their understanding and skills. It is designed for students and busy professionals alike. Each book marries practice issues and challenges with the latest theory and research in a compact and applied format. The authors represent a wide variety of experience both as educators and practitioners. Taken together, the books set a standard in their clarity, relevance and rigour.

A list of new and best-selling titles in this series follows overleaf. A comprehensive list of titles available in the series, and further details about individual books, can be found online at :
www.palgrave.com/socialworkpolicy/basw

Series standing order **ISBN 0–333–80313–2**

You can receive future titles in this series as they are published by placing a standing order. Please contact your bookseller or, in the case of difficulty, contact us at the address below with your name and address, the title of the series and the ISBN quoted above.

Customer Services Department, Macmillan Distribution Ltd, Houndmills, Basingstoke, Hampshire RG21 6XS, England

Practical social work series

New and best-selling titles

Robert Adams *Social Work and Empowerment* *(3rd edition)*

Sarah Banks *Ethics and Values in Social Work (3rd edition)* **new!**

James G. Barber *Social Work with Addictions (2nd edition)*

Suzy Braye and Michael Preston-Shoot *Practising Social Work Law (2nd edition)*

Veronica Coulshed and Joan Orme *Social Work Practice (4th edition)* **new!**

Veronica Coulshed and Audrey Mullender with David N. Jones and Neil Thompson
Management in Social Work (3rd edition) **new!**

Lena Dominelli *Anti-Racist Social Work (2nd edition)*

Celia Doyle *Working with Abused Children (3rd edition)* **new!**

Tony Jeffs and Mark Smith (editors) *Youth Work*

Joyce Lishman *Communication in Social Work*

Paula Nicolson and Rowan Bayne and Jenny Owen *Applied Psychology for Social
Workers (3rd edition)* **new!**

Judith Phillips, Mo Ray and Mary Marshall *Social Work with Older People
(4th edition)* **new!**

Michael Oliver and Bob Sapey *Social Work with Disabled People (3rd edition)* **new!**

Michael Preston-Shoot *Effective Groupwork*

Steven Shardlow and Mark Doel *Practice Learning and Teaching*

Neil Thompson *Anti-Discriminatory Practice (4th edition)* **new!**

Derek Tilbury *Working with Mental Illness (2nd edition)*

Alan Twelvetrees *Community Work (3rd edition)*

neil thompson

anti-discriminatory practice

fourth edition

macmillan

First edition 1993
Reprinted five times
Second edition 1997
Reprinted four times
Third edition 2001
Reprinted five times
Fourth edition 2006

Published by
PALGRAVE MACMILLAN
Houndmills, Basingstoke, Hampshire RG21 6XS and
175 Fifth Avenue, New York, N.Y. 10010
Companies and representatives throughout the world

PALGRAVE MACMILLAN is the global academic imprint of the
Palgrave Macmillan division of St. Martin's Press, LLC and of
Palgrave Macmillan Ltd. Macmillan® is a registered trademark in
the United States, United Kingdom and other countries. Palgrave is a
registered trademark in the European Union and other countries.

ISBN-13: 978–1–4039–2160–4
ISBN-10: 1–4039–2160–1

This book is printed on paper suitable for recycling and
made from fully managed and sustained forest sources.

A catalogue record for this book is available from the
British Library.

A catalog record for this book is available from the
Library of Congress.

10	9	8	7	6	5	4	3	2	
15	14	13	12	11	10	09	08	07	06

Printed in China

for Susan and Anna

Contents

Preface to the fourth edition   xi
Acknowledgements   xv

1 Introduction   1
The historical background   3
What is discrimination?   12
Good practice is anti-discriminatory practice   14
Multiple oppressions   15
Structure and outline   17
Points to ponder   18
Guide to further learning   19

2 The theory base   21
Social divisions and social structure   21
PCS analysis   26
Structured inequalities and institutional
     oppression   30
Ideology: the power of ideas   33
The role of language   37
Commonalities and differences   42
Points to ponder   46
Guide to further learning   46

3 Gender and sexism   48
What is sexism?   49
The implications for social work   52
The feminist response   61
Sexism and men   66
Towards anti-sexist practice   68
Points to ponder   70
Guide to further learning   70

4 Ethnicity and racism   72
What is racism?   73
The implications for social work   78
The anti-racist response   86
Race, class and gender   90
Towards anti-racist practice   92
Points to ponder   96
Guide to further learning   96

5 Ageism and alienation   98
What is ageism?   99
The implications for social work   102
The anti-ageist response   110
Multiple oppressions   113
Towards anti-ageist practice   116
Points to ponder   120
Guide to further learning   120

6 Disability and social handicap   122
What is disablism?   122
The implications for social work   126
The anti-disablist response: the Disabled
    People's Movement   135
Multiple oppressions   138
Towards anti-disablist practice   142
Points to ponder   146
Guide to further learning   147

7 Diversity and oppression   148
Aspects of oppression   149
Sexual identity   152
Religion   156
Language, nation and region   159
Mental health problems   163
Mental impairment   167
Diversity and multiple oppressions   170
Points to ponder   171
Guide to further learning   172

8 Conclusion   173
The main themes   174
The way forward   176

Bibliography   182
Index   204

Preface to the fourth edition

When a book reaches its fourth edition, it is a sure sign that it has achieved a significant measure of success. One reason for this success is no doubt the continued widespread commitment to ensuring that social work practice contributes more to challenging discrimination and oppression than to perpetuating them. This new edition responds to that commitment by providing a basic introduction to this very complex field of theory and practice. It builds on the success of the previous editions by retaining their strengths but also incorporating discussions of developments in the theory base and the policy and practice context, extending and updating the 'Guide to further learning' sections, extending and improving some sections of the text and adding 'Points to ponder' sections at the end of each of the main chapters.

It is now almost thirteen years since the first edition of this book was published. Times have changed a great deal during that period and we have made some significant advances in tackling discrimination and oppression. However, the challenges we face remain enormous and represent a long-term project. At the time of writing the first edition I was a team manager in a social services department and in daily contact with many of the issues covered in this book. My current role as a trainer and consultant brings me into almost daily contact with practitioners, managers, students and educators who are wrestling with the challenges of ensuring that social work interventions are positive and empowering rather than disempowering and demeaning. The feedback I have received has been very gratifying in confirming that the earlier editions have succeeded in their aim of presenting a clear and accessible introduction to tackling discrimination and oppression. I now hope that this latest incarnation of the book will also achieve my aim of making a positive contribution to understanding the key issues the book addresses.

Important notes

1. It has become the practice in recent years for some commentators to distinguish between anti-discriminatory and anti-oppressive practice. For such commentators, the former is reserved for a narrow, legalistic perspective that does not take on board wider sociopolitical concerns. It is therefore important to clarify, right from the start, that this is not a distinction I shall be drawing here. As the arguments presented in this book should make very clear, I see anti-discriminatory practice as a broad undertaking that needs to incorporate sociological, political and economic concerns above and beyond narrow legal requirements. In my view, discrimination is the process (or set of processes) that leads to oppression. To challenge oppression, it is therefore necessary to challenge discrimination. Anti-discriminatory and anti-oppressive practice are therefore presented here as more or less synonymous on the grounds that a legalistic perspective is too narrow to challenge discrimination and the ensuing oppression, and does not therefore merit the title of 'anti-discriminatory'. I shall revisit this point in Chapter 1.

2. The term 'client' is one that I use throughout this book and indeed in many of my writings. It is important to recognise that this is a contested term. Many people have abandoned it in favour of 'service user'. However, many people object to this latter term, especially when it is shortened to 'user'. In my view, client is a term of respect and is consistent with the notion of professionalism (see Thompson, 2005, for a fuller discussion of this).

3. This book was written specifically with a social work readership in mind. However, I have become aware that it is also widely used by others within the human services or helping professions (for example, nurses, advice workers and youth and community workers). If you are in this latter category, then I hope that the constant references to social work are not too discouraging for you. You may find it helpful, every time you encounter the term 'social work' to stop and think about how the point being made applies to your own professional discipline. In many cases it may be very similar, but in others it may be very different. Making these comparisons between social work and your own discipline can be an important part of your learning.

4. In the Preface to the third edition of this book, I made the following comment:

> Throughout the process of writing this book there has been no doubt in my mind that its role is as an *introductory* text, a gateway to the broader and more advanced literature. It is certainly not intended as an 'all you need to know on the subject' type of book. I have therefore found it quite sad, especially as an external examiner at various universities, to note so many students using the book as if it were the only one available on the subject! I am, of course, pleased that the book has become established as a key text, but this does not alter the fact that it is a key *introductory* text and should therefore not be used as a substitute for reading more widely or for engaging with the more advanced texts available. Partly in response to this problem I have added a 'Further reading' section at the end of each chapter. But, again it should be recognised that these are just suggestions and not a definitive or finite reading list.
>
> If you find this book helpful, then that's great, but please use any benefits you have gained from it as a launch pad for further learning, and not as a source of complacency that stands in the way of further development.

I now wish to reinforce that message as I continue to see the potential problem of the book's strengths becoming a weakness by discouraging further reading and learning. I hope that tutors, trainers and practice teachers will play their part by emphasising this point.

5. Each of the main chapters ends with a 'Guide to further learning' section. Please note that the inclusion of particular publications or websites in these sections means that I feel they are worth consulting. However, this does not mean that I necessarily agree with and endorse everything the authors concerned put forward in their writings or on their websites.

6. In between the publication of the first and second editions of this book I was approached by a number of people who urged me to write a follow-up text, a more advanced book which examined in more depth and detail some of the key issues outlined here. This led to the publication in 1998 of *Promoting Equality: Challenging Discrimination and Oppression in the Human Services*. A second

edition was published by Palgrave Macmillan in 2003. References below to *Promoting Equality* relate to this book. It is perhaps helpful to see *Anti-Discriminatory Practice* as a first-level, introductory text, while *Promoting Equality* is a more advanced, second-level text.

NEIL THOMPSON

Acknowledgements

In preparing this text I have once again had the support and assistance of a good many people. My thanks go yet again to those who provided helpful comments in the development of the first edition – their contributions continue to be of value.

It has become something of a habit for me to express my gratitude to Susan Thompson for her unwavering support – moral, practical and intellectual. However, it is not just a habit – it is a heartfelt vote of thanks. Her commitment to helping me see this project through, in all four of its incarnations, has been of immense value. I have also continued to benefit greatly from the advice and guidance of Jo Campling in her role as series editor and beyond this as a trusted adviser and friend.

Other friends who continue to help in the development of my thinking and whose influence can be seen here are my good friend, Denise Bevan, John Bates of North East Wales Institute, Bernard Moss of Staffordshire University and Colin Richardson, Fellow of Keele University.

Catherine Gray, Beverley Tarquini and Sheree Keep at the publishers have continued to be very helpful whenever called upon, and can always be relied upon to respond in a friendly and supportive way. I continue to be very grateful to them for that.

A big vote of thanks goes to Judy Marshall for her excellent copy-editing work.

I would also like to say thank you to the very many participants on courses I have run in recent years who have shared their experiences and views with me and who have reaffirmed my commitment to developing forms of education and training geared towards tackling discrimination and oppression which are not in themselves oppressive.

This edition follows the pattern of the first three in that it is dedicated to Susan and Anna, the two most important people in my life.

NEIL THOMPSON

1 | Introduction

During the late 1980s social work education became increasingly aware of the impact of oppression and discrimination on clients and communities. There was a growing awareness and recognition of the relative neglect of such issues in traditional approaches to social work. For example, in 1989, the former governing body for social work education, the Central Council for Education and Training in Social Work (CCETSW), laid down its regulations and requirements for the then newly formulated Diploma in Social Work (DipSW) and included these references to anti-discriminatory practice:

> Social workers need to be able to work in a society which is multi-racial and multi-cultural. CCETSW will therefore seek to ensure that students are prepared not only for ethnically sensitive practice but also to challenge institutional and other forms of racism . . . CCETSW will also seek to ensure that students are prepared to combat other forms of discrimination based on age, gender, sexual orientation, class, disability, culture or creed.
> (CCETSW, 1989, p. 10)

This emphasis on combating discrimination is part of the process of establishing these issues as fundamental building blocks of qualifying training and subsequent practice. They were therefore seen as an essential part of the curriculum and the evaluation process and continue to be regarded as such, as is shown by their inclusion in the curriculum for the degree in social work which has replaced the diploma as the primary qualification.

This major development in social work education and training has also been reflected more broadly, to a certain extent at least, in social work policy, theory and practice (although it would be naïve not to acknowledge that much progress remains to be made in these respects). Anti-discriminatory practice has therefore been featuring as a regular and high priority item on the social work agenda for some time now, although there sadly continues to be a great deal of misunderstanding and oversimplification of the issues (see Thompson, 2003a, Chapter 5, for a discussion of this).

But it is not only students as new entrants to the profession who need a grounding in the theory and practice of anti-discriminatory social work. There remain very many practitioners, managers and trainers schooled in more traditional approaches to social welfare who want or need a better understanding of the theory base and practice implications of a social work based on the principles of anti-discrimination. For example, it is not uncommon for practice teachers to experience a degree of anxiety about anti-discriminatory issues because of this 'generation gap'. They are working with students who are likely to have had a far greater amount of teaching on these issues and may therefore, at times, feel relatively ill-equipped to deal with these matters (Thompson *et al.*, 1994a).

The primary aim of this book is to provide just such a grounding – for qualified staff, for those seeking qualification, for practice teachers, trainers and managers and for others with a general interest in modern social work, equality and diversity or related issues. The text seeks to clarify and to answer, in part at least, a number of important questions:

● What are the factors underlying discrimination and oppression, especially as they relate to social work theory and practice?
● What are the common concepts and issues across the various forms of discrimination – sexism, racism, ageism and so on? What are the key differences?
● Why is the development of anti-discriminatory practice so important?
● What are the necessary steps towards constructing a social work practice based on principles of anti-discrimination and the promotion of equality?

Before beginning to tackle these questions, it would be helpful to outline the recent history of anti-discriminatory practice in order to be able to locate the analysis which follows within its historical context. I shall therefore sketch out some of the broad issues which have contributed to the current emphasis on anti-discriminatory practice in its various forms: anti-racism, anti-sexism and so on.

The historical background

The 1960s was a significant decade in a number of ways. Feminist thought took major steps forward (for example, Friedan, 1963) and also gained major recognition in popular consciousness as the 'Women's Liberation Movement'. Issues of equal rights and equality of opportunity for women became much more firmly established on the political agenda. At this stage, however, evidence of the impact of this on social work is rather hard to find.

Also during the 1960s issues of racial discrimination and the oppression of ethnic minorities achieved a higher political, media and public profile. This was particularly the case in the United States of America, especially in relation to such issues as segregated transport and schooling (Polenberg, 1980). A similar process of consciousness raising also occurred in the UK, although again there is little evidence of the impact of this on social work.

Indeed, it was a decade characterised by the notion of 'consciousness raising' in terms of both increased political radicalism and the emerging psychedelic drug culture. The radicalism was particularly apparent in the latter part of the sixties, as evidenced by student protest, occupations and so on. It was a time of idealism and anti-establishment challenge of the status quo. This was accompanied by an increased emphasis on humanitarian values and liberation. It was a time in which progressive movements flourished and the breaking down of traditional barriers was being pursued on a large scale.

The liberated, flower-power sixties also saw the growth in popularity of writers such as R. D. Laing (1965, 1967), who challenged orthodox notions of psychiatry and propounded a radical alternative – an alternative vision which did seep in to social work thinking (Thompson, 1991a). This further contributed to a spirit of liberation and a cry for the removal of oppression (Cooper, 1968).

Whilst this process was underway in wider society, social work continued to be dominated by the influence of psychodynamics, although the beginnings of a sociological approach were starting to become evident (Leonard, 1966). Rojek *et al.* (1988) wrote of:

> the deep influence of psychoanalytical thought with a focus on the relationship to the external world and the ego reactions to the drives of the id and the demands of the superego. Psychoanalytic ideas were seen as the only effective

method of altering personality structure; and insight at that time was seen as primary goal and major strategy of intervention.

(p. 21)

The grip of psychodynamic influence was indeed strong, but was already beginning to yield, to a certain extent at least, to the wider focus of sociology, with its emphasis on social processes and institutions (Heraud, 1970). The 'sociological imagination' (Mills, 1970) was beginning to be recognised as a valuable approach to social work education and practice.

---

practice focus 1.1

Lynne was a psychology graduate who had recently begun her social work training on a postgraduate course. From the sociology component of the course, she began to appreciate how narrow her perspective had previously been. She began to realise that, although her psychological perspective was very important and valuable, she also needed to understand the wider sociological issues that were so relevant to the life experiences of social work clients, relationships between social workers and clients and so on. She had begun to develop the 'sociological imagination'.

This 'imagination' was more than a widening of the focus to include social, as well as psychological, factors. It embraced a new emphasis, a more critical approach geared towards 'debunking' taken-for-granted assumptions (Berger, 1966) and questioning dominant views and values. Sullivan (1987) exemplifies this in relation to poverty:

The worker . . . may have exploited a sociological imagination to question commonsense understandings of poverty and to perceive poverty's objective and subjective meanings. The result may be to lead him/her to a conceptualization of poor people as victims of a social system predicated on inequality.

(p. 161)

The influence of sociological thinking had the effect of producing a more critical and socially and politically aware social work with a stronger emphasis on social structure, deprivation and inequality. The seeds of a radical social work were being sown.

The second half of the 1960s also saw the introduction of anti-discrimination legislation in Britain – for example, the Race Relations Acts of 1965 and 1968. These acts constituted a recognition, partially at least, of the discrimination experienced by black and ethnic minority people in, for example, employment and housing. They were an attempt to outlaw unfair treatment of people on racial/ethnic grounds, although, as many critics have pointed out, they amounted to a very limited and largely ineffectual attempt.

In 1989 Solomos expressed condemnation of the functionalist emphasis in the race relations literature, with its implied goal of integration and assimilation. In this context, anti-discrimination laws can be seen as a 'mixed blessing' – on the one hand, a move in the right direction towards anti-racism but, on the other hand, a potentially oppressive policy premised on the denial or abandonment of cultural identity (assimilation). Solomos links this mixed blessing to the two different interest groups reflected in the legislation: 'Legislation is a compromise between demands of those who are worried about immigration and those worried about racial discrimination' (1989, p. 81).

The 1970s saw the introduction of further anti-discriminatory legislation – another Race Relations Act (1976) plus, in relation to gender discrimination, the Equal Pay Act 1970 and the Sex Discrimination Act 1975.

Again, as with the 1960s legislation, there has been much criticism of sex discrimination laws for failing to address the fundamental bases of discrimination. They were also criticised for being unduly complex and for having too many exceptions (Pannick, 1985).

These legislative changes were part of a liberal programme of reform. They were liberal in the sense that they sought to humanise or ameliorate the existing social system without calling for a radical change in the structures and social arrangements in which racism and sexism could be seen to operate. There was therefore a significant gap, both politically and conceptually, between the class focus of the radicals and the race and gender focus of the liberal reformers. Both sets of people were striving for a less oppressive society but were approaching the issues from different angles and with different long-term aims.

It was not surprising, therefore, that the school of radical social work, which began in the late 1960s but emerged in a more influential form in the mid- to late seventies, focused primarily on a class-based analysis (the critique of capitalism) and only tangentially covered issues of race and gender. For example, two of the key radical texts clearly display this pattern: Bailey and Brake (1975) is a collection of eight essays but none relates primarily to race or gender (although one, Milligan, discusses what would today be referred to as 'heterosexism' – see Chapter 7 below); Brake and Bailey (1980) do, however, reflect some movement forward and, within their ten essays, include one on feminism (Wilson) and one on racism (Husband).

Peter Leonard, in his foreword to Dominelli and McLeod (1989) acknowledges the failure of earlier radical social work, premised on classical marxism, to take account of issues of gender and patriarchy. Issues of race/ethnicity and racism were similarly paid little or no attention. The critique of capitalism, a central plank of radical social work, necessarily hinged on notions of class conflict and exploitation. This was not to deny the oppression associated with race and gender; the problem was the lack of scope within the analysis to incorporate these concerns.

The emergence of radical social work drew attention to the structural and political context of social work and the key part played by concepts such as ideology, oppression and discrimination:

> In assessing their clients and delivering their services, social workers are undertaking a profoundly ideological task on behalf of the established structures: at the same time they are often trying to help clients to resist the most oppressive and discriminatory features of the welfare system.
> (Corrigan and Leonard, 1978, p. viii)

Radical social work was therefore premised on the following arguments (amongst others):

● Social workers need to recognise the sociopolitical context of the life experience of their clients and of their agency role and function;

● The dangers of social work practice contributing to and reinforcing oppression and discrimination must be recognised and
guarded against; and
● Opportunities for emancipation of clients from oppressive and
damaging circumstances should be seized upon as part of a
project which alerts clients to the social and political basis of
their problems and difficulties.

As we shall see below, these are also essential building blocks of
anti-discriminatory practice.

---

practice focus 1.2

Tim had many years' experience as an unqualified worker before
commencing his professional training. That experience, though, was
entirely in a fieldwork team where he dealt exclusively with individuals
and families on a casework basis. On the first placement of his
course, however, he worked on a community development project
where, for the first time, he was able to see the shared problems, the
commonalities of poverty, deprivation, racism and so on. With the
help of his practice teacher he was able to understand the structural
dimension of social problems and to appreciate the need to go
beyond individual or family problems.

Although radical social work achieved a higher profile in the
mid- to late 1970s, there were elements of such an approach apparent before this time. Hearn (1982) sees its roots as extending back
to the previous decade, to the 'protest and alternativism of the
sixties' (p. 22). Simpkin (1989) is more specific in linking the movement to the political upheavals of 1968:

> The events of 1968 released an energy which manifested
> itself in a variety of social and cultural forms, one of which
> was a political activism which became more and more inde-
> pendent of the traditional parties. This consciousness was
> fed by a generalised sense of injustice which sought both
> inspiration and justification from the now burgeoning acade-
> mic industry of social analysis. A growing acquaintance with
> the hypocrisy, injustice and repression which characterised

the machinery of the state created a wider and more recep-
tive audience for class-based doctrines of revolt.
(Carter *et al.*, 1989, p. 160)

The radical social work of the 1970s was therefore a development of the emancipatory and progressive ethos of the 1960s but
linked specifically to class analysis and class struggle.

The increasing influence of sociology on the social work education curriculum had also no doubt made inroads into the traditional, psychologically based infrastructure of social work theory
and practice and thus paved the way for a more radical approach.

But even this sociological influence was primarily class-based
and lacked much of the width of other forms of sociology which
also noted the relevance of gender, race, religion and so on. In
short, despite the impact of sociology, the radical social work of the
1970s centred on the critique of capitalism, but with only the faint
beginnings of a critique of patriarchy and imperialism.

Simpkin (1989) relates this to the specific political tactic, dating
from 1974, of concentrating on trade-unionism and class struggle
which entailed 'downgrading' issues of women's and gay rights
(ibid., p. 166). For this reason, amongst others, radical social work
remained locked into class without acknowledging the role of other
social divisions in the oppression and dehumanisation of social
work's clients.

It was only in the 1980s that the primacy of class was seriously
challenged and issues of gender and race began to be taken firmly
on board by radical social work – by this time a much weakened
movement made distinctly less popular by the emergence, and
dominance, of New Right ideology with its promotion of individualism and its mistrust of all forms of collectivism.

The influence of feminism in sociology was now beginning to
extend to social policy in general and social work in particular. A
number of key anti-sexist texts became available – including
Ungerson (1985) and Pascall (1986/1997) on social policy; Brook
and Davis (1985) and Gittins (1985) on the family and welfare and
Hanmer and Statham (1988/1999) and Dominelli and McLeod
(1989) on social work practice from a feminist perspective (for
developments in the literature base since then, see the 'Guide to
further learning' sections at the end of this chapter and also
Chapter 3).

For a profession whose basic grade workforce and clientele are both predominantly female and in which a major focus is on 'the family', the feminist plea for an anti-sexist approach to social work was long overdue. It is an indication of the strength and dominance of patriarchal ideas that the 'gendered' nature of social work should have been neglected for so long.

The development of interest in issues of race and racism within sociology has also permeated into social work and the thrust towards an anti-racist social work has steadily gained ground. The Association of Black Social Workers and Allied Professionals (ABSWAP) was formed in 1983 and consistently argued for more black social workers, a greater understanding of the nature and impact of racism and a firmer commitment to the development of anti-racist social work.

But this is only one example of the increased recognition of racism as a social problem and the dangers of an uninformed social work practice reinforcing its effects. As with anti-sexism, the 1980s saw the publication of a number of key texts which have played a part in the strengthening of the anti-racist movement, with further developments in the literature base in the 1990s – see the 'Guide to further learning' sections at the end of this chapter and also Chapter 4).

A further aspect of the historical development of anti-discriminatory practice is the movement away from an individualistic, pathological approach to disability towards a social model which takes account of the wider social context in which disability is experienced and indeed constructed (see the discussions in Chapter 6).

Radical social work has therefore taken on wider issues of race and gender and, albeit to a lesser extent, age, disability and sexual identity. However, as these become more established, they also become less radical – they become part of the establishment framework. This is an example of the reform versus revolution dilemma highlighted by Pritchard and Taylor (1978) in which piecemeal reformist improvements, whilst welcome in their own right, may reduce the impetus towards more radical solutions. Jones and Novak (1980) argued that social reformers have bolstered ruling class interests by introducing measures which, though reducing discontent, inhibit or obstruct radical social change. Whether antidiscriminatory practice can keep in touch with its radical roots or whether its potential for social change will become diluted (by its incorporation into mainstream policy and practice) remains an open question (see Penketh, 2000, for an interesting discussion that touches on these issues). In the 1990s we reached the stage where greater consciousness of oppression and discrimination had been achieved, as reflected in the range of literature and training courses available, the development of equality and diversity policies (in embryo form at least) and the regulations relating to social work qualifying courses (CCETSW, 1989, 1991a, 1995).

One unfortunate development that accompanied the growing awareness of, and commitment to, anti-discriminatory practice, was a strong tendency towards oversimplification or 'reductionism' – reducing a complex, multi-level phenomenon to a simple, single-level issue. For example, to many people, the complexities of the relationship between language use and discrimination became reduced to 'political correctness' – a reliance on a list of taboo or 'non-PC' words (Thompson, 2003b). This was also accompanied in many quarters by a very crude approach to education and training in relation to discrimination and oppression, a point to which we shall return in Chapter 2. This crude reductionism, while a significant problem in its own right, also led to another major concern – the development of a culture of fear and blame in which defensiveness became a very common response. It is understandable that, if students and in-service course participants were being told in effect that they were 'oppressive', they were likely to perceive this as an attack and thus respond in a defensive manner. Key features of this defensiveness have been:

● A tokenistic 'lip-service' approach caused by people's understandable reluctance to engage firmly and closely with what they perceived as such dangerous, threatening issues.
● A tendency to avoid the subject where possible – a 'Let's not go there' mentality.
● A tense and anxious approach which in itself could lead to oversimplification (when we feel tense, anxious and threatened, we are not likely to be eager to engage with very complex and intricate concepts and issues).
● In some cases, a long-standing lack of confidence in dealing with these issues as a result of the painful experiences of being exposed to some very crude and ill-thought-through approaches to teaching and learning.

In running courses on the subject of anti-discriminatory practice I have come across large numbers of people who have given me very worrying examples of earlier experiences that were extremely unhelpful in contributing to their understanding of the complexities or in equipping them to deal with such issues effectively in practice. This is a sad legacy of a rapid change from an education and training system which largely neglected discrimination and oppression to one in which such concerns very quickly became central. It is to be hoped that we have managed to learn the lessons from that period and are now adopting much more sophisticated approaches not only to anti-discriminatory practice itself, but also to how such matters are addressed through education and training.

One development in recent years that has given us a foundation from which to counter such defensiveness is the emergence of the 'diversity approach'. This new way of addressing inequality has become a mainstream approach in many areas, both within and outside social work. It is characterised by two main themes:

1. It adopts a *positive* approach by emphasising that diversity (that is, variety and difference) is not only a very real characteristic of contemporary social and organisational life, it is also a *valuable* characteristic. Diversity is seen as an asset, a positive feature of society that enriches our experience – it is something that should be valued, affirmed and even celebrated. The fact that there are different ethnic groups, different identities, different approaches and perspectives should be seen as a good thing, a source of learning, variety, stimulation and interest, rather than a source of unfair discrimination based on 'punishing' some people for being different from the perceived mainstream.
2. It adopts a broad approach by arguing that any form of unfair discrimination is a problem to be tackled (this is a point to which we shall return below), regardless of whether the discrimination in question is illegal or not. In this respect, the diversity approach goes far beyond the traditional equal opportunities approach which tends to limit itself largely to ensuring legal compliance with anti-discrimination legislation.

By adopting a positive focus and not limiting itself to legal compliance, the diversity approach has the potential to offer in part at least an 'antidote' to the negative and defensive approach which has been allowed to develop in many organisational settings. In this respect, it can be seen as a positive step forward.

However, we should not too enthusiastic in our embracing of this approach, as it has its down sides too. First, it has the potential to become a return to multiculturalism, in emphasising the positives of cultural diversity but without acknowledging the realities of how oppressive discrimination can be – that is, it rightly values *diversity* but without paying adequate attention to the realities of *adversity* for those people subjected to unfair discrimination.

Second, the diversity approach has so far tended to have a very individualistic focus. There is a danger that the gains made in moving away from a psychological approach based on notions of prejudice to a more sophisticated sociological one, based on personal, cultural and structural factors (see Chapter 2) will be lost by an overemphasis on individual factors.

To be fair to the diversity approach, there is nothing inherent within it that makes these problems inevitable – they are dangers rather than necessary flaws. It has to be recognised that the diversity approach is still in its infancy and is in a relatively underdeveloped state. How it develops in the coming years will be very significant.

Another development in the recent history of anti-discriminatory practice in the UK is a new wave of anti-discrimination legislation. This includes: the introduction of the Human Rights Act 1998 which is part of a broader movement towards a culture based on human rights (Crompton and Thompson, 2000); the implementation of the Race Relations (Amendment) Act 2000; and the regulations governing discrimination on the grounds of sexual orientation and religion, which were implemented in December 2003. While these are positive developments and very much to be welcomed, we have to bear in mind that the role the law can play is quite limited. As we shall see in the chapters that follow, a genuine commitment to anti-discriminatory practice must go far beyond the confines of a narrow, legalistic approach.

What is discrimination?

The literal meaning of to discriminate is to identify a difference. As such it is not necessarily a negative term. For example, being able to discriminate between safe food and harmful poison is clearly a good thing. However, when the term is used in a legal, moral or political sense (as in this book), it is generally used to refer to *unfair* discrimination. That is, it refers to the process (or set of processes) through which (i) a difference is identified; and (ii) that difference is used as the basis of unfair treatment. To use the technical term, a person or group 'suffer a detriment' (that is, experience a disadvantage) because they are identified as 'different' (in terms of gender, race/ethnicity, sexual identity and so on).

Instead of differences between people being seen as positive (as per the diversity approach discussed above), they become the basis of unfair discrimination, a basis for disadvantaging certain groups of people. This discrimination then becomes the basis of oppression. It is through the process of identifying some people as 'different' that they receive inhuman or degrading treatment (see the definition of oppression in Chapter 2) and are thus oppressed.

While this is a satisfactory basic definition of discrimination, what it does not do is indicate the important role of power involved. Anyone can discriminate against anyone else. However, where the impact will be of major proportions will be in those cases where relatively powerful groups will be in a position to discriminate systematically against those in relatively powerless groups. Such power can arise because of personal circumstances or characteristics, cultural norms or structural position (see the discussion of PCS analysis in Chapter 2). This is where established *patterns* of discrimination have become ingrained in social practices – racism, sexism, ageism and so on, and are not simply examples of individual preference or prejudice. Discrimination is therefore a sociological and political phenomenon as well as a psychological one.

Note that, in referring to power, I was very careful to use the term 'relatively'. This is because, as we shall see below, there has been a tendency to oversimplify issues of power and reduce them to a simple dichotomy of two groups in society: the powerful and the powerless. Power is a much more complex phenomenon than this, and so it is important, at this early stage in our discussions, not to fall into the trap of presenting it too simply.

A key point to note is that the model of anti-discriminatory practice presented here is not a narrow one that ignores wider sociopolitical concerns. Differences between this book and the work of authors who distinguish between anti-discriminatory and anti-oppressive practice are primarily semantic rather than theoretical or ideological. In order to promote forms of practice that are genuinely *emancipatory*, it is necessary to address the processes of discrimination that give rise to oppression. So, whether we refer to such endeavours as anti-discriminatory or anti-oppressive practice, is in my view not a significant issue. What is significant is that we seek to reduce oppression by tackling the processes of discrimination that give rise to it.

Good practice is anti-discriminatory practice

Social workers can be seen as mediators between their clients and the wider state apparatus and social order. This position of 'mediator' is a crucial one, as it means that social workers are in a pivotal position in terms of the relationship between the state and its citizens.

The relationship is a double-edged one, consisting of elements of care and control. It is also double-edged in the sense that it can lead to either potential empowerment or potential oppression – social work interventions can help or hinder, empower or impress. Which aspect is to the fore, which element or tendency is reinforced depends largely on the actions of the social workers concerned. As long ago as 1975, in the era of radical social work, Peter Leonard captured this point in relation to class and capitalism, although much the same can be said of gender and patriarchy, race and imperialism and so on:

> In capitalist society, social work operates as part of a social-welfare system which is located at the centre of the contradictions arising from the dehumanising consequences of capitalist economic production. Social workers, although situated in a largely oppressive organisational and professional context, have the potential for recognising these contradictions and, through working at the point of interaction between people and their social environment, of helping to increase the control by people over economic and political structures.
> (in Bailey and Brake, 1975, p. 55)

What this entails, in effect, is that there can be no safe middle ground, no liberal compromise. Social work is not, as Halmos (1965) would have it, a matter of the personal detached from the political (Pearson, 1975).

As I have argued previously (Thompson, 1992a):

There is no middle ground; intervention either adds to oppression (or at least condones it) or goes some small way towards easing or breaking such oppression. In this respect, the political slogan, 'If you're not part of the solution, you must be part of the problem' is particularly accurate. An awareness of the sociopolitical context is necessary in order to prevent becoming (or remaining) part of the problem. (pp. 169–70)

In short, a social work practice which does not take account of oppression, and the discrimination which gives rise to it, cannot be seen as good practice, no matter how high its standards may be in other respects. For example, a social work intervention with a disabled person which fails to recognise the marginalised position of disabled people in society runs the risk of doing the client more of a disservice than a service (see Chapter 6 below).

I hope this principle – that good practice must be anti-discriminatory practice – will become more clearly and firmly established in the chapters that follow.

Multiple oppressions

There are many texts available which concentrate on a particular aspect of anti-discriminatory practice, whether this be anti-racism, anti-ageism and so on. This book, however, is not intended simply as an introduction to each of the discrete areas. There is an underlying thread of 'multiple oppression', the interaction of various sources and forms of oppression.

Oppression and discrimination are presented as aspects of the divisive nature of social structure – reflections of the social divisions of class, race, gender, age, disability and sexual identity. These are dimensions of our social location (where and how we fit into society) and so we need to understand them as a whole – facets of an overall edifice of power and dominance, rather than separate or discrete entities. To use an existentialist term, they are 'dimensions of our lived experience'.

At the Critical Social Policy conference on 'Citizenship and Welfare' (London, March 1991) two of the papers presented made reference to the need for an integrated approach, a framework which recognises the interactions of multiple oppressions. Amina Mama stressed the need for a 'politically holistic approach – a politics of alliance' based on an integrated analysis. Race, class, gender and so on are separated out for analytical purposes but they are not entirely separate processes; they occur simultaneously and affect people in combination. They are related dimensions of our complex existence rather than discrete entities.

Fiona Williams expressed similar views in advocating a wider analysis which goes beyond class, race and gender to include marginalisation on the grounds of age, disability and sexuality. She argued for a theoretical approach which recognises diversities in patterns of power and inequality, but one which does not fall into the trap of establishing a 'hierarchy of oppressions'. The task, she affirmed, is to relate the diversity and differences between forms of oppression, on the one hand, to a need for an anti-oppression alliance on the other (see also Williams, 1992).

Both Mama and Williams were advocating an *integrated* approach, one which recognises the reality of multiple oppressions but which seeks to concentrate on the commonalities and shared aspects of alienation, marginalisation and discrimination. In short, political energies should be directed towards fighting oppression in its various forms rather than in-fighting between different anti-discrimination interest groups.

This is, of course, more easily said than done, but the argument does have implications for social work policy and practice, as Chapters 5–7 will indicate. The notion of an integrated analysis is a central one to this book, as my focus will be very clearly on the conception of anti-discriminatory practice as a unitary whole (rather than simply the sum total of anti-sexism plus anti-racism plus anti-ageism and so on). It has to be recognised that the combination of oppressions and their interaction is a complex, intricate and relatively under-researched area (Stuart, 1992; Morris, 1991; Williams, 1992) but one which none the less needs to be addressed (see Thompson, 2003a). This is a topic to which we shall return in Chapter 7.

Discrimination and oppression are multifaceted phenomena and so it is important to gain an understanding of both the common themes across areas and the key differences between them.

---

practice focus 1.3

Sue was keen to work in an anti-discriminatory way in assessing Mrs Desai's needs under the NHS and Community Care Act 1990 and therefore paid close attention to Mrs Desai's cultural background and needs and her experiences of racism. However, it was only in a subsequent supervision session that she realised that her anti-discriminatory focus had been one-dimensional. That is, she had neglected to consider issues of gender and sexism or, indeed, the profound effects of ageism on Mrs Desai. Sue was fortunate in having a team leader who had a good understanding of anti-discriminatory issues, and who was able to help her develop her understanding and skills in this demanding aspect of practice.

Structure and outline

Chapter 2 examines the theoretical concepts and framework which underpin anti-discriminatory practice. The major themes will be explained and links with social work practice drawn in order to begin to build a bridge between theory and practice. Indeed the need for a clear practice focus, illuminated by theory, will be a primary concern throughout the book (Thompson, 2000a). This chapter will also tackle the thorny issue of language. The topic will be approached from two angles; first to understand the role played by language in constructing and reinforcing discrimination; and, second, to clarify the terminology used in this text – that is, to define the key terms and concepts.

This chapter sets the scene for the following analysis of the various forms of oppression and processes of discrimination. This is achieved by explaining the common theory base which acts as a framework for understanding the complex issues discussed in ensuing chapters. Chapter 3 is the first of four chapters to explore a specific area of discrimination, in this case gender. The theory of patriarchy is explained and the steps towards an anti-sexist practice are sketched out. Chapters 4 to 6 follow a similar structure and pattern. Chapter 4 addresses issues of race/ethnicity and racism. Imperialist ideology and notions of cultural superiority are explored and rejected as a first step towards building a social work practice based on principles of anti-racism. In Chapter 5 the less publicised and less well-established concept of ageism is the object of our attention. The issues of discrimination on the grounds of age are considered and a framework for developing anti-ageist practice is presented. Chapter 6 adopts a similar approach in exploring the marginalisation of disabled people. Discriminatory attitudes, policies, structures and practices are identified and the oppression inherent in catering only for the able-bodied majority is recognised as a target for change.

In addition to these four main areas, there exist a number of other, less well-publicised forms and sources of oppression and discrimination. These are the subject matter of Chapter 7, in which attention is paid to discrimination on the grounds of sexual identity (heterosexism), culture and language, religion and so on. A major feature of this chapter is the need to emphasise the point that unfair discrimination is something that needs to be tackled in all its forms and not only the more well-established ones or more fully documented ones. Anti-discriminatory practice is a matter of a principled commitment to social justice rather than simply following political or other fashions.

Chapter 8 is the concluding chapter. It summarises seven main themes and examines possible ways forward, divided into seven positive steps to be taken and seven pitfalls to avoid. The focus here is on the need to develop critically reflective practice (Thompson, 2000a) – that is, forms of practice that incorporate a critical evaluation of our own actions. This is necessary, as was suggested above, to ensure that social work is part of the solution rather than part of the problem.

points to ponder

➤ Have you ever experienced unfair discrimination?
➤ How might your experience(s) help you as a social worker?
➤ What problems would you envisage if a social worker were to ignore or disregard clients' experiences of discrimination?
➤ How confident do you feel about tackling discrimination and oppression?
➤ Who can help and support you in developing your knowledge, skills and confidence in this area?

Guide to further learning

The historical development of radical social work and its more modern manifestations are covered in a number of texts, including the following: Langan and Lee (1989); Mullaly (1993); and Langan (1998).

The law relating to discrimination is well covered in Preston-Shoot (1998) while Blakemore and Drake (1996) provide a useful discussion of related matters. The Human Rights Act 1998 is covered in a training pack form in Crompton and Thompson (2000) and in book form in Wadham and Mountfield (1999) and Watson and Woolf (2003). Useful information on the Act can also be downloaded from www.dca.gov.uk/hract/hramenu.htm

The regulations relating to discrimination on the grounds of sexual orientation and religion are helpfully explained in documents that can be downloaded from the ACAS website: www.acas.org.uk

In terms of gender issues, the 1990s saw a further development in the anti-sexist literature base: Elliot (1996) on the family; Arber and Ginn (1991, 1995) in relation to old age; Busfield (1996) in relation to mental health and Cavanagh and Cree (1996) on the subject of sexism and men. This has now continued into the new century – see, for example, Fawcett *et al.* (2000); Pizzey *et al.* (2000). See the 'Guide to further learning' section at the end of Chapter 3 for further details.

In relation to race and racism, Ahmad (1990) provides a very useful text with a clear practice focus, as does the set of readings produced by CCETSW (CD Project Steering Group, 1991); Dwivedi and Varma (1996) address child care issues, Littlewood and Lipsedge (1997) mental health and Blakemore and Boneham (1993) old age. Robinson (1995) provides an anti-racist perspective on psychology for social workers and Bowser (1995) provides an international perspective on racism and anti-racism. A longstanding classic text on racism (Solomos, 1989) is now available in a revised third edition (Solomos, 2003). Also, Luthra (1997) is a useful information source on demography and related issues. See the 'Guide to further learning' section at the end of Chapter 4 for further details.

For a general introduction to issues relating to discrimination and oppression, the following are relevant: Jordan (1990); Mullaly

(1993); Braye and Preston-Shoot (1995); Dalrymple and Burke (1995); Adams (2003); and Tomlinson and Trew (2002). Fook (2002) is an exceptionally good book that is highly recommended. More advanced treatment of the issues is to be found in Humphries (1996); Lešnik (1998); and Thompson (1998a; 2003a).

2 | The theory base

Social work theory derives from a wide range of sources although, traditionally, the social work literature owes much to social science thinking. In particular, the theory base outlined here draws heavily on sociology and social psychology.

This is not of course primarily a theoretical text – the major focus is on anti-discriminatory *practice*. But an understanding of the underlying conceptual framework, and the themes and concepts of which it consists, *is* necessary to ensure that such practice is based on intelligent and informed debate, rather than dogma, fad or ignorance. Indeed, discrimination and oppression as a field of study has been prone to more than its fair share of dogma and over-simplification over the years (Thompson, 1998b).

I shall therefore present an exposition of some of the key themes and issues and sketch out some of the linkages between the theoretical concepts and the social work concerns they are intended to illuminate. This will, of course, be a far from comprehensive account – a text of this size devoted entirely to such issues would still barely do justice to the complexity and scope of the subject matter (see Thompson, 2003a for a more detailed exposition of the theory base). This chapter is therefore very much an *introductory* exploration of the theory base. It is a beginning which, I hope, will have the effect of both equipping and motivating the reader to build on these foundations through further reading, discussion and above all, relating such theory to practice.

Social divisions and social structure

Societies are not, of course, simply amorphous masses of people. A society comprises a diverse range of people and is therefore characterised by differentiation – people are categorised according to social divisions such as class and gender. These divisions then form the basis of the social structure – the 'network' of social relationships, institutions and groupings – which plays such an important role in the distribution of power, status and opportunities.

It has long been recognised that people can be 'located' within the social structure in terms of the intersection of different social divisions (Berger, 1966). That is, who we are depends to a large extent on how and where we fit into society. And this, in turn, depends on the complex web of social divisions or social 'strata' (hence the term 'stratification'). These strata are many and varied but the emphasis here will be on the major social divisions, those of class (Roberts, 2001), gender (Richardson and Robinson, 1997), race/ethnicity (Skellington, 1996), age (S. Thompson, 2005) and disability (Oliver, 1996). This is not to deny the importance or relevance of other social divisions such as sexual identity, creed or linguistic group. It is simply a matter of having to be realistic in restricting the scope of the analysis for reasons of space (see Chapter 7).

Let us look briefly at each of these dimensions of the social structure before considering their significance for social work.

Class

There is a longstanding major debate within sociology concerning the definition of class (Roberts, 2001). There are those who, following Marx, define class in relation to ownership or control of the means of production (specifically, the means of producing wealth – land, factories, machinery and so on). There are others, who, following Weber, relate class to 'relations of exchange' (that is, buying power) rather than relations of production. (See Giddens, 1997, for an overview of these issues and Giddens, 1971, for a fuller discussion.)

Within social work the term tends to be used loosely, in a broadly Weberian sense, to indicate different levels of economic power. Low class position (equals low economic power due to low pay or reliance on benefits) is associated with poverty, poor quality housing, poor health and a general lack of opportunity. Dobelniece (1998) highlights the consequences of living in poverty:

> Poor people get less of everything that is considered important and necessary for a decent life, that is, less money, food, clothing, shelter. The deprivation experienced by poor people is pervasive. Children brought up in poverty are more likely to fail in school, to drop out of school. They are more

likely to develop mental health problems, are more suscepti-
ble to chronic illnesses, and are less likely to be covered by
health insurance. They are more likely to lose jobs and to
drop out of the labour force. They are more likely to experience hostility and distrust. They are less likely to participate
in meaningful groups and associations. As the ultimate
deprivation, they are likely to die at a younger age.
(pp. 5–6)

The relationship between class, poverty and social work is therefore
a very significant one (Jones and Novak, 1999).

Gender

There are distinct and relatively fixed biological differences
between men and women. These are *sex* differences. However,
when we ascribe particular social significance to these differences,
and allot roles accordingly, they become *gender* differences. That is,
it becomes a matter of social construction rather than biological
determination (Burr, 2003).

Boys and girls are socialised into differential patterns of behaviour, interaction, thought, language and emotional response.
Different roles are assigned, according to gender, and so differential sets of expectations are established. These expectations are
constantly reinforced through social interaction and the influence
of the media, the education system and so on. Where people deviate from these gender expectations, sanctions are applied – boys
who stray into feminine territory are labelled 'cissy' or 'effeminate'
whilst girls who transgress are seen as 'butch' or a 'tomboy'. These
childhood patterns become deeply ingrained and persist through to
adulthood.

Gender expectations can also produce a situation whereby the
same characteristic can be interpreted differently according to
whether it applies to a man or a woman. For example, assertiveness in men can be seen as strength of character, whereas in
women it can be seen as bossiness (Thompson, 2002a). The cycle
is complete when biological sex differences are used to justify or
'legitimate' the inequalities inherent in social differences based on
gender. This is an important point and so this link between the
biological and the social will feature again below in the discussion
of ideology.

Race and ethnicity

'Race', like sex, is often assumed to be a biological matter, but this is a misleading assumption to make. Blackburn (2000) argues that the assumed biological basis of 'race' is a common fallacy and goes on to point out that: 'biologically, there is one race – the human race – in its modest variety and overwhelming commonality' (p. 19). Similarly, Muldoon (2000), in discussing the history of slavery, argues that:

> The relationship between slave and master was fixed by a biological imperative. It was a law of nature that could not be repealed. The medieval notion that humanity was one and that humankind had the same capacity for transformation was replaced by a pseudoscientific view that people existed as biologically different races, the mental and moral capacities of which were fixed for all time.
> (p. 92)

It is partly for this reason that the term 'race' often has the word 'ethnicity' attached to it – to emphasise that it refers to a social grouping rather than a biological one. That is, it is the equivalent of gender rather than sex. For the same reason, many authors consistently place inverted commas around the word ('race') in order to indicate that it is not being used in its literal, biological sense.

Race is therefore a socially constructed way of categorising people on the basis of *assumed* biological differences. As with socially constructed gender distinctions, the notion of race entails:

● *Inherent inequalities.*   Racial categorisation involves not only *difference* but also implies relations of superiority/inferiority. This is the basis of *racism* (see Chapter 4).
● *Biological legitimation.*   The biological aspect of this social division is used as a justification for discrimination and inequality.

Some people might argue that, because it does not have a biological basis, race does not exist. It *does* exist, but it is a social construction, rather than a biological entity.

Age

The problems associated with sexism and racism have long been recognised and are relatively well documented. Discrimination on the grounds of age, or 'ageism', as it has become known, is a relatively new addition to anti-discriminatory discourse. Fennell *et al.* (1988) define ageism in the following terms: 'Ageism means unwarranted application of negative stereotypes to older people' (p. 97). As we shall see in Chapter 5, old age is strongly associated with notions of frailty, mental and physical debility and dependency. This association is greatly exaggerated by common (mis)-conceptions about the nature of old age and the incidence of problems. This tendency to devalue older people and overemphasise the negative aspects of later life is characteristic of ageism. The distribution of power, status and opportunities is therefore dependent upon not only class, race and gender but also age. Age is therefore an important social division, a significant dimension of the social structure. The main focus of anti-ageism is old age but when we consider that very similar issues apply to children (Thompson, 1997; 2002b), the impact of ageism takes on additional significance. Indeed, we could go beyond Fennell *et al.*'s definition of ageism to include children: 'discrimination against any individual or group on the basis of age'.

Disability

Disability is a concept which distinguishes a certain proportion of the population (those with some degree of physical impairment) from the 'able-bodied' majority. Again, this is not simply a biological/physiological matter but has major social implications. By defining disability as primarily a physiological matter, the issues are personalised and individualised. In this way the social and political dimensions are overlooked. This leads Oliver (1989a) to comment:

> The growth of the disabled people's movement and, especially, its redefinition of the problem as social oppression has given rise to the concept of disablism which is inherent within the individual model of disability.
> (p. 192)

Thus it is argued that traditional, individualised approaches to disability mask the inherent marginalisation and dehumanisation involved in attitudes and policies in relation to people with disabilities. Once again, the biological level is used as a means of legitimating unequal power relations at the social and political levels.

Disablism is the term used to describe the oppression and discrimination implicit in this situation – the social division of disability.

---

practice focus 2.1

Pearlene was an experienced social worker whose work had mainly been in the field of mental health. However, her new post was in a disability team. As part of her induction programme she attended a meeting of the local disability forum. This was to be a significant event for her as she was amazed to see how much anger there was against local service providers and how patronised the disabled people at the forum felt by medically oriented social work and nursing staff. She realised that her common-sense views of disability and disabled people's needs would have to be reconsidered.

The psychodynamic focus of traditional social work has been criticised for its failure to take account of the social dimension. From this critique, systems theory developed with its explicit emphasis on social systems. This, in turn, has been criticised for ignoring the importance of conflict, structure and social divisions. Social work theory has now progressed to a level of sophistication at which the part played by social divisions and social structure is receiving increasing attention. However, what is needed is a conceptual framework which will enable us to develop a clearer understanding of how the problems social workers and their clients face can be located in this wider, structural context. PCS analysis, which I shall explain below, can take us some way towards this.

PCS analysis

In order to understand how inequalities and discrimination feature in the social circumstances of clients, and in the interactions between clients and the welfare state, it is helpful to analyse the situation in terms of three levels. These three levels (P, C and S) are closely interlinked and constantly interact with one another (see Figure 2.1).

P refers to the *personal* or *psychological*; it is the individual level of thoughts, feelings, attitudes and actions. It also refers to *practice*,

Figure 2.1 PCS analysis

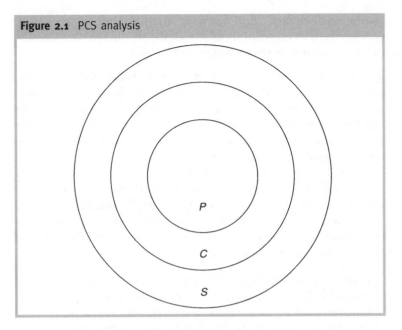

individual workers interacting with individual clients, and *preju-dice*, the inflexibility of mind which stands in the way of fair and non-judgemental practice. Our thoughts, feelings and attitudes about particular groups in society will, to a certain degree at least, be shaped by our experiences at a personal level.

C refers to the *cultural* level of shared ways of seeing, thinking and doing. It relates to the *commonalities* – values and patterns of thought and behaviour, an assumed *consensus* about what is right and what is normal; it produces *conformity* to social norms, and *comic* humour acts as a vehicle for transmitting and reinforcing this culture. It is therefore primarily a matter of shared meanings. It includes conventional notions of culture, such as religion, belief systems and nationality, but goes beyond these. The cultural level is a complex web of taken-for-granted assumptions or 'unwritten rules'. Culture is very influential in determining what is perceived as 'normal' in any given set of circumstances.

S refers to the *structural* level, the network of *social divisions* and the power relations that are so closely associated with them; it also relates to the ways in which oppression and discrimination are institutionalised and thus '*sewn in*' to the fabric of society. It denotes the wider level of *social forces,* the *sociopolitical* dimension of interlocking patterns of power and influence.

The *P* level is, as Figure 2.1 illustrates, embedded within the cultural or *C* level – that is, the *C* level forms the context in which our personal experience occurs. Our thoughts, actions, attitudes and feelings are to a certain extent unique and individualised, but we must also recognise the powerful role of culture in forming our opinions, guiding our actions and so on.

The *C* level represents the interests and the influence of society as reflected in the social values and cultural norms we internalise via the process of socialisation – for example, manners, etiquette and rituals (such as to how to behave towards someone when it is their birthday or they have just become engaged). Peter Berger (1966) captures this point well:

> Only an understanding of internalisation makes sense of the incredible fact that most external controls work most of the time for most of the people in a society. Society not only controls our movements, but shapes our identity, our thoughts and our emotions. The structures of society become the structure of our own consciousness. Society does not stop at the surface of our skins. Society penetrates us as much as it envelops us.
> (p. 140)

This passage is particularly relevant to the cultural influence of forms of discrimination on individual consciousness. It lays the foundations for understanding the various forms of discrimination not simply as personal prejudice (the *P* level) but, more realistically, the discriminatory and oppressive culture base manifesting itself in and through individual thought and action. It is therefore a more complex situation involving the interaction of the *P* and *C* levels.

Humour is an example of how a discriminatory culture can subtly but powerfully influence individual thoughts and actions. For example, racist jokes can be seen as a vehicle for reinforcing and legitimating notions of racial superiority. The fact that humour is so highly valued as a social quality means that it is both a highly potent influence and relatively well defended from attack. Comments such as 'it's only a joke' or 'it's only a bit of fun' act as

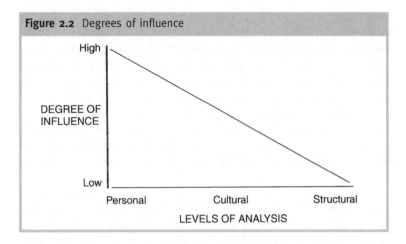

Figure 2.2 Degrees of influence

effective defences and help to maintain the discriminatory power of humour. This is not to say that humour is necessarily discriminatory – far from it – but where it does have oppressive potential we need to be wary of allowing ourselves to be seduced by it.

To say that the *P* level is embedded within the *C* level is not to suggest that the thoughts and actions of individuals are simply a 'reflection' of society or culture. PCS analysis is not deterministic; it does not imply that culture 'causes' our actions, but rather that individual behaviour has to be understood in the wider social and cultural context.

But even this cultural context needs to be understood in terms of a wider context – the structural. That is, the *C* level is embedded within the *S* level. It is no coincidence that we have the cultural and social formations that currently exist. These owe much to the structure of society – the interlocking matrix of social divisions and the power relations which maintain them. To understand the *C* level we need to relate it to the *S* level, the structure of society.

Marx argued that the economic base or 'infrastructure' conditions the 'superstructure' – that is, the political, social and cultural aspects (the *C* level). This is an argument about *class*, the class conflict in the economic base of capitalism. But, as was argued in Chapter 1, class is not the only structural dimension which merits our attention.

Feminists have convincingly argued the case for recognising the importance of gender in mapping out the social structure whilst the anti-racist movement has built on the foundations of a plea for understanding the racially structured nature of modern western societies. These will both be discussed further in Chapters 3 and 4 respectively. The significance of age and disability as relevant dimensions of the social structure is also being increasingly recognised, as some of the discussions in this text will confirm.

Marx's analysis does not, therefore, take us far enough, but it is, none the less, a useful beginning. Indeed, I would contend that it is a grave mistake to reject marxism – a case of throwing the baby out with the bath water. I shall return to this point in the concluding chapter.

PCS analysis shows the different levels at which discrimination operates and how these levels reinforce each other. What is also worth noting, however, is that the degree of control and impact a worker can have on tackling discrimination is also related to the three levels, as is shown in Figure 2.2.

The further away one moves from the personal level, the less impact an individual can have. It therefore becomes necessary to move beyond the personal level, not only in terms of *understanding* discrimination but also in terms of tackling it. This involves individuals playing their part in collectively *challenging* the dominant discriminatory culture and ideology and, in so doing, playing at least a part in the undermining of the structures which support, and are supported by, that culture.

Structured inequalities and institutional oppression

One of the advantages of using PCS analysis is that it shows the inadequacy of explanations which stop short at the individual level. For example, it is not enough to explain racism as a personal prejudice or the wicked misdeeds of a bigoted minority such as members of extreme right-wing organisations. In fact, this more overt type of racial discrimination is referred to by many as 'racialism' (Nelson, 1990) to distinguish it from the wider concept of racism. As we shall see in Chapter 4, racism can be by omission as well as commission. It is not simply a matter of prejudicial beliefs.

If we accept that we live in a racist society (that is, a society that is geared to the white majority and thus discriminates against ethnic minorities – see the discussion of institutional oppression below and of institutional racism in particular in Chapter 4), then it is not surprising that racist beliefs and practices will have been learned and 'taken on board' as parts of our personalities and what Berger and Luckmann (1967) call 'the taken-for-granted-ness of everyday life'. Even if we are full of good intentions in relation to anti-discriminatory practice, unless we are actively seeking to eliminate racist thoughts and actions from our day-to-day dealings, they will 'filter through' from the culture and structure into which we were socialised and which constantly seek to influence us (through the media, political propaganda and so on). It is in this sense that we cannot remain 'neutral'. As the political slogan would have it: 'if you're not part of the solution, you must be part of the problem'. That is, the tide of discrimination (the C and S levels) is so strong that, unless we actively swim against it, it is more or less inevitable that we will be carried along with it.

I have used the example of racism but much the same can be said of the other forms of discrimination. For example, in terms of sexism, it is not simply a matter of a relatively small number of men who are overtly sexist or 'male chauvinist pigs'. Sexism subtly pervades our thoughts and actions and very often influences us in ways which we do not recognise until somebody points them out to us. (It is for this reason that 'Awareness Training' is an important prerequisite for anti-discriminatory practice – see Chapter 8.)

Oppression and discrimination cannot be explained simply by reference to personal prejudice. Katz's (1978) notion of 'prejudice plus power' takes us in the right direction but ultimately confuses the issue more than it clarifies it (Sibeon, 1991a). Discrimination is a reflection (and a reinforcer) of structured inequalities. The fact that we live in such a highly stratified society means that inequalities are part and parcel of the social order – there are inevitably winners and losers. Again, this is not an individual matter, as such inequalities are 'sewn in' to the fabric of society – they underpin social order.

This introduces the notion of 'institutional oppression'. Oppression does not derive simply from individual actions or 'praxis'. It can be, and often is, built in to structural and institutional patterns and organisational policies. Rooney (1987) gives a good example of how this operates. He describes how one local authority used to recruit its home-help staff by word of mouth. When vacancies arose, the existing (predominantly white) work-force would be asked to let people know of such vacancies. They would, of course, pass this information on to their (predominantly white) circle of friends, some of whom would then be recruited. Consequently, this form of recruitment systematically marginalised and excluded potential black staff, albeit perhaps unintentionally.

There are many aspects of social work which run this risk of institutional oppression (the inherent sexism of some forms of family therapy, for example – see White, 1997). The concept is therefore an important part of the theory base of anti-discriminatory practice. An important point to bear in mind is that discrimination is a matter of outcomes rather than just intentions. That is, even where no discrimination is intended, if certain individuals or groups of people experience an unfair disadvantage, the discrimination has taken place and oppression is likely to be experienced as a result of it. Unwitting discrimination can be just as damaging (if not more so) as intentional discrimination.

PCS analysis: A note of caution

Since I first introduced PCS analysis in the first edition of this book and developed it in other publications (*Promoting Equality*, 2003a, for example), it has become very well established and widely used. While this can clearly be seen as a positive development, it has left me with two concerns:

1. In my role as an external examiner at a number of universities I have come across many examples of students simply referring to PCS analysis without showing any real understanding of it or how it can be used. It is as if it has become a 'mantra' to be uttered, rather than an analytical framework that can help us make sense of the complexities of discrimination and oppression. I am concerned to ensure that it should not be used in an unthinking or uncritical way. It should be used as a basis of critically reflective practice not as an alternative to it. Critically reflective practice will be discussed in Chapter 8.
2. I have encountered examples of PCS analysis being distorted and used inappropriately. For example, one group of participants on a training course I ran told me that a trainer on a

previous course had presented PCS analysis to them (without acknowledging its source) and had argued that, because racism exists at a structural and cultural level, then white people in this country *must* be racist at a personal level. This represents a gross distortion of PCS analysis, as it conflates the different levels. Personal racism and cultural and structural forms of racism are very different entities. Although they can be interrelated, it would be a grave mistake to equate them. Care should therefore be taken to ensure that the complexities of PCS analysis are appreciated and not allowed to form the basis of a reductionist approach.

Ideology: the power of ideas

An ideology is a set of ideas which are associated with a particular set of social arrangements. The ideology has the effect of 'legitimating the status quo' and thus justifies, protects and reinforces those social arrangements and the power relationships inherent within them. For example, patriarchal ideology promotes traditional notions of the respective roles of men and women and strongly discourages any deviation from these. The power interests inherent in patriarchy are therefore well served by the ideology of patriarchy. In short, the ideas base safeguards the power base. In fact, this is what characterises ideology – the *power of ideas* operating in the interests of *power relations*:

> Ideology refers to the power of ideas to maintain existing structures and social relations. For example, patriarchal ideology (patriarchy means 'the law of the father' – that is, male dominance) serves to maintain existing power relations between men and women by presenting gender roles as natural and inevitable (despite the considerable evidence to the contrary). Ideology is closely linked to power relations because it is largely through the role of ideology that power is exercised. That is, the subtle, often unquestioned, workings of ideology can be far more effective in maintaining power structures than the overt and explicit use of power, for example through force or coercion.
> (Thompson, 2000b, p. 56)

There are various ideologies at work in society but it tends to be the ideas of powerful groups which become dominant or, to quote the marxist dictum: 'The ideas of the ruling class are, in every age, the ruling ideas' (quoted in Bottomore and Rubel, 1963, p. 93). The ideologies of capitalism, patriarchy and imperialism are examples of such dominant ideologies.

Ideology can be seen to operate in a number of ways – that is, a number of 'ideological devices' can be identified. The setting up of 'norms' is an important part of this. An ideology will establish what is 'normal' and, therefore, by extension, what is 'abnormal'. Ideology therefore defines deviance. 'Norm', however, is an ambiguous concept in so far as it can refer to a *statistical* norm, a quantitative measure. For example, heterosexuality can be seen to be 'normal' in so far as the majority of people are heterosexual. However, 'norm' can also be used in an idealised sense to reflect what 'ought to be', that is, an *ideological* norm. It is a common ideological device for the two types of norm to be conflated – for an ideological norm to masquerade as a statistical norm. For example, the ideological norm of the nuclear family is often presented as if it were a statistical norm whereas, in fact, only 22 per cent of households follow the nuclear family pattern of biological parents with their dependent children (*Social Trends,* 2005).

Another very common primary device is that of presenting particular goals or values as 'natural'. The use of the term 'natural' is a very powerful way of gaining approval – it is a form of legitimation. To describe, for example, the traditional male role of breadwinner as 'natural' adds a false, pseudo-biological air of legitimacy. This is a particularly significant device in terms of the ideological justification of oppression. Racism is premised on the false notion of biological/natural racial categories, sexism on the reduction of social gender roles to biological sex roles. Similarly, disablism hinges on a medical (hence biological/ natural) model of disability (Oliver and Sapey, 1999) and there is an almost direct parallel here with ageism. Indeed, the masking of the economic and sociopolitical dimensions (of old age) under the guise of a biological or natural decline is an ideological device, parallel with the 'biology is destiny' axiom of sexism and the 'racial superiority' fallacy of imperialism (Thompson, 1992b).

---

practice focus 2.2

Phillippa was the head of care at a large residential school where she was charged with implementing the organisation's equal opportunities policy. However, she found considerable resistance on the part of many staff. After months of trying to persuade her colleagues of the value of challenging discrimination, she began to recognise a pattern, a set of common themes that she kept encountering. She realised that biology was the reason commonly given for not promoting equality. Race, gender and so on were all seen as biological differences and therefore natural and not open to change. Phillippa therefore decided that she would need to think of ways of convincing them of the flaws in their argument, ways of showing them that biology was only one factor in a very complex situation.

The terms 'normal' and 'natural' both tend to have strong ideological overtones and so we should be very careful in using them and sensitise ourselves to their use by other people. The logic of discrimination is perpetuated by ideology and so we should be very wary of these common ideological devices. Ideology refers to both the set of ideas which 'serve as weapons of social interests' (Berger and Luckmann, 1967, p. 18), that is the ideas themselves, *and* this very process of serving such interests – reinforcing the power base of the status quo. A significant part of this is the process of 'stereotyping'.

An important distinction can be drawn between 'archetypes' and 'stereotypes'. An archetype is a 'typification' – that is, a set of typical characteristics and expectations we associate with a particular person, group or thing. It is a helpful way of simplifying the complexity of social reality and thus making sense of the world. It introduces and maintains a degree of stability and predictability. However, this helpful and constructive process can easily spill over into the much more harmful and destructive process of stereotyping.

A stereotype is a fixed set of ideas that come as a 'package'. A set of characteristics is assumed to apply in total to a person or group that is stereotyped. For example, stereotypical ideas about older people include assumptions that they are deaf, inactive, dependent and incapable of making their own decisions. Not only are such assumptions patronising, they are also very problematic in so far as they distort reality by presenting oversimplified images of a complex reality.

What distinguishes an archetype from a stereotype is that we are likely to abandon an archetype as soon as we encounter information that negates our assumptions, whereas stereotypes tend to persist regardless of evidence or experience to the contrary. For example, someone who holds negative stereotypes about black people who meets a black person they get on with and feel positive towards, is likely to see that particular black person as an 'exception to the rule' and continue to hold negative views about black people in general, rather than abandon the stereotype.

This is a matter of assumptions. In forming a typification we make certain assumptions – often ideological assumptions – and, if we refuse to allow logic or evidence to challenge these, we run the risk of stereotyping, as we are more prepared to reject evidence than we are to reject our own ideology.

This concept of stereotyping is a particularly important one in relation to discrimination and oppression. Dominance, inequality and injustice are often maintained by reference to stereotypes, for example of disabled people, gay men, lesbians or bisexuals. Stereotypes are therefore powerful tools of ideology, and are thus significant obstacles to the development of anti-discriminatory practice.

In terms of PCS analysis, ideology can be seen as the 'glue' which binds the levels together. It is ideology which acts as the vehicle of 'cultural transmission' between the C and P levels. Similarly, it is ideology which explains how the C level reflects, maintains and protects the S level by presenting social divisions as 'natural' and 'normal' and thus desirable. In short, the relationship between the levels is an *ideological* one, a reflection of the meeting point of the idea of power and the power of ideas.

Before leaving the topic of ideology, it is as well to point out that ideology is not an abstract force unconnected with human actions. Indeed, it is in and through human action that ideology comes into being. It is part of the complex interplay of individual and wider social forces, it is the bridge between the external objective world of social circumstances and the internal subjective world of meaning. As such, it is an *existential* concept, a dimension of human existence rather than an abstract form in its own right (Thompson, 1992a).

The role of language

As ideology involves the communication of ideas, language is a central part of this process. It is therefore important to develop an understanding of the role of language in constructing and maintaining discrimination and oppression. It is a major subject in its own right and so the discussion here is necessarily selective (see Thompson, 2003b for a detailed discussion of the significance of language). I shall focus on just two aspects, firstly the discriminatory nature of some language forms and secondly a clarification of the terminology used in constructing a basis for anti-discriminatory practice.

Many words and expressions have derogatory, or overtly insulting overtones whilst others are more subtle and less obvious in producing a discriminatory effect. For example, the British Sociological Association (BSA) has produced a set of guidelines on anti-sexist language which states: 'When reference to both sexes is intended, a large number of phrases use the word man or other masculine equivalents (e.g. 'father') and a large number of nouns use the suffix 'man', thereby excluding women from the picture we present of the world.' Thus the use of 'masculine' language to refer to both men and women contributes to the 'invisibility' of women and thereby facilitates the persistence of the gender imbalance in terms of status and power. This is 'exclusive' language, as it has the effect of excluding women.

Similarly, the BSA has produced a set of guidelines on anti-racist language indicating which terms are appropriate and which are likely to have racist overtones. However, it is acknowledged that tackling these issues is difficult and far from straightforward:

> The issues are not always clear cut. There is disagreement as to whether some terms are acceptable or not and different political positions are aligned with different terms. Consequently, this guidance can only aim to promote an awareness of the issues in many instances rather than to prescribe or reinforce the use of particular terms.

The debate over terminology and racial discrimination will no doubt continue, and it is likely that a definitive lexicon of anti-racism will remain elusive. Indeed, it is not simply a matter of distinguishing between 'taboo' words and 'OK' words, as in the sense of 'political correctness'. What is needed is not a simple list of proscribed words but, rather, an awareness of, and sensitivity to, the oppressive and discriminatory potential of language. This must be a fundamental part of anti-discriminatory practice, as the tendency to oversimplify language issues stands in the way of recognising, and dealing with, the complexities of the power of language and their role in perpetuating patterns of discrimination and oppression.

Language is also a key aspect of ageism. As I have argued previously:

> Terms such as 'the elderly', 'the old', 'EMI' are commonly used but are, none the less, very dehumanizing – they 'depersonalize' the people to whom they refer; language can also patronize older people through the use of terms such as 'old dear', or by using first names without checking that this is acceptable. . . . Language therefore plays a pivotal role with regard to dignity – it can either enhance it or act as a barrier to its realization.
> (Thompson, 1995a, pp. 11–12)

This passage is a good example of how the C level (culture as embodied in language) has a significant impact on the P level of our day-to-day practice. Furthermore, as Hugman (1994) comments, referring to the work of Featherstone and Hepworth (1990): 'the language which surrounds old age and older people tends not to provide the materials with which to construct a positive identity' (p. 78).

Much the same can be said of the language of disability. Whilst depersonalised terms such as 'the elderly' are frowned upon by the anti-discriminatory movement, so too is the term 'the disabled'. A more appropriate term is 'disabled *people*' or 'people with disabilities' (see Chapter 6).

Language therefore needs to be used sensitively and critically in order to avoid negative connotations. Davis (1988) points out that even officially defined terms can be discriminatory. For example, he distinguishes between the World Health Organisation (WHO, 1980) definitions of impairment and disability (with their individualistic emphasis) and those of The Union of the Physically Impaired Against Segregation (UPIAS) which underline the social nature of disability – the restrictions caused by *social organisation*, rather than the impairment itself (UPIAS, 1976). This will be an important aspect of the discussions in Chapter 6.

Language therefore plays a significant part in the construction and maintenance of discriminatory and oppressive forms of practice. However, it has often been argued that the use of language is secondary to the good intentions of those using these terms. The argument goes: 'If people use such terms in good faith without intending any ill-will towards the groups concerned, surely it is petty to make an issue of the use of such language?'

This seems a reasonable argument on the surface but, when we look at it more closely, the pitfalls become visible. The major point we need to recognise is that language is not simply a reflection of oppression (and thus an innocuous route if paved with good intentions, it could be argued) but actually *constructs* such oppression. Foucault uses the term 'discourse' to refer to the way in which language and other forms of communication act as the vehicle of social processes (see Foucault, 1977, 1979). For example, medical discourse not only reflects the power of the medical profession but actively contributes to constructing, re-enacting and thus perpetuating such power.

Discriminatory language therefore both reflects the discriminatory culture and social structure in which we live, and also contributes to the continuance of such discrimination. Language is not a passive receptacle; it is an active encounter with the social world. Freire (1972) draws a similar conclusion:

> Human existence cannot be silent, nor can it be nourished
> by false words, but only by true words, with which men
> transform the world. To exist, humanly, is to *name* the
> world, to change it. Once named, the world reappears to the
> namers as a problem and requires of them a new *naming*.
> (pp. 60–1)

Language is part of the social world; indeed, it is one of the bridges between the personal and the social and, as such, it cannot be neutral (see Fook, 2002). The language we use either reinforces discrimination through constructing it as 'normal' or contributes, in some small way at least, to undermining the continuance of a discriminatory discourse.

Rojek *et al.* (1988) also stress the importance of language and its discriminatory potential when they argue that, 'the language which social workers are trained to use in order to free clients very often has the effect of imprisoning them anew' (p. 1). This further under-lines the need for a sensitivity to language and a critical approach to the forms of communication we commonly use. Indeed, it is largely for this reason that I shall now move on to clarify some of the key terms used in current attempts to promote anti-discrimina-tory practice. This is not intended as a glossary and is far from comprehensive in its coverage. However, I hope it will lead to a clearer understanding of some of the central issues, and thus make it easier to get to grips with the complexities of this intricate and thorny subject.

Discrimination

Unfair or unequal treatment of individuals or groups based on an actual or perceived difference; prejudicial behaviour acting against the interests of those people who characteristically tend to belong to relatively powerless groups within the social structure (women, ethnic minorities, old or disabled people and members of the work-ing class in general). Discrimination is therefore a matter of social formation as well as individual or group behaviour.

Oppression

Inhuman or degrading treatment of individuals or groups; hardship and injustice brought about by the dominance of one group over another; the negative and demeaning exercise of power. It often involves disregarding the rights of an individual or group and is thus a denial of citizenship. Oppression arises as a result of unfair discrimination – that is, the disadvantages experienced as a result of discrimination have oppressive consequences.

Anti-discriminatory practice

An approach to practice which seeks to reduce, undermine or elim-inate discrimination and oppression, specifically in terms of chal-lenging sexism, racism, ageism and disablism (these terms will be defined in subsequent chapters) and other forms of discrimination or oppression encountered in practice. Social workers occupy posi-tions of power and influence, and so there is considerable scope for discrimination and oppression, whether this be intentional or by default. Anti-discriminatory practice is an attempt to eradicate discrimination and oppression from our own practice and challenge them in the practice of others and the institutional structures in which we operate. In this respect, it is a form of emancipatory practice (Thompson, 2002c).

Equal opportunities

A generic term for various forms of anti-discrimination, particularly with reference to employment-related issues – recruitment, promotion and so on. Implicit in the concept is the notion of *disadvantage* and the need to guard against it – by avoiding disadvantaging certain people (for example, through restrictive employment practices) and by promoting greater access to employment, training and promotion opportunities for members of disadvantaged groups (affirmative action). Equality of opportunity is closely linked to the notion of anti-discrimination and the anti-discrimination legislation (discussed in Chapter 1) which underpins it.

Diversity

A term increasingly being used to emphasise the differences between individuals and across groups *and* the fact that such differences are best seen as assets to be valued and affirmed, rather than as problems to be solved. Diversity and difference are the roots of discrimination, in the sense that it is through the identification of differences that discrimination (and thus oppression) takes place. The 'diversity approach' seeks to tackle discrimination by presenting differences as positives to be benefited from, rather than the basis of negative, unfair discrimination.

Prejudice

An opinion or judgement formed without considering the relevant facts or arguments; a biased and intolerant attitude towards particular people or social groups; an opinion or attitude which is rigidly and irrationally maintained even in the face of strong contradictory evidence or in the persistent absence of supportive evidence; a rigid form of thinking based on stereotypes and discrimination. Although prejudice operates primarily at the P level, it is closely linked with, and informed by, the C and S levels. Prejudices do not occur at random but, rather, reflect particular social divisions and social processes.

Radical social work

An approach to social work which seeks to locate the problems experienced by clients in the wider social context of structured inequalities, poverty, inadequate amenities, discrimination and oppression – to recognise the sociopolitical 'roots' of clients' problems, hence the term 'radical' which means 'at the root'. It sees social work as primarily a political venture, a *struggle* to humanise, as far as possible, the oppressive circumstances to which clients are subject. It is premised on the key notion of *empowerment,* the process of helping clients gain greater control over their lives in whatever ways possible – resources, education, political and self-awareness and so on.

Definitions can, of course, obscure as much as they clarify but the discussions and analyses in subsequent chapters will continue to cast light on these seven terms and related concepts and issues.

Commonalities and differences

There are many common themes across the various forms of oppression. These include:

● prejudice and judgemental attitudes towards particular individuals and/or groups;
● stereotypes;
● the dynamic interplay of the P, C and S levels;
● inequality and the denial of rights;
● power relations; and
● ideological legitimation based on biology.

There are also a number of others which have not been discussed here. For example, the concept of 'hegemony' is applicable across the board. This refers to the ideological dominance of one group over another or over a range of groups. One group, or 'social collectivity' (for example, men, white people, able-bodied people) gain power, status, position, prestige or some other advantage at the expense of other, less socially favoured groups (women, black or disabled people) and continue to maintain such dominance through the power of ideas which reinforce the 'naturalness' of the status quo.

Hegemony is therefore closely linked to the notion of exploitation, although not necessarily in any deliberate or intentional sense. It is also closely linked with ideology for it is primarily through the vehicle of ideology that hegemony operates. Clarke and Cochrane (1998) explain the link between ideology and hegemony when they comment that ideologies:

> try to organize and mobilize elements of common-sense knowledge as part of their world view and in support of the social interests they represent. Thus, dominant social classes will refer to, and make connections with, aspects of common-sense knowledge that reflect and support existing patterns of inequality and which legitimate the economic or political power of these dominant groups. Counter-ideologies will want to build connections with those other elements of common-sense thought that object to or are sceptical about the existing social order. . . . The aim is to ensure that there appears to be no alternative to the vision of society being presented that is capable of winning tacit or active support from people across a wide social spectrum. Gramsci used the term *hegemonic* to describe a political project that achieved these ends.
>
> (p. 33)

Part of the ideological basis of hegemony is the idea of an 'out group', a group of people defined in negative terms and assigned an inferior status. This can be recognised as part of the process of discrimination and oppression and is thus a further commonality.

It is important that social workers are aware of the common threads and are able to respond to them accordingly – through resisting or weakening their influence and softening or preventing their impact. The commonalities are also an important part of avoiding the development of a divisive 'hierarchy of oppressions', as discussed in Chapter 1. Understanding the common themes is a major aspect of fighting the common enemies, those of discrimination and oppression. However, there are also significant differences between the multiple forms of oppression. It would be a mistake, both analytically and tactically, to concentrate exclusively on the commonalities without paying due heed to the important differences.

---

practice focus 2.3

Darren had worked in a day centre for disabled people where he took a keen interest in issues of rights and equality. When he moved to a centre for older people, he expected to be able to continue his work on empowerment and was looking forward to challenging ageism in much the same way as he had tackled disablism in his previous job. However, he was soon to be disappointed as he found that many of the older people showed little or no interest in rights issues. At first, Darren was very worried by this as he felt that he would not be able to achieve any progress in his new job. However, after a little while, he regained his confidence and came to the conclusion that empower- ment was not impossible, but he would have to make adjustments. His experience of dealing with one form of oppression could not be imported wholesale and uncritically into working with people experi- encing another form of oppression.

It is beyond the scope of this book to give a detailed and thorough exposition of the differences and so I shall restrict myself to a small selection by way of illustration of the wider field. Race and gender issues can be contrasted with age issues in at least two ways:

1. In the former cases, people subject to oppression have recourse to the law whereas, in the latter in UK at least, there is no equivalent anti-discrimination legislation (although, at the time of writing, there are plans to develop such a legal framework).
2. The people affected by discrimination on the grounds of age (or disability) are subject to the dangers of 'medicalisation'. That is, old or disabled people are construed as 'ill' (and thus 'invali- dated' Laing, 1967; Laing and Cooper, 1971) in a way which women and black people are generally not.

There are also varying levels of publicity given to the areas and different levels of public awareness of the issues, both within social work in particular and within the wider community at large.

There are also differences in the ways in which racism and sexism are experienced and combated. For example, womanhood is not a totally homogeneous, undifferentiated entity (it intersects with class, race/ethnicity, age and so on). However, it is a much more homogeneous concept than that of race. There is, for example, no consensus as to which groups should be classified as 'black' – or 'Black' with a capital 'B' to emphasise that it is a political, rather than descriptive term (Williams, 1989, p. ix). The BSA guidelines on anti-racist language note, for example, that: '. . . some Asians in Britain object to the use of the word "black" being applied to them and some would argue that it also confuses a number of ethnic groups which should be treated separately'. There is a danger, however, of overemphasising the differences and we should be clear about the need to focus on the commonalities and thus the common steps that can be taken to challenge oppression and fight discrimination.

There is a danger in placing too much emphasis on the disparate elements of oppression and thus failing to see the links between, for example, racism and sexism (Bayne-Smith, 1996) sexism and ageism (Arber and Ginn, 1995) and so on. We can fail to see the patterns and common threads and thereby miss an opportunity for moving forward together as part of a wider anti-discrimination movement. It should also be remembered that the various oppressions are separated out for purposes of analysis and clarity of exposition but are, in fact, dimensions of the same existence. People do not feel oppressions in isolation but, rather, as different but related aspects of what Sartre called 'lived experience' ('le vécu', Sartre, 1976).

This is a point which is particularly worthy of note in relation to the following chapters where the focus of attention falls on a particular form of oppression (beginning in Chapter 3, with sexism). The point again needs to be made that sexism, racism, ageism, disablism and so on are analytical categories and thus part of a wider and deeper social process (that of hegemony, social division and exploitation) rather than distinct and unrelated forms of discrimination.

Although substantially different, quantitatively and qualitatively and in both a historical and contemporary sense, these forms of oppression share enough in common to justify a unified theoretical approach to tackle the relevant issues in each of these areas.

This chapter has contributed towards the task of establishing such a theory base. However, it would be naïve in the extreme to assume that the theoretical tools given here are sufficient for the task of developing a genuinely anti-discriminatory practice. This chapter, and indeed this book as a whole, can only be a beginning, a few relatively small, but none the less important steps in the right direction.

points to ponder

> Can you identify aspects of the culture you were brought up in that have discriminatory connotations (for example, in relation to gender roles)?
> How might these affect the way you practise as a social worker?
> Where would you locate yourself in terms of the structure of society (class and race/ethnicity, for example)?
> Can you identify ways in which the structure of society might affect clients, their circumstances and their problems?
> In what ways might you take these structural factors into consideration in your practice?

Guide to further learning

Social divisions are a major feature of the sociological literature and so a great deal has been written about them. For an introductory overview, see Abercrombie *et al.* (2000) or Giddens (2001). See also Payne (2000). Class in particular has a large literature base. General texts include Crompton (1993) and Devine (1997). Roberts (2001) is particularly clear and helpful. Literature relating specifically to social work includes Jones (1998) and Jones and Novak (1999). Donnison (1998) is also an important text.

PCS analysis is discussed at a more advanced level in Thompson (2003a) and, specifically in relation to older people and anti-ageist practice, in Thompson (1995a) and S. Thompson (2005). Bevan (2002) provides a worked example of PCS analysis in relation to loss and grief issues.

Diversity is discussed briefly in Thompson (2003a) and more fully in Kandola and Fullerton (1998). The importance of language in social work is explored in Parton and O'Byrne (2000) and is further emphasised in Taylor and White (2000). Thompson (2003b) is devoted to an extensive discussion of communication and language and makes frequent reference to issues of discrimination and oppression. In particular, it warns of the dangers of over-simplifying these issues.

An interesting discussion of stereotyping is to be found in Pickering (2001).

Ideology and hegemony are discussed at an introductory level in McLellan (1995). Fook (2002) is a very helpful text in this respect. Thompson (2003b) also contains discussion of these topics.

3 | Gender and sexism

Gender is a fundamental dimension of human experience, revealing an ever-present set of differences between men and women. As Simone de Beauvoir puts it in her classic text:

> In truth, to go for a walk with one's eye open is enough to demonstrate that humanity is divided into two classes of individuals whose clothes, faces, bodies, smiles, gaits, interests and occupations are manifestly different. Perhaps these differences are superficial, perhaps they are destined to disappear. What is certain is that they do most obviously exist.
> (1972, pp. 14–15)

But it is not simply a matter of difference, of interesting and benign diversity. Abercrombie *et al.* (2000) argue that issues of gender (and gender inequality) now occupy a central place in sociological discussion:

> Gender is the social aspect of the differentiation of the sexes. Sociological discussion in this area recognizes that social rather than biological processes are the key to understanding the position of women (and of men) in society. Notions that a woman's biology, such as her capacity to bear children, determined the shape of her life have been replaced by complex debates as to how different social processes interact to produce a great variety of patterns of gender relations. Emphasis has shifted towards understanding the diversity of the social practices which constitute gender in different nations, classes and generations.
> (p. 193)

This notion of 'not just different but unequal' introduces the concept of *sexism*: inequality, discrimination and oppression on the grounds of gender – in short, male hegemony. But what exactly is sexism? What are its constituent parts and what impact does it have on social work? These are important questions and open up a number of significant issues which can be seen as central to the theory and practice of social work. It is therefore important to clarify the basis and dimensions of sexism and it is with this task that we begin.

What is sexism?

A longstanding but none the less apt definition of sexism is that of:

> a deep-rooted, often unconscious system of beliefs, attitudes and institutions in which distinctions between people's intrinsic worth are made on the grounds of their sex and sexual roles
> (in Bullock and Stallybrass, 1977, p. 571).

The reference to 'beliefs, attitudes and institutions' indicates that sexism operates at all three levels: *P*, *C* and *S*. The beliefs and actions of individuals, the cultural values and norms and the institutional or structural patterns all tend to display an inherent bias against women, producing a situation in which women:

- earn less than men and are more vulnerable to unemployment;
- tend to be concentrated in less prestigious and less secure forms of employment;
- do considerably more housework than men; and
- experience substantial inequalities in relation to housing, welfare benefits and health (see Abercrombie *et al.*, 2000).

Sexism is closely linked to the concept of *patriarchy*, literally 'the law of the father'. Weber (1947) used this concept to refer to the dominance of men within the family. Its use, however, has been extended to refer to the dominance of men in general, as reflected in the distribution of power in society. Millett (1971) captured this point well when she argued that: 'the military, industry, technology, universities, science, political office, and finance – in short, every avenue of power within the society, including the coercive force of the police, is entirely in male hands' (p. 25). Perhaps 'entirely' is an overstatement but it none the less remains the case that power at a structural level is predominantly a male phenomenon.

Sexism is therefore a set of beliefs, practices and institutional structures which reinforces, and is reinforced by, patriarchy. The two concepts are mutually supportive. In particular, patriarchal ideology promotes the traditional model of the family, with the male breadwinner as provider, head of the household and defender of his territory, the wife and mother as nurturer and carer and their dependent children whom they socialise into following in the footsteps of the appropriate role model – boys to grow up like daddy, girls to grow up like mummy.

In fact, the links between patriarchy and the nuclear family are so great that the term 'familial ideology' has been coined to refer to the ideas base which seeks to legitimate these social relations. Helen Lentell (1988) describes the concept in the following terms:

> Familial ideology in our society asserts that the co-resident nuclear family is a universal and desirable way to live, and that the prevailing sexual division of labour, in which the woman is housewife and mother and primarily located within the private world of the family and the man is the wage-earner and breadwinner located in the public world of work, is universal and normatively desirable.
> (p. 46)

From this she goes on to depict the family as: 'the ideological site in which gender differences are constructed' (p. 46). The emphasis on the nuclear family as 'normal' thus defines other family forms as 'deviant' and undesirable. The pressure to conform to sex-appropriate roles within the patriarchal family is both a major part of the socialisation process and a significant aspect of sexism.

A further constituent part of sexism, as referred to above by Lentell, is that of the sexual division of labour. Work tasks, both within and outside the home, tend to follow a gender-specific pattern. Women tend to be involved primarily in the domestic sphere of housework and childcare, while men are more closely associated with the public sphere of paid work and political life (Lister, 1997). The allocation of pay, status, leisure time and other rewards shows a distinct bias in favour of men at the expense of women.

Rowbotham (1973) was amongst the first to link this to capitalism and the marxist notion of men as *producers* (that is, workers producing material wealth) and women as *reproducers* (that is, childbearers and nurturers of the workforce). However, Pascall

(1997), while recognising the contribution of this marxist analysis to social policy, bemoans the overemphasis on production and thus relative neglect of reproduction. She therefore argues for a greater understanding of the role of the family in the sexual division of labour. In particular, there is a need for greater attention to be paid to the ways in which the Welfare State reinforces familial ideology and the sexism inherent within it. Pascall (1997) comments:

> Support for the breadwinner/dependant form of family has entrenched the dependency of women in marriage as well as the difficulties of living outside such families, of forming different kinds of relationships, and of leaving particular unhappy marriages.
> (p. 25)

This is an important point and will be relevant to the discussions below of the interrelationships between social policy, social work and sexism/patriarchy.

---

practice focus 3.1

Frank was an experienced social worker who specialised in family work. He took great pride in his work and tried very hard to make sure that he did a good job. He was therefore very disconcerted when one of the families he worked with made a complaint against him. A single mother had complained about his 'old-fashioned' attitude towards women and his apparent disapproval of single-parent families without a traditional 'breadwinner'. This came as a complete surprise to Frank and forced him to rethink his views about women and families and the assumptions he had been making.

A further aspect of sexism relates specifically to sexuality and the implicit (or sometimes explicit) assumption that male sexuality is a strong and 'difficult to resist' force. This assumption is then often used, in part at least, to justify or excuse male aggression against women. Weeks (1986) refers to this as the 'Biological Imperative' and it is yet another example of a biological argument being used as a basis for legitimating social relations, power and dominance. Weeks comments:

The idea that there are differences between peoples is not in itself dangerous. What is peculiar about sexuality is that certain differences have been seen as so fundamental that they become divisions and even antagonisms. At best, there is the argument that though men and women may be different they can still be equal. At worst, assumptions about the forceful nature of the sexual drive have been used to legitimize male domination over women.
(p. 47)

This 'dominance' can be seen to go a step further and emerge as sexual violence. The seriousness of violence against women is something that has not yet been fully appreciated in social work (Mullender, 1996; Radford, 2001). For a variety of reasons, including the less than helpful response of the law enforcement agencies, a major proportion of these incidents go unreported and do not therefore appear in the crime statistics (see also Mama, 1989b, for a study which focuses particularly on the experiences of black women).

These issues are also relevant to our understanding of, and response to, child sexual abuse as will become clear in the next section concerning the implications of sexism.

Patriarchy, then, is one of the *structural* dimensions of society which is strongly associated with the sexist *culture* which demeans and disempowers women and thus sows the seeds for the cultivation of *personal* prejudice in terms of both attitudes and behaviour. The taken-for-granted nature of sexism at an individual level thereby promotes and protects the patriarchal structure. Thus, sexist ideology keeps the wheels of oppression turning.

But what impact does this have on social work? In what ways does social work fit into this picture? It is these issues I shall now address.

The implications for social work

One of the major implications for social work is the need to rethink radically the male-dominated and masculine-orientated basis of traditional social work theory. As Mullender (1997) comments:

It is not possible to understand the personal or social world without taking a gendered perspective. We are not able as professionals to intervene appropriately or justly in people's

lives unless we perceive the ways in which women are disadvantaged by an unequal dispersal of power, and in which both men and women are constrained by over-rigid and falsely dichotomized role and relationship expectations.
(p. 42)

Sexism raises many issues for social workers seeking to develop anti-discriminatory practice. While this text cannot address all of them, we can at least begin to explore some of them.

Social work operates at the boundaries of 'normality' and 'deviance' (Pearson, 1975) and so it is important that we recognise that our conceptions of normality are 'gendered'. That is, we need to become sensitive to the gender issues involved in the notion of 'normal'. For example, the concept of a 'normal' family, as commonly used, is likely to be a patriarchal family; 'normal' child-rearing practices are also gender-specific – when we speak of 'good-enough parenting', we are, more often than not, talking of 'good enough mothering', father remaining relatively invisible (Hanmer and Statham, 1999).

It is therefore an easy step from taking 'normality' for granted to reinforcing stereotypical expectations of men and women. Carlen and Worrall (1987) comment on the expectations of a 'normal' woman:

Being a normal woman means coping, caring, nurturing and sacrificing self-interest to the needs of others. It also means being intuitively sensitive to those needs without them being actively spelt out. It means being *more than man,* in order to support and embrace Man. On the other hand, femininity is characterised by lack of control and dependence. Being a normal woman means needing protection . . . It means being childlike, incapable, fragile and capricious. It is being *less than man* in order to serve and defer to Man.
(p. 3)

A clear implication for social workers, therefore, is the need to develop a *critical* approach which questions and challenges everyday assumptions and thereby gets underneath the ideological gloss of 'normality'.

The converse of this situation also applies. That is, not only can social work be seen to reinforce sexism if a critical approach is not adopted, but sexism can also be seen to be a major factor underpinning many of the problems social workers are asked to tackle. The discrimination and oppression inherent in sexism are, of course, not without cost to the women concerned.

Poverty is one example of this, as women have more restricted access to resources than men. This produces a situation which has come to be known as the 'feminisation of poverty' (Spicker, 2001), as so many women are reliant upon either men or state benefits for financial support: in 1995, 70 per cent of the world's poorest people were women (United Nations, 1996, cited in Bryson, 1999). A related concept is that of 'secondary poverty', the fact that women, even in relatively financially secure households, are often starved of resources – the man of the household taking a disproportionate amount of the family income to follow his leisure interests or other pursuits (Bryson, 1999).

Glendinning (1987) makes a similar point when she argues that:

> women bear the burden of managing poverty on a day-to-day basis. Whether they live alone or with a partner, on benefits or low earnings, it is usually women who are responsible for making ends meet and for managing the debts which result when they don't. Indeed, the lower the household income, the more likely it is that this responsibility will rest with women.
> (p. 60)

The links between poverty and the problems social work clients experience have been clearly established and are well documented. The fact that women constitute the majority of social work clients adds weight to the 'feminisation of poverty' thesis and also underlines the linkages between gender, oppression and social work (Langan and Day, 1992).

Poverty has also been associated with mental health problems and with depression in particular. Depression is also significant in terms of gender: women are heavily over-represented as far as this disorder is concerned (Busfield, 1996). This is relevant for social workers at two levels:

1. Specifically in terms of mental health social work and the significance of gender for this type of work; and
2. More generally in relation to a range of social work situations in which depression plays a part: childcare (including child protection); loss and grief; work with older people and so on.

Brown and Harris (1978) undertook what has come to be recognised as a classic study of the incidence of depression in women and sought to uncover the underlying factors. They were surprised by the relatively high frequency of depression amongst women, especially in urban areas. A number of 'vulnerability factors' were identified, for example, a low level of intimacy with one's husband/partner and these, in turn, tend to lead to low self-esteem. The low self-esteem of many women therefore leaves them much more prone to depression.

But Brown and Harris emphasised that these are sociological factors, to do with the position of women in society, rather than purely psychological. They comment that depression is not only relatively common but also:

> fundamentally related to social values since it arises in a context of hopelessness consequent upon the loss of important sources of reward or positive value. A woman's own social milieu and the broader social structure are critical because they influence the way in which she *thinks* about the world and thus the extent of this hopelessness; they determine what is valued, as well as what is lost and how often, and what resources she has to face the loss.
> (p. 270)

Although Brown and Harris did not refer specifically to sexism, it is clear that the same issues are applicable. Indeed, PCS analysis is highly compatible with their work – the psychological level being embedded within the wider cultural milieu and social structure.

Reference was made above to child protection work, and once again gender issues can be seen to be relevant here too. Parton and Parton (1989) refer to the concept of 'dangerous *families*', but argue that, in reality, the focus is on 'dangerous *mothers*'. Mothers are seen to have primary responsibility for children (this is a key part of patriarchal ideology) and are therefore held responsible when things go wrong. Even when the mother herself is not the abuser, she is deemed to be culpable by virtue of the fact that she has failed to protect the child. Parenting is seen primarily as mothering. Poor parenting, neglect or abuse are therefore construed mainly as a failure on the part of women.

Despite the fact that the majority of sexual abuse cases involve male perpetrators, the focus remains on the role of the mother. It is her role to protect the child in general and this includes protection from a 'driven and uncontrollable' male sexuality (MacLeod and Saraga, 1988, quoted in Hudson, 1989). Implicit blame therefore tends to be attributed to the female's 'failure to protect', rather than the male's proclivity to abuse. Saraga (1993) captures these points well in the following passage:

> If abuse is seen as something wrong in the family, then deci-
> sions about 'protection' of the child focus on whether or not
> the family is or can be helped to become a safe place, or
> whether the child should be removed from home. In practice,
> much of the discussion focuses on the mother's role, in
> particular asking whether she 'knew' about the abuse,
> whether she 'colluded' and whether she 'failed to protect' her
> child. By conveying a meaning that she *should* have known,
> the intervention may serve to strengthen her denial. In
> contrast, a practice influenced by a feminist perspective
> emphasizes the responsibility of the individual abuser, and
> therefore aims to remove him rather than the child from the
> home, so that the child can remain in the non-abusing part
> of the family. It also recognizes that the mother has herself
> suffered a loss and betrayal, that she may need help in her
> own right to accept what has happened in order to be able
> to make decisions, and to support her child.
> (p. 77)

The prevalence of the viewpoint Saraga is rejecting here is a clear example of the strength and depth of the influence of patriarchal ideology. Women are cast as primary carers and so, in situations of child abuse, they find themselves in a 'no-win' situation. If they are the abusers (and we shall come on to discuss this below), they have failed as mothers and thus failed as people. Where it is the menfolk who are the abusers, the women have failed in their duty to protect (and, in the eyes of some, also failed to 'keep their man happy'). Men, by contrast, tend not to be charged with a failure to protect and, even where they are the perpetrator, some allowance is often made for their behaviour, based on essentialist notions of male aggression and unrestrained sexuality being 'natural' (the 'Biological Imperative').

Physical abuse of children has often been described as an abuse of parental power, or the power of adults over children in general. In sexual abuse, the gender dimension is more apparent as the choice of a child as a sexual partner can be seen as an example of male sexuality as a form of power (see, for example, Lees, 1997) and sexual abuse as an abuse of such power. Indeed, in 1989, Corby argued that it was only the efforts of feminists that had brought the problems of child sexual abuse to light and he referred to Rush (1981) who had contended that issues such as child sexual abuse and child pornography were not being tackled because men in power did not take them seriously.

Ong (1985) also made an important contribution in discussing the concept of 'wonderful children' which refers to the tendency to idealise children and concentrate on the positive aspects of bringing them up. The pressures, stresses and pains are paid scant attention and tend to be 'swept under the carpet', thus placing immense additional pressure on women to conform to the idealised norm of a happy, contented mother. In reporting her study of mothers and children at a family centre, she comments:

> [Mothers] are often feeling guilty that they cannot perceive their children in positive ways, and fail to see that this is largely related to factors outside their personal power. Taking women's own experiences as a point of departure, investigating the limitations in their mothering context, can probably instigate more positive change than insisting that all children are wonderful.
> (p. 105)

The common ideological view of children as 'wonderful' is therefore an additional source of oppression for women.

---

practice focus 3.2

Liz had been keen to become a mother, even though she was only 17. However, she had not thought through the consequences and was not prepared for what it would entail. Her boyfriend, Steve, was horrified to find she was pregnant and very quickly disappeared from the scene. Liz's parents were very annoyed with her and offered her only very limited support. Within six months of giving birth, Liz felt under immense pressure with the very limited support and she became increasingly withdrawn and uncommunicative. The health visitor was sufficiently concerned to make a referral to Social Services.

A further implication of sexism for social work is the casting of women in a caring role. In 1983 Finch and Groves presented an argument for seeing community care of disabled, mentally disordered or elderly people as primarily care by the family which, in turn, amounts to care by women, and there is little to suggest that this has changed. As Finch (1984) commented:

> In recent years, feminists have increasingly insisted on making explicit the true meaning of 'community care' as it applies to elderly or handicapped [sic] people, i.e. for community read family, and for family read women, and have rightly been suspicious of attempts to increase such 'community' provision, seeing them as part of the political agenda of getting women out of the labour market and back into the home, to provide unpaid health and welfare services for members of their own family.
> (p. 6)

There is therefore a clear need to avoid making the assumption that women's roles as carers are 'natural' or that men are not 'cut out' for caring. As Fisher (1994) argues, the assumption that men will find caring difficult:

> allows service providers to cite the carer's masculine gender as evidence of the need for service. It allows the myth of the incompetent man to be reproduced, and to be imposed on male carers and on care receivers.
> (p. 673)

Patriarchal ideology is therefore very significant in relation to caring roles and something that we should be very wary of reinforcing.

The Equal Opportunities Commission established quite some time ago that reinforcing the caring role of women is a financially more attractive option than institutional care or care based on comprehensive state services (EOC, 1982). The report discussed the narrowing of opportunities (for example, for paid employment) experienced by those women who act as carers. The ideological assumption that caring is primarily a female role therefore has profound and far-reaching implications for women in terms of restricted opportunities or life-chances. The discriminatory and oppressive impact of this assumption is therefore of major proportions.

This is a good example of how the familial ideology implicit in social policy manifests itself. Whilst the family as a set of living arrangements has a number of advantages, we should not forget:

1. Men derive more benefits from family life than do women. For example, the statistics for suicide attempts show that marital status is very relevant for both men and women – but in opposing ways: the rates for women are *higher* if married but for men the reverse is true as married status indicates a *lower* rate. The clear implication here is that marriage offers more positives and fewer negatives for men than is the case for women.
2. Traditional family roles and the patriarchal assumptions on which they are based, can have a profoundly alienating effect on women by restricting life-chances, imposing high and often unrealistic expectations in terms of undertaking caring duties and so on.
3. As Dallos and Sapsford (1997), amongst others, have argued, the family is a potentially very destructive institution and, given that women act as the lynchpin of the family in the domestic sphere, it is likely that they will suffer the greatest effects and, indeed, be allocated the greater share of the blame. This is particularly significant for social work, operating as it does, at the intersection of conflicting forces, within the family and the wider social sphere.

Social workers therefore need to adopt a critical stance towards the family, as the traditional social policy eulogy of the family conceals a large number of patriarchal assumptions which fuel the sexism which oppresses women by chaining them to the domestic sphere of caring and nurturing. But social work also needs to look at itself to see sexism as, for example, in the sexual division of labour to be found within social work organisations. Women form the majority of social work clients and social work staff, and yet they form a relatively small minority of senior managers (Coulshed *et al.*, 2006).

Hanmer and Statham (1999) argue that women managers face additional pressures in so far as they have to operate within a predominantly masculine environment and ethos in which leadership skills can be seen as 'unfeminine'. Women managers are also expected to prove themselves to justify their place in the 'man's world' of management, and this, of course, adds to the pressures of coping with the demands of the job (Grimwood and Popplestone, 1993 – see also Colgan and Ledwith, 1996).

The Social Services Inspectorate report on women in Social Services (SSI, 1991) argues that there are many reasons for the under-representation of women in management, not least of which is the stereotyping of women implicit in sexist ideology:

> Women may . . . experience the insidious effects of gender stereotyping, which will not have been such a noticeable feature of their earlier professional careers, when to be a woman was the norm. Examples such as the assumption that a woman is at the meeting to take the minutes, that she will not be able to understand financial matters . . . and she may be considered 'humourless' when she fails to laugh at, or draws attention to, sexist comments.
> (p. 27)

Social work agencies are very clearly not immune from the workings of patriarchy and, indeed, very much reflect them. Occupational segregation in social work is based on a 'sexual division of labour', with women occupying the majority of lower status, lower paid jobs whilst men occupy the majority of more highly paid, higher status posts (Coulshed et al., 2006).

This has major implications for attempts to develop anti-sexist practice. It needs to be recognised that such endeavours involve 'swimming against the tide' within a masculine-dominated organisational structure and ethos. And it is this which prompts Dominelli and McLeod (1989) to argue that it is necessary for women to seek support – from like-minded colleagues and managers, trade unions and politicians – if the marginalisation of women is to be countered. Change must therefore take place at an organisational as well as individual level (Vince, 1996).

There are, of course, very many other implications for social work deriving from sexism but space does not permit a more extensive exposition of the issues. However, I hope the examples given here have raised awareness sufficiently for readers to pursue other issues through further reading and discussion.

The question of how we take forward anti-sexist practice is of course a major one and follows on from the discussion here. However, before tackling these issues, we need to be clear about the contribution of feminist theory to this area of social work. In short, it would be unwise to begin to address practice issues without first exploring the theory base – the theoretical formulations of a now well-established tradition of feminist thought. There is now a clear basis for the further development of anti-sexist practice as the emergence of a specifically feminist school of social work has shown (see Langan and Day, 1992). It is therefore important to understand at least the basics of feminist theory.

The feminist response

Williams (1989) presents an account of six different forms of feminism and draws out some of the similarities and differences. This indicates that there is no one consistent and uniform feminism, no simple consensus on the factors underlying male domination and the strategies required to tackle these.

However, this is not to say that there are no common themes or points of agreement. Indeed, they all share a focus on the critique of patriarchy and the need to establish a fairer society in which women are no longer marginalised, alienated and pushed into secondary roles. They also share the belief that 'the personal is political'. This has several levels of meaning:

1. The domestic private sphere also contributes to the wider public and political sphere. For example, housework and child care are not marginal to the economy but do, in fact, play a key role in maintaining the workings of economic structures and processes.
2. The personal sphere is one dominated by issues of power. Power is not simply a matter of macro structures relating to large-scale social issues; it also revolves around personal relationships, identity and other such microstructural aspects of social life.
3. The family is the locus of political struggle. Power, conflict and domination are common aspects of family life. In particular, the power of men over women manifests itself most clearly in the family home in terms of the sexual division of labour, the allocation of leisure time and so on.
4. Gender is *socially constructed* (that is, it hinges on the social significance attached to the differences between men and women), rather than biologically determined. Gender therefore has wider social and political connotations.

5. The oppression of women, and the problems they experience arising from this, are not only 'private troubles' but also 'public issues' (Mills, 1970).
6. Personal problems have their roots in political structures and political structures are reinforced by a particular form of personal relations (patriarchy).

Feminism therefore seeks to:

1. *Politicise the personal*: to draw attention to the political nature and basis of the alienation and oppression of women; and
2. *Personalise the political*: to engage women in the collective political struggle for equality of opportunity and equal rights.

The latter is, of course, premised on the heightened awareness achieved by the former. How this struggle should be taken forward is the subject of fierce debate and will no doubt continue to be for some time yet.

The early form of feminism has been labelled 'liberal feminism' and its basic tenets continue to be adhered to by a number of theorists and activists. The emphasis in liberalism is on the individual (Coates, 1990). Individuals are expected to attain differing levels of achievement within social life and the marketplace. This is felt to be natural and desirable provided that no individual or group of individuals is unfairly disadvantaged. And this is where liberal feminism comes in – women are felt to be handicapped in competing for jobs, status, power and so on as a result of sexism.

Liberal feminism therefore sees the way forward as a combination of campaigning for equal opportunities generally, educating people about the problems of discrimination and generally allowing a fairer basis on which women can compete, on an individual basis, with men. Change is seen as gradual, incremental and based on specific targets for reform.

The liberal feminist focus is, in terms of PCS analysis, very much at the P level, the personal or individual. And it is this which has been the major source of criticism of this approach. The individualism inherent in liberal feminism is castigated for failing to take account of the wider aspects, particularly the structural nature of power relations and the institutional, rather than personal, sources of discrimination and oppression. It is seen as rather a naïve approach which tinkers with superficial aspects of the problem rather than tackling the social and political roots. This is sometimes expressed in comical (but none the less serious) terms as 'rearranging the deckchairs on the *Titanic*', that is, maintaining a blinkered view of a structurally based problem.

However, we should not dismiss liberal feminism altogether. It is more helpful to see it as not going far enough, rather than going in the wrong direction. The need, therefore, is not to reject liberal feminism, but rather to transcend it. Indeed, liberal feminists could argue that they have achieved significant steps forward in terms of anti-discrimination legislation and a higher level of awareness of gender inequality whilst more structurally based approaches have achieved little or nothing. This is an important argument for anti-sexist social work and one to which I shall return below.

An alternative perspective is that of radical feminism. By contrast with liberalism, radical feminism focuses on underlying structural and power issues which are seen to hinge on the key concept of *patriarchy*. In radical feminism the dominance of men is seen as a historical constant, a ubiquitous feature of male-dominated relations. Regardless of the type of society – capitalist, pre-capitalist, communist or whatever – men are everywhere to be found in positions of power, including central and local government, economic institutions, the judiciary, the professions and so on.

Crowley (1992) makes apt comment when she argues that:

Sociology has analysed a wide range of institutional aspects of the family, including the organization of the household economy, the consumption, work and leisure activities of women and men, intersexual relations and intrafamily dynamics. However, woman's place in the family – a factor which links these aspects of the family together – has been assumed to be 'given' and not to require a sociological explanation. Thus, Durkheim, for example, noted that while 'man is almost entirely the product of society', woman is 'to a far greater extent the product of nature' (Durkheim, 1952, p. 385). Such an ideology not only makes women's labour in the private sphere appear to be natural, it also strips it of its status as *labour,* because women's work in the family is separated from the public domain of waged work. Consequently, a polarized view of the division between women and men has emerged as a division between non-work and work, and between the natural and the social. (pp. 71–2)

This assumed natural or biological dimension of women's oppression is a key part of radical feminism. It emphasises the part played by reproduction and the family structures and ideology that have been constructed around the notion of women as primarily mother figures thus allowing men to take up the powerful father role (hence the word *patriarchy*).

The strength of the radical perspective is that it recognises the structural dimension of women's oppression and therefore goes much further than the liberal approach which would leave existing power structures relatively untouched. Radical feminism, as the name implies, identifies the need to tackle the problems *at the root,* to redress the power balance between men and women, and this cannot be done by piecemeal reform alone. A more comprehensive programme of social change is called for.

The weakness of this approach is its ahistorical nature. It sees the dominance of men as universal – both across cultures and through history. Thus it has been criticised for placing too much emphasis on the biological underpinnings of sexism and not enough on historical, sociopolitical factors. This leads Walby (1990) to comment as follows:

> The main problems that critics have raised about radical feminism are a tendency to essentialism, to an implicit or explicit biological reductionism, and to a false universalism which cannot understand historical change or take sufficient account of divisions between women based on ethnicity and class.
> (p. 3)

Marxist-feminism – or socialist feminism as it is often called – shares radical feminism's emphasis on the structural and power base of the oppression of women. However, unlike the radical approach marxist-feminism focuses not on the biological roots of sexism but rather its historical and political roots.

Marxist-feminism sees patriarchy as a structure which supports and reinforces capitalism. The family is seen as a microcosm of wider society in which women represent the proletariat (the exploited class) and men the bourgeoisie (the exploiters) (Engels, 1976/1844). A central part of this is the sexual division of labour, as discussed earlier in this chapter. Men are socialised into the role of workers in the public sphere – *the producers* – whilst women are socialised into the roles of wives and mothers in the private sphere – *the reproducers*. This arrangement is well suited to capitalism as it produces a workforce which is 'serviced' from within the family. In addition, it provides a 'reserve army of labour', a secondary (female) workforce which can be recruited when the economy expands or in exceptional circumstances (for example, men going off to war) and dispensed with when they are no longer required. This is facilitated by the fact that women tend to be located lower down the occupational hierarchy (Bryson, 1999).

Marxist-feminism recognises the dual oppressions of capitalism (related to class) and patriarchy (related to gender) and the interrelationship between the two. As Williams (1989) puts it: 'there can be no socialism without women's liberation, and no women's liberation without socialism' (p. 57). The marxist version of feminism seeks to locate patriarchy within the context of a materialist analysis. That is, patriarchy is not simply a reflection of biological differences between men and women. Rather, it is closely related to the production of material life – that is, the economic base.

This link with the economy is precisely one of the strong points of marxist-feminism. It succeeds in relating the power of men over women to that of the capitalist class over the working class.

This emphasis on class is perhaps also its main weakness. The main focus of explanation is the economic base and the class divisions on which it rests. This leads to a relative weakness in terms of explaining the dominance of men over women in non-capitalist societies, for example, agrarian societies.

In recent years a further approach to feminism has become more firmly established, namely postmodernist feminism. This approach follows postmodernist thought in challenging the notion of fixed identities. It argues the case for seeing gender identities as socially constructed, rather than biologically fixed – see Waugh (1998) for further discussion.

There are, of course, other forms of feminism which have something to offer to an understanding of women's oppression. But what is clear is that there is no one right answer, no definitive feminist school of thought. The debates and struggles continue and, from a social work point of view, the positive thing to note is that the issues are now more firmly established on the professional agenda than ever before.

The approaches to feminism are not static and fixed. Literature on this subject continues to be published. And, what is perhaps most significant is that there is now a growing body of literature on feminism and social welfare – see the 'Guide to further learning' section below.

Sexism and men

There are two aspects to the question of men and sexism: first, what impact does sexism have on men? And second, what part can men play in undermining, reducing or eliminating sexism?

Whilst the actions and attitudes of men are often a significant source of pressure and difficulty for women as a result of the potent and far-reaching influence of sexist ideology, it cannot be said that sexism is unproblematic for men. There are clearly many ways in which men do benefit from the power and privilege invested in them by patriarchy. However, it must also be recognised – and this is a very important potential source of change – that men also suffer as a result of sexism (although clearly not to the same extent or depth as women, see Thompson, 1995b). The negative impact of sexism on men can be seen to include the following elements:

- certain emotions are regarded as feminine and thus 'off limits' to many men (Jansz, 2000);
- many men die as a result of not seeking medical help in the early stages of a life-threatening illness (see O'Brien, 1990);
- many people die or are injured as a result of ritualised displays of masculinity – high-speed car chases, for example;
- many men are drawn into a life of crime because, in part at least, they are misguidedly expressing their masculinity;
- divorced fathers are far less likely to gain custody of their children; and
- men, like women, can feel alienated and disaffected as a result of culturally defined gender role expectations and the limitations they impose.

Nelson (1990) uses the dehumanisation inherent in sexism as the basis of an argument for men adopting a pro-feminist stance in opposing sexism. As Nelson puts it, the aim is not to 'let men off the hook'. It is, rather, to recognise that anti-sexism is a battle to be fought not only by women but also by men, partly for their own emotional emancipation and partly for humanitarian reasons as a step towards the dissolution of oppressive structures and practices. It would be naïve indeed to assume that men would readily give up the advantages of patriarchy but this should not deter us from seeing the benefits of anti-sexism for both women and men. As Segal (1999) comments:

> Why feminism? Because its most radical goal, both personal and collective, has yet to be realized: a world which is a better place not just for some women, but for all women. In what I call a socialist feminist vision, that would be a far better world for boys and men, as well.
> (p. 232)

Men therefore have a part to play in furthering the cause of anti-sexism. A major aspect of this is the need to become sensitive to the part we play in reproducing sexist structures and cultural patterns in and by our actions and attitudes. In short, both men and women need to be aware of how their actions (the P level) can avoid falling into the trap of reinforcing and reproducing the sexism inherent in the C and S levels – and, indeed, can even go so far as challenging those patterns and structures.

---

practice focus 3.3

Pearlene found working in a male-dominated team quite trying at times. She grew tired of some of the comments and sexist assumptions that were commonly made. She did not complain about this situation, however, until one particularly difficult day when she felt the need to express her anger. Some of the men in the team became very defensive but, to her great surprise and relief, two of her male colleagues were very supportive indeed and made strenuous efforts to rid the team of its sexist overtones and tendencies. She recognised that men too had a part to play in challenging sexism.

Towards anti-sexist practice

Although there is a growing body of literature on anti-sexist theory and policy, this is unlikely to have an impact unless it is put into practice. It is therefore necessary to focus on some of the ways in which anti-sexist practice can be made a reality. Of course, there can be no single 'formula' approach to putting anti-sexist theory into practice, but identifying some broad principles can hopefully help us move in the right direction.

1. The aim of social work intervention is empowerment, *not* adjustment. The social work task should not be to help women to adjust to their 'rightful' place in the family but rather to assist them in gaining the power to overcome or challenge the oppression they experience. The personal is, after all, political.

2. An important, indeed major, part of this is the need to avoid stereotypical assumptions. We should not assume, for example, that the male is the head of the household and the primary decision maker in a two-parent family. If we are not careful, assessing family dynamics can be reduced to jumping to sexist conclusions.

3. Similarly, in child care cases, in addition to focusing on the child(ren), work should be directed towards *parents* rather than simply mothers. If not, we run the risk of 'mother-blaming' and reinforcing the notion that women carry the primary responsibility for the family.

4. The sexist implications of the notion of 'community care' need to be addressed. This entails resisting the pressure to push women into caring roles. Sexist ideology leads us to believe that it is 'natural' for women to be carers and this can, unless we guard against it, allow us to ignore or marginalise the intense pressures which can be inherent in the caring role.

5. Familial ideology reinforces sexism by emphasising the positives of family life and playing down the negatives. Social workers are likely to be well aware of the destructive capabilities of families, but may none the less be seduced by familial ideology into uncritically promoting the value of the family. Social work practice needs to be based on a balanced view of the family which recognises both its strengths and its weaknesses.

6. Clients too are strongly influenced by familial ideology in particular and sexist ideology in general. Whilst the primary task of social work is not the dissolution of sexism, consciousness raising is often necessary to help service users understand how sexism may be contributing to their problems or acting as a barrier to the solution of their problems. This parallels the radical social work principle of helping people recognise the political basis of many of the problems commonly experienced (poverty, bad housing, alienation and so on).

7. It has been argued that social workers often portray women in unduly negative terms as 'helpless' or 'not coping' (Rojek *et al.*, 1988, p. 93) in order to gain additional resources for them. This tactic has the effect of producing enforced dependency and is therefore one to be avoided.

8. Women are 'invisible' within a male-dominated society in so far as their achievements and contributions are rarely given due credit. Social workers need to avoid this trap and appropriately value women, their thoughts, feelings and work. At a micro level social work can contribute to enhanced self-esteem for women clients (and staff) and at a macro level play at least a small part in the breaking down of the sexist devaluation of women.

9. Sexual harassment is also an important issue: 'Unwelcome sexual comments, looks, actions, suggestions or physical contact can cause great distress to women and damage confidence, job performance and promotion prospects' (SSI, 1991, p. 53). This can be applied to both women colleagues and clients. Although much sexual harassment is unintentional, based on an insensitivity to women's needs and feelings (and thus a reflection of cultural assumptions about women as sexual objects), it is none the less oppressive (Thompson, 2000c). Anti-sexist social work must challenge intentional forms of harassment and develop sufficient sensitivity to avoid unintentional forms.

10. Anti-sexist practice involves challenging dominant discriminatory attitudes, values, practices and structures. It entails 'problematising' – that is, taking everyday, apparently unproblematic matters and showing just how problematic they are, highlighting just how discriminatory and oppressive

they really are. This includes Berger's (1966) notion of 'debunking' or Mills's (1970) 'sociological imagination'. In short, it amounts to questioning assumptions about men and women in society and involves adopting a *critical* approach.

There are many more points and examples which could be given to build on these basics. Indeed, it should be recognised that sexism is so pervasive and so deeply ingrained in society in general and social work in particular that we should develop as extensive a repertoire as possible of strategies for promoting anti-sexist practice (Hanmer and Statham, 1999).

---

points to ponder

➤ Consider your own gender. How might the way you have been brought up as a woman or a man influence your practice as a social worker?

➤ Can you identify any ways in which gender can be a key factor in the problems social workers attempt to deal with?

➤ The majority of policy makers and senior managers are men. What difference might this make in relation to how social work services are delivered?

➤ Sexist stereotypes can be very damaging. Can you identify a number of common stereotypical assumptions about men and women?

➤ How might you ensure that you avoid relying on such stereotypes?

Guide to further learning

Mullender (1997) is a very good short introductory account. Langan and Day (1992) provide a very good analysis of a wide range of issues relating to gender and social work, as do Gruber and Stefanov (2002). Grimwood and Popplestone (1993) address gender in relation to management in a social care context, while Wilson (2003) explores gender and organisational behaviour. Elliot (1996) discusses gender and the family, as does Featherstone (2004). Bell (1993) relates the theories of Michel Foucault to gender. This is not a straightforward or introductory text but it is an important one.

Bernard and Meade (1993) provide a very illuminating account of women, and old age, as do Arber and Ginn (1995), while Busfield (1996) explores the gender dimensions of mental health problems. Morris (1991) addresses disability issues and gender, as does Lonsdale (1990). Cohen and Mullender (2002) discuss gender in the context of groupwork. Cavanagh and Cree (1996) provide an interesting discussion of gender in examining social work with men. Christie (2001) also provides an interesting set of readings on the subject of men and social work. Lister (1997) presents an important account of feminist perspectives on citizenship. Muncie *et al.* (1997) offer a very helpful set of discussions of the family.

General texts on feminism and gender include Jackson and Jones (1998), Richardson and Robinson (1997), Bryson (1999), Segal (1999), Connell (2002) and Cranny-Francis *et al.* (2003), while Hallett (1996) and Pascall (1997) address gender issues in relation to social policy.

Thompson (2003b) discusses gender issues in relation to communication and language. Riches (2002) focuses on gender issues in relation to loss and grief.

Relevant websites include:

The Commission for Racial Equality   www.cre.org.uk
The Disability Rights Commission   www.drc.org.uk
The Equal Opportunities Commission   www.eoc.org.uk

4 | Ethnicity and racism

The UK, it is often said, is a multicultural society. That is, it is composed of a variety of ethnic groups, each with different characteristics and patterns. How important this is for social work forms the major analytical focus of this chapter. Storkey (1991) defines ethnicity as:

> all the characteristics which go to make up cultural identity; origins, physical appearance, language, family structure, religious beliefs, politics, food, art, music, literature, attitudes towards the body, gender roles, clothing, education.
> (pp. 109–10)

The term is particularly significant when used to describe minority groups within a society – that is, ethnic minorities. As Storkey suggests, it is often forgotten that all people are 'ethnic' – that is, belong to a cultural group, and so it is both inaccurate and misleading to refer to members of ethnic minorities as 'ethnics' or 'ethnic people'. This implies that to be a member of the ethnic majority is 'normal' and so members of ethnic minorities are by definition deviant. This, as we shall see below, is a form of racism.

But ethnicity is only one part of the situation; it is by no means the whole story. Ethnicity implies *difference* whereas the dominant notion social workers encounter is that of *deficit*. Members of ethnic minorities are often perceived as inferior and are thus subject to discrimination and hence oppression. Ethnic minority groups are presented, ideologically, as biologically different from and, by implication, inferior to, the ethnic majority. In this way, ethnic difference (characterised by solidarity, shared values and positively valued cultural identity) is constructed as racial inferiority (characterised by exclusion, marginalisation and oppression). It is therefore important to see ethnicity and race in conjunction, as the cultural differences of ethnicity are used as a political weapon to reinforce the power of the dominant majority, in so far as these differences are seen as deviations from the ethnocentric norm.

Failure to recognise this covert shift from ethnicity to race serves to mask racism and its subtle influences. Rex (1986) comments: 'The attempt to assimilate racial to ethnic problems, therefore, often led to the interpretation of racial problems not as forms of conflict but as benign phenomena of difference' (p. 19). In short, the UK, the USA and other western countries are indeed multicultural, but to focus exclusively on cultural or ethnic patterns without taking account of 'race' is indeed a naïve mistake. Race is not a biological category, it is a process – a social and political process whereby ethnic differences are translated into pseudo-biological racial deficits. In this way, the seeds of racism are sown. Discrimination against black and ethnic minority peoples is legitimated on the basis of assumed racial inferiority. This is a point to which I shall return below.

Social workers dealing with a wide range of ethnic communities therefore need to be aware of ethnic differences (ethnically sensitive social work) and the commonalities across minority groups – that is, oppression, discrimination and relative powerlessness (anti-racist social work). This chapter seeks to establish a clearer understanding of the racial dimension of social work and take steps toward the development of an anti-racist social work practice base. The first step towards this must be a clarification of the central concept of racism.

What is racism?

Burke and Harrison (2000) define racism in the following terms:

> Racism is a multidimensional and complex system of power and powerlessness. It is a process through which powerful groups, using deterministic belief systems and structures in society, are able to dominate. It operates at micro and macro levels, is developed through specific cognitions and actions, and perpetuated and sustained through policies and procedures of social systems and institutions. This can be seen in the differential outcomes for less powerful groups in accessing services in the health and welfare, education, housing and the legal and criminal justice systems.
> (p. 283)

This is a most helpful definition that incorporates some very important elements. It is very compatible with PCS analysis in so far as it shows that racism is not simply a matter of individual prejudices – it is far more complex and multi-layered than that. Another definition is offered by Chakrabarti (1990) when he argues that:

> Racism is, first a set of beliefs or a way of thinking within which groups identified on the basis of real or imagined biological characteristics (skin colour, for example) are thought necessarily to possess other characteristics that are viewed in a negative light . . . It is rooted in the belief that certain groups, identified as 'races', 'ethnic minorities' or by some more abusive label, share characteristics such as attitudes or abilities and a propensity to certain behaviour. The assumption is made that every person, whether man, woman or child, classified as belonging to such a group, is possessed of all these characteristics.
> (p. 15)

This definition includes a number of key elements:

1. Beliefs and values are a basic part of racism; that is, racism is an *ideology*.
2. It relates to 'real or imagined biological characteristics'. Racism is therefore socially constructed rather than biologically given (Soydan and Williams, 1998).
3. Racism is a negative term: it has strong negative connotations and is used as a form of abuse (and, by extension, discrimination and oppression).
4. Stereotypical assumptions are used to sustain this negativity and thus to maintain the dominance, power and privilege of the white majority.

A simpler and more well-known definition is that of Katz (1978): 'prejudice plus power'. This is useful in so far as it points out that racism is more than just a matter of personal prejudice but is indeed a much wider issue. However, this definition and the approach of Katz in general have been discredited as we shall see in our discussion below of 'Race Awareness Training'.

Racism can be seen to operate at all three levels of PCS analysis:

P – personal prejudice is an important part of the complex matrix of racism. Many people hold explicitly racist views and may even be members of racialist organisations. However, personal prejudice also manifests itself much more subtly and we are not likely to be aware of it unless and until we are confronted.

C – racist jokes, cultural stereotypes and assumptions of white superiority are all to be found at the *C* level. Popular notions of black and white are imbued with racism as cultural or ethnic differences are reframed as examples of cultural deficit. Patterns, values, behaviours or any kind of norm which differs from that of the white majority are construed as inferior.

S – race is an important aspect of social stratification and the differential allocation of power to individuals and groups in society. Racism is built in to the structure of society and its dominant institutions. The discrimination and oppression experienced by people from ethnic minorities is not simply individual prejudice, but rather a reflection of discriminatory structures and institutional practices.

There are a number of implications arising from this. First, we must be aware of the mistake so often made in the past – that is, to focus too much attention on the individual level and see prejudice as the basis or 'cause' of racism. It takes one part of the whole, separates it from the wider context in which it is embedded and presents it as the 'whole story'. Bryson (1999) makes apt comment when she argues that:

> It is also important to see that race, like gender, is not simply a matter of individual attributes or identity, but that it is a source of social identity and power which involves relations of domination and oppression. Such relations are often invisible to white people, who may be reluctant to recognise racial differences lest this be seen as a form of 'prejudice'. Thus a recent study of white American women found that many insisted that they personally were not racist, and that skin colour could therefore have no significance for them: a frequently used phrase was 'I don't care if he's Black, brown, yellow or green' (. . .). Such a perspective is, however, one of privilege, for those who are racially oppressed know that their skin colour is often of profound significance. Even when white people can see the racial disadvantages experienced by black people, they are frequently unable to see that this also means that they themselves are privileged by their whiteness, and that racial

advantage is not simply the product of individual racist acts, but of a whole system of racial hierarchy.
(p. 52)

Similarly, Sivanandan (1991) points out the weakness inherent in the Scarman Report of 1982 which also laid too great a stress on the *P* level. He puts this point across quite strongly in the following passage:

Basically, Scarman said there is no institutional racism but there is racial prejudice. He took away the objective facts of institutional racism and made them subjective. So that what we had to tackle was not the system, not the power, not the police on the streets, not the immigration officers who examined my sister to see if she was a virgin. What we had to change was the immigration officer's mind, so that he would not dislike my sister. That is nonsense.
(p. 42)

PCS analysis also alerts us to the fact that racism is not necessarily intentional. In reflecting dominant cultural values or carrying out routine institutional practices, we may actually be perpetrating acts of racism unwittingly. For example, working on the premise that Asian families 'look after their own' may prevent Asian clients from receiving the service they require (Atkin and Rollings, 1996). Although this may not be racist in *intention,* it is none the less racist in *effect* or *outcome* and is likely to be experienced as oppressive.

This relates closely to the important concept of 'institutional racism' which was defined in the Macpherson report as the:

collective failure of an organisation to provide an appropriate and professional service to people because of their colour, culture or ethnic origin. It can be seen or detected in processes, attitudes and behaviour which amount to discrimination through unwitting prejudice, ignorance, thoughtlessness and racist stereotyping which disadvantage minority ethnic people.
(Macpherson, 1999, 6.4)

Racism can be, and often is, deeply ingrained in the culture of an organisation and will therefore often manifest itself even if individuals are not deliberately perpetrating overtly racist acts. Institutional racism therefore refers to racism at the cultural and structural levels. It is a concept that reinforces the importance of recognising the complexity of discrimination and oppression and not simply reducing them to personal prejudice.

In this respect, and indeed many others, racism can be seen to parallel sexism. For example, Shah (1989) argues that: 'Racism and sexism work in similar ways by discriminating against people and by reinforcing stereotyping' (p. 179). There are indeed important parallels in the processes which underpin both sexism and racism. Thus, in seeking to understand racism, looking to our knowledge of sexism can help us move forward. However, we must none the less avoid the mistake of allowing the similarities to distract us from the significant differences (for example, the role of sexuality in sexism or the legacy of imperialism in racism).

Racism serves to 'pathologise' black individuals and families, to present them as inferior to, and therefore less worthy than, their white counterparts. This tendency is also visible in social work and therefore has major implications for practice. As Ahmed (1991) puts it:

> Negative images of black family life have crept into social work and social policy analysis. The Afro-Caribbean family is often seen as a tangle of pathology, virtually non-existent as a unit or rapidly falling apart, with mothers being seen as too strong and committed to wage-earning. On the other hand, the Asian family is seen as problematic because the mother's position is considered weak and uninfluential.
> (p. 174).

practice focus 4.1

Jill was a newly qualified social worker in a child care team. At an allocation meeting she was very interested in the case of the Bhogal family where there had been suspicions of neglect. Jill therefore expressed a willingness to take the case. However, to her great surprise and consternation, her team leader, Mike, commented that it would be better suited to a more experienced worker '. . . considering this is a black family'. When challenged about this, Mike found it very difficult to explain or justify his remarks. He could only reiterate that the case needed a more experienced worker. Jill therefore remained concerned about Mike's apparent negative assumptions about black families.

Such negative stereotypes serve to reinforce the process of pathologising individuals, families and cultures who 'deviate' from the dominant white norm. This is one example amongst many of the implications of racism for social work policy, theory and practice. It is a discussion of these issues which forms the basis of the next section.

The implications for social work

One very clear implication to be drawn from the literature on racism and social work is that traditional social work has seriously neglected the racial dimension of the social problems it seeks to tackle and the impact of racism on ethnic minority communities.

It even goes beyond this to the point where social work practice can itself be racist, whether by acts of omission or commission, whether deliberate or unwitting. In the past twenty years or so, social work has had to re-evaluate its assumptions about race, culture and ethnicity and to become more alert to the presence and impact of racism. This is not to say that social workers are 'racists' who deliberately try to short-change their black clients – that would be to confuse the *P* level with the wider levels of *C* and *S*. The actions of social workers need to be seen in their wider cultural and structural context, but we should not make the mistake of assuming that the *C* and/or *S* levels *determine* our actions at the *P* level.

Rooney (1980) captures the point well in the following passage:

> And it's hard to accept that in the work we do daily, with its humanitarian and Christian ethics, we may be a part of a process of institutionalised racism. But hard though that may be, it is too easy to disassociate ourselves in clear conscience from the part that we play in the subtle, sophisticated strategies of racial discrimination, which despite apparent well-meaning and good intent at every level, still leaves blacks worse off by the time the process works its way through.
> (p. 51)

At one level, it is indeed hard to believe that 'nice people' such as social workers could contribute so strongly to discrimination and oppression. However, at another level, they are part of a wider framework which reflects power and privilege differences and which hinges on social divisions. This therefore brings us back to the point emphasised earlier, namely: if you are not part of the solution, you must be part of the problem. While our actions are not determined by wider forces, they can, if we are not careful, reinforce those wider forces – for example, by relying on racist stereotypes, we are not only reflecting the cultural level, but also reproducing it.

Racism operates via acts of omission as well as commission, and so the excuse that we were not aware of 'the problem' is not a valid one. When we become aware of the racism inherent in the culture and institutions of social work (the C and S levels), our own actions (the P level) will either reflect, reinforce and consolidate such racism, or may go at least some small way to challenging and undermining it. There can be no neutral territory.

One way in which racism manifests itself in social work is in the over-representation of black people in 'control' situations and under-representation in 'care' situations. The criminal and youth justice fields provide many instances of racist assumptions serving to prejudice black defendants' treatment in the courts (Smith, 1995). For example, Whitehouse (1986) undertook a study of social inquiry reports prepared in respect of black clients. He cites many examples of reports which are premised on racist assumptions and therefore increase the chances of a harsher sentence being imposed. He describes the situation whereby stereotypical assumptions can trigger off a process which can have very negative consequences for the client:

Thus if the social worker has stereotypical expectations and attitudes he or she will tend to select information to confirm them. If the persons under assessment perceive themselves to be the object of categorical or stereotypical assessment, they will tend to withdraw from the interaction, to give as little information and collaboration as possible. This may well be interpreted by the more powerful in the interaction as uncooperative behaviour or having 'something to hide'.
(p. 117)

Hutchinson-Reis (1989) gives similar examples and adds that, while social work is perhaps no more racist than other state institutions, the 'progressive facade' of social work enables it to obscure or conceal the underlying racism (p. 171). The power of the social worker or probation officer in court is considerable, given the high percentage of report recommendations accepted by the courts. Where this power is premised on racist assumptions, unwitting stereotypes or other such aspects of institutional racism, the disservice to the black clients is likely to be of major proportions.

Ahmad (1990) makes similar points concerning mental health social work in relation to black people. She points to the growing literature on the subject and comments that:

> It is well acknowledged that Mental Health services are involved in social control and as such Mental Health professionals have power to enforce controlling functions, including the law. The correlation between over-representation of Black people in Mental Health services and exposure to social control is not hard to identify.
> (p. 31)

There are (at least) two key aspects to this: first, misdiagnosis through a lack of cultural understanding or even overt racism (Littlewood and Lipsedge, 1997; Watters, 1996; Iley and Nazroo, 2001) and, second, the fact that: 'Many black people become mentally ill as a result of the systematic erosion of their capacity to deal with multiple oppressions' (Pennie Pennie, chair of ABSWAP, quoted in Whyte, 1989, p. 24).

In relation to the first point, Francis (1991a) comments on the need for the Afro-Caribbean Mental Health Association to provide a legal advice and representation service, such are the numbers of black people who feel they have been wrongfully detained in hospital under the Mental Health Act 1983 (see also Browne, 1996).

Many studies refer to the over-representation of black and ethnic minority people in terms of the diagnosis of schizophrenia (Littlewood and Lipsedge, 1997). A frequently cited explanation of this is the tendency to 'over-diagnosis' brought about by a lack of understanding of the patient's culture and the ways in which distress and emotion are handled. As Whyte (1989) puts it: 'How can a white, middle-class male psychiatrist know how a young

Afro-Caribbean man expresses grief or how an Asian woman deals with depression?' (p. 23). This has become the basis of what is known as 'transcultural psychiatry' (Acharyya, 1996), and it is an important step towards ethnically sensitive practice – a practice which seeks to avoid the pitfalls of a distorted diagnosis based on an inadequate appreciation of cultural patterns, values and norms. This is a *necessary* condition for anti-racism but, as we shall see below in our discussion of multiculturalism, it is not a *sufficient* condition.

Inappropriate use of powers under the Mental Health Act 1983 is an easy trap for social workers to fall into if they are not sufficiently aware of the racial dimension of psychiatry, their own potential for racism and that of other professionals within the mental health field.

In relation to the second point, the impact of racism on mental health, Pennie's comments draw a clear causal link between racism and mental disorder. Burke (1986), however, takes a more cautious view. He argues, in relation to second and third generation West Indians in Britain, that: 'High rates of unemployment . . . together with inadequate housing and education, will have the effect of identifying a socially deprived group that is likely to be over-admitted to mental hospital facilities' (p. 179). Whether these social circumstances lead to more psychiatric admissions by 'causing' mental health problems or by triggering racial prejudice within the psychiatric system remains an open question. This is indeed a complex area (see Burke, 1984, for further discussion of this debate), but one thing which is clear is that racism plays an important part in the over-representation of black people within the statutory mental health field.

Similar arguments apply to the over-representation of black children in care (Barn, 1993). We can but speculate as to the precise reasons for such over-representation, but these are likely to include:

- a lack of effective preventative work due to the reluctance or inability of white social workers to work with black families;
- the reluctance of black families to engage in preventative work due to their mistrust of (potentially) racist social work organisations; and
- the tendency to pathologise black families (Ahmad, 1990).

These examples of the over-representation of black people in 'control' situations are paralleled by an equivalent under-representation in 'caring' or supportive services. Numerous sources refer to the relative neglect of black communities in terms of the provision of supportive social services (Ahmad, 1990; Ahmad, 1993; Robinson, 1995).

Social work has long been recognised as a mixture of care and control and, to a large extent, the two elements represent two sides of the same coin (Thompson, 2005). However, the situation in relation to black and ethnic minority clients is that there is a distinct imbalance. The control element is very much to the fore, while the caring element features far less than is the case with white clients.

What this demonstrates is that racism not only acts as a barrier to good practice but actually 'uses' social work as a vehicle for further discrimination and oppression. In the wake of the Macpherson report, there has been a major focus on institutional racism in the police force. However, we should certainly not be complacent enough to assume that social work is free of such problems (Penketh, 2000).

This relates to the point made in Chapter 1 – that good practice must be anti-discriminatory practice; a social work which is unaware of its potential for discrimination and oppression is a dangerous social work. These issues are particularly pertinent to the process of assessment – gauging the nature and extent of the problems and the resources available or needed. There are two main sets of issues involved. First, there is the cultural dimension. There is a danger that assessment will be based on dominant white norms without adequate attention being paid to cultural differences. Failure to take such differences into account will not only distort, and thereby invalidate, the basis of the assessment but will also serve to alienate clients by devaluing their culture (Thompson, 2002a).

But this means more than distinguishing between white culture and 'black culture' for there is no one single black culture (as indeed there is no one 'white' culture). Black cultures are many and varied and to ignore this is to operate at a stereotypical level, to oversimplify a complex picture. Ethnically sensitive social work involves developing at least a basic understanding of local ethnic minority communities and cultures. Social work assessment needs to be based on understanding and analysis rather than ignorance and assumptions.

Henley (1986) discusses Asian communities in Britain and comments that:

> Each group tends to see itself as separate and distinct from the others, and the different groups originally settled separately, drawn to different employment offers and prospects. Lumping people together and seeing them as a single, culturally homogeneous group is therefore very misleading. It is about as useful as lumping people together as Europeans. A Sikh from Punjab and a Muslim from Bangladesh are likely to have as much and as little in common as a Catholic from Spain and a Protestant from Sweden.
>
> (p. 37)

And, of course, the cultural pluralism is further extended by the fact that a significant and growing proportion of black people (between 26% and 87%, according to ethnic group – *Social Trends,* 2003) were born in Britain and have therefore been brought up under the influence of the culture of their parents and the dominant white culture as transmitted by the media, the education system and so on.

Black communities are therefore different, both from each other and from the white majority – this is the dimension of *ethnicity*. What social work assessment also needs to take into account is what black communities have in common – their experience of *racism*. As Ahmed (1987) puts it:

> I am not against better cultural understanding but I am against an *over-reliance* on cultural explanations which distract attention both from significant emotional factors as well as structural factors such as class and race. This important point is that for Black clients, the centrality of racism needs to be more explicitly acknowledged in the assessment process and cultural explanations need to be considered in the context of racism.
>
> (p. 6)

practice focus 4.2

Steve was a very competent student on placement in a specialist team for older people. In response to a referral from a local GP, he was asked to undertake an assessment of Mrs Jordan, a woman of West Indian origin. He set about his task with enthusiasm and did a lot of background reading. He interviewed Mrs Jordan on three separate occasions and was very thorough in gathering information about her life, her background and her needs, paying particular attention to the cultural aspects of the situation. Steve's practice teacher congratulated him on the quality of his work and his success in working in an ethnically sensitive way. However, she had to point out to him that, despite this, he had failed to address issues of racism. He had not taken into account what part racism had played in shaping her current circumstances or how racism may affect her current and future needs. His work was therefore ethnically sensitive but not anti-racist.

It is perhaps easier and less uncomfortable for us to take on board cultural diversity without going a step further and acknowledging racism and the need to challenge it. There are times when we can indulge in seeing the rich variety of cultural patterns as a contribution to social life, an 'entertainment' to make white lives more interesting but without also recognising the disadvantages and discrimination ethnic minority communities experience (Cheetham, 1981, p. 6).

Fernando (1989) warns of the dangers of reducing race to culture and thereby side-stepping the difficult and painful task of challenging racism. He comments:

> An emphasis on culture, however well-intentioned, may lead to a racist approach in practice . . . the promotion of cultural sensitivity without challenging racism may result in the reinforcement of racism by masking it and thereby inducing complacency.
> (p. 167)

Cultural awareness promotes ethnically sensitive practice and thus helps to avoid the problems of devaluing minority cultures or seeing them as inferior to white culture and thereby alienating the people who share those cultures. This is a valuable step forward but, as Fernando warns, it is also necessary to take the further step of recognising elements of racism in ourselves, our practice and our agencies. It is only then that we can move towards *anti-racist* practice.

One aspect of the relationship between racism and social work which is often not appreciated is that the foundations of anti-racist social work are actually enshrined in legislation:

> The Race Relations Act 1976 makes discrimination on racial grounds unlawful, and places a statutory duty on local authorities to make appropriate arrangements to ensure that their functions are carried out with due regard for the need to eliminate unlawful discrimination and to promote equality of opportunity and good relations.
> (Woolfe and Malahleka, 1990, p. 5)

And, in addition, as we noted in Chapter 1, we can now also add the Race Relations (Amendment) Act 2000 and the Human Rights Act 1998. But, of course, it would be naïve to assume that such a broad legislative statement could ensure a firm foundation for anti-racist practice. A tighter and much more specific set of policy guidelines and regulations would be necessary to provide such a baseline for anti-discriminatory policies which can readily be translated into practice.

Ahmad (1990) makes a similar point when she comments that:

> No legislation alone can make social workers anti-racist. Much depends on how they interpret the laws or even abuse them to reinforce racism. Much also depends on how legislations are used as a tool to tackle racism in social work.
> (p. 5)

Racism is a powerful force in society. It subjects one portion of society – black and ethnic minority groups – to oppression, degradation and discrimination on the grounds that they are deemed to be inferior, by virtue of biology and/or culture, to the white majority.

When we consider this carefully, it becomes clear that this situation has major implications for social work in terms of policies, theory base, practice, training, recruitment and management. Space does not permit a detailed analysis of these issues (see the 'Guide to further learning' at the end of the chapter), but I shall return later in this chapter to focus specifically on some of the practice implications.

Having drawn, albeit rather sketchily, some of the links between racism and social work, let us now consider some of the factors leading to the development of the modern approach to anti-racism.

The anti-racist response

Although there have been black communities in Britain for centuries, it was in the late 1940s and early 1950s that race relations issues began to take on increasingly major significance as a result of specific historical developments at that time.

In the years following the end of the Second World War there were labour shortages which, it was felt, would hold back the promised new age of prosperity and post-war reconstruction. It was therefore felt necessary to seek out new sources of labour to expand the workforce and thus sustain economic development. The New Commonwealth countries were seen as a rich seam of potential workers and so these areas were targeted for an intensive advertising and promotional campaign to persuade possible recruits to emigrate to Britain. This campaign was largely successful and led to a rise in Britain's black population (although not as great as contemporary media reports suggested; see Miles and Solomos, 1987).

However, what this campaign did not emphasise was that the jobs available were the lowest paid and the least popular. It was also not made clear that no additional, health or educational facilities would be provided. In particular, the failure to consider housing need exacerbated the existing housing shortage which meant that the vast majority of the invited immigrants lived in very poor quality conditions in seriously overcrowded accommodation.

The link between race and class became strongly established as black people very quickly became over-represented at the lower levels of Britain's socioeconomic class system (the relationship between class and race is an important one, and one to which I shall return later). It was not long before black people were seen not as the victims of poverty, inadequate housing and so on but as a significant part of the *cause* of such problems.

An attitude of racial superiority among the white 'hosts' was instrumental in translating the structurally based problems experienced by black people into matters of personal failing, weakness or inadequacy – poverty caused by 'not working hard enough', poor housing by having 'lower standards' and so on. The next step was to blame black people for the problems experienced by white people: 'they take our jobs', and 'they cause trouble'. This was the emergence of racism on a much wider scale than ever before. The focus was not on the problems of black people brought about by the Government's poorly thought-out migrant labour policy but rather on black people *as a problem*. This pattern persists to this day: the problem of racism is conveniently reframed as the problem of race.

An early response to this situation was the development of what became known as the *assimilationist* approach. The proposed solution was that black people should integrate as far as possible into mainstream white society so that they did not attract hostility by being 'too different'. In short, the answer to white hostility was seen as black people becoming 'white' in all but skin colour. Once again we see an implicit notion of racial superiority – adopting white norms is seen as advantageous to black people. The loss of ethnicity and cultural 'belongingness' is not considered important and the development of positive black identities is obstructed. According to this model, the best that a black person can become is 'almost white'. Penketh (2000) summarises the situation as follows:

> Assimilationist perspectives are based on the belief in the cultural and racial superiority of white society and the associated belief that black groups should be absorbed into the indigenous homogeneous culture. That is, they are expected to adopt the British 'way of life' and not to undermine the social and ideological bases of the dominant culture. Integrationist perspectives also subscribe to assumptions of cultural superiority, and therefore place the responsibility on black communities to learn 'new customs' and ways of behaving in order to be accepted by the indigenous population.
>
> (p. 24)

A significant aspect of this approach is the attempt to seek to minimise differences between black and white. The assimilationist approach is therefore characterised as 'colour blind'. In social work this amounts to ignoring the different needs of ethnic minority groups (brought about in no small part by the impact of racism) and treating them in a uniform, undifferentiated way – a far cry from the notion of valuing and affirming diversity.

A very different but similarly problematic approach which follows a different logic is that of *multiculturalism*. The emphasis here is not on minimising differences between black and white but rather on *cultural diversity*. The differences between white 'mainstream' culture and the various black cultures are given due regard, in theory at least, and such differences can actually be celebrated as enriching the cultural life of all. Ethnicity is positively valued and diversity is presented as a potential benefit rather than a problem.

Up to a point, this is a significant improvement on the assimilationist position, as it does avoid the problems of sweeping ethnic differences under the carpet. However, it does not go far enough and, albeit unintentionally, can actually allow racism to persist, but in a more respectable form. As Ahmed (1991) comments:

> This perspective regards other cultures as valuable and interesting but ignores the fundamental fact that cultures are ranked in order of merit in British society and black cultures are ranked very low indeed . . . This model aims to promote better understanding but demonstrates little regard for racial justice. It ignores the power relations between black and white people in history and in the present.
> (p. 168) (See also Sivanandan, 1991.)

An approach which did not ignore power was that of Race Awareness Training or 'RAT' as it became known. RAT was based on Katz's (1978) definition of racism as 'prejudice plus power'. However, the sort of power to which it referred was that of individuals by virtue of their job or status (Sivanandan, 1991, p. 43), rather than social or political power on a wider structural basis. A further problem with this approach was that its attempts to tackle racial prejudice were based on an aggressive, confrontational approach and, as Gurnah (1984) points out, this was in fact counterproductive in so far as it resulted in helping 'white liberals to cope better with their guilt without making any real changes in their behaviour' (Ferns, 1987, p. 21). Or, as Husband

(1986) puts it: 'Race awareness training can produce a socially competent non-racist performance; it does not produce an anti-racist practice' (p. 11).

---

practice focus 4.3

Karen was an experienced trainer who frequently ran courses on equality issues. On one particular course she was concerned that Phil, one of the participants, became very distressed and anxious when the subject of racism was raised. Consequently, during the coffee break she had a word with him to check that he was all right. He apologised for possibly disrupting the course but he was experiencing very painful memories of a course he had attended some ten years earlier where a highly confrontational approach had been adopted. For Phil, and so many others, the experience had left him feeling confused and anxious and had encouraged him to adopt a defensive attitude towards the whole subject area.

These various approaches to 'race relations' have all failed to address the central feature of the problem, namely *racism*, premised on:

1. The hostility of many white people to black;
2. The assumed superiority which legitimates this; and
3. The unequal distribution of power, privilege, resources and life-chances which such hostility sustains.

Roys (1988) makes apt comment:

> The difficulties faced by the black population are the result not only of migration and differences in culture and language but also of living in a society which is hostile to black people, denies them equal life chances and can expose them to enormous material and psychological pressure. The clients of social services present with not only linguistic and cultural complexities but also with the profound effects of racism.
> (p. 221)

Modern anti-racism dismisses the oppression and 'cultural imperialism' of assimilationism and transcends the cultural pluralism of multiculturalism. It recognises the structural basis of racism and how this underpins the cultural and personal dimensions of racial discrimination.

How anti-racism can possibly be made a reality in social work practice will be discussed below, but we must first clarify, to a certain extent at least, the relationships between race and class on the one hand and race and gender on the other.

Race, class and gender

The presence of black communities in Britain is an issue not only of race but also of class. The primary reason for the initial migration of black people was the capitalist economy's need to boost its workforce – to extend the working class. Also, as was noted above, the jobs that were available to be filled were low paid and of low status and thus at the bottom of the class hierarchy.

There are close links between race and class. Indeed, racism can be seen as an ideology which divides the working class by setting worker against worker and thereby contributes to the continuance of capitalism by discouraging working-class solidarity. However, it is a mistake to see the social division of race as a subcategory of class. Class and race articulate together; that is, they are interrelated. Williams (2000) captures this point when he argues that:

> race is defined not as a 'natural' or biological attribute but as a socially and historically constructed concept by which members of society endow skin color variations, which have no intrinsic meaning, with meanings that reinforce a hierarchy of privilege and power in society. Class is defined as a system of stratification in which unequal allocation of resources and opportunity for social advancement is supported by cultural myths that naturalize inequality. Although these concepts are conceptually distinct, they are related in interesting and complicated ways. . . . [C]lass issues are often concealed in racially coded language and meanings. Racial stereotypes are frequently used to reinforce a system of class inequality while class stereotypes are used to reinforce a racial hierarchy.
> (p. 215)

Similarly, Miles (1989) argues that 'contextualising the impact of racism within class relations' has the effect of demonstrating the linkages with other forms of oppression or 'exclusion' (p. 134). In short, racism should not be seen in a vacuum, separate from class and economic factors, but nor should it be seen as simply a by-product or subcategory of the social division of class (Roberts, 2001).

This parallels the debate in the previous chapter about the relationship between capitalism and patriarchy. But what we now need to consider is the third aspect of the class, race, gender triangle – the relationship between race and gender.

Feminism, in its earlier formulations at least, has been characterised by an emphasis on the common oppression of women, the shared experience of 'sisterhood'. However, the appropriateness of such an emphasis has increasingly been called into question. It is argued that the tendency to focus almost exclusively on the commonalities of women's experience leads to a disregard for significant differences between women, particularly in terms of race. As King (1993) comments:

> Many white feminist activists have often assumed that their antisexism stance abolished all racial prejudice or discriminatory behaviours . . . At best, this presumption is naïve and reflects a serious ignorance of the pervasiveness of racism in this society.
> (p. 229, cited in Bryson, 1999, p. 61)

Ramazanoglu (1989) extends this argument to include other divisions between women – for example, sexual orientation – and this reinforces the critique of an oversimplified analysis of women's experience of oppression. Ramazanoglu also points to the class dimension inherent in the attack on white feminism when she underlines the highly educated middle-class ethos of the movement (p. 129), which no doubt further fuelled the anger of the critics.

The theme of anti-sexism failing to take on board issues of anti-racism has been a recurring one. It features in the work of hooks (1982, 1986), Amos *et al.* (1984), Foster-Carter (1987), Bhavnani and Coulson (1986), Williams (1987), as well as the authors already mentioned. In sum, 'a feminism which ignores racial divisions is open to serious criticism' (Allen, 1987, p. 174). However, there is clearly a growing awareness of the need for feminism to incorporate an anti-racist perspective and the implications of this are in the process of being worked out – see, for example, Langan and Day, 1992).

It has been recognised that it is not simply a matter of 'tagging on' racism to sexism as the complex interactions of the two need to be explored and clarified (Mullender, 2002). For, as Bryan *et al.* (1985) point out, racism can actually change the nature of how sexism is experienced: 'Our relationships with men – both Black and white – have meant that in addition to racism, Black women have had to confront a form of sexism and sexual abuse which is unique to us' (p. 212).

The dynamic interplay of class, race and gender is indeed complex and multifaceted. And, indeed, it will continue to be so, as this is an ongoing dynamic – historically variable and far beyond a simple once-and-for-all solution. Although very complex, this is an area where social workers need to have at least a basic grasp of the fundamental issues in order to construct an adequate theoretical basis for anti-discriminatory practice.

Towards anti-racist practice

Distilling the principles of anti-racist social work is by no means an easy task, especially as this is a rapidly changing area and one prone to considerable political conflict and widely differing sets of values. None the less, the remainder of this chapter is an attempt to crystallise some of the basic tenets of anti-racist social work as I see it. Given the nature of the subject matter, this attempt can be neither definitive nor comprehensive. The aim is to inform, raise consciousness and thus promote further study and debate rather than to provide 'the answer'.

1. The first step towards anti-racism is to recognise and eradicate any tendencies towards racism that may be present in our own practice (for example, as a result of relying on stereotypes). This is not a RAT-style guilt trip but an acknowledgement (in line with PCS analysis) of the structural and cultural influences on our behaviour and attitudes. If we are not sensitive to these issues, if we do not attempt to swim against the tide of racism, then we will be carried along by the strong current, knowingly or otherwise. Denney, as long ago as 1983, was therefore right to argue that: 'Above all is

the importance of recognising racism in one's own practice. Failure to act against racism is in itself a form of unintentional or negative racism' (p. 172).

2. For many years now there has been considerable rhetoric about anti-racism and the notion of equal opportunities in general. There is therefore a danger that anti-racism remains at a rhetorical level only. It is much more comfortable for people to deal with it at this level without actually engaging with the issues. As Ahmad (1990) argues, anti-racist social work must be premised on more than just good intentions. There must be a real commitment to tackle some difficult and painful issues. The rhetoric is only of value if it is backed up by reality.

3. Social work with black and ethnic minority clients must operate on the basis of cultural *difference* and not *deficit*. All steps must be taken to ensure that assessment and intervention do not hinge on negative stereotypes – assumptions need to be checked out. The common ethnocentric tendency of pathologising black families, individuals or even whole communities is a very serious danger which must be avoided. For example, the ideological tendency to assume a higher level of criminality amongst black people (Marlow and Loveday, 2000) is a very destructive trap to fall into.

4. Following on from this is the need to help develop positive black identities. This applies particularly to areas such as fostering and adoption (Kirton, 2000), although this remains a contentious area. The issue of positive black identities is, however, a much wider one and would apply, for example, to social work with black elders (see Chapter 4). Maxime (1987) argues the point strongly: 'one's identity is like the foundation stone of a building, if you don't have a solid foundation, you don't have a building at all' (quoted in Zacune, 1991, p. 43). This is not to say that *all* black clients will need help in developing a positive identity, as that would be a reductionist oversimplification of a complex situation. It is none the less important to recognise the need to counter the potentially damaging effects of negative racist stereotypes. As Robinson (1995) puts it in making a case for black perspectives to be incorporated into social work's use of psychology:

Much more must be written, researched, and published in order that all of us may better understand what experiences are necessary and therefore should be provided to every black child and adult in order to facilitate the development of a positive black identity. Social workers have still much work ahead in the area of fostering healthy, positive, self-images in black children and adolescents.
(p. 112)

5. Affirmative action is a principle endorsed by Ahmad (1990) and she defines it in the following terms: 'Affirmative practice is not about discriminating in favour of Black clients and disfavouring white clients and "reversing discrimination". On the contrary, it is about condoning and ensuring equity in social work planning for practice' (p. 75). This involves recognising the accumulation of disadvantage black people have suffered as a result of racism and developing policies and practice which will help to overcome the difficulties this causes. Ignoring the need for affirmative action amounts to adopting a colour-blind approach.

6. Combating racism is not simply a matter of purging one's own practice of discriminatory elements. It involves challenging racist comments, actions or attitudes in others and creating anti-racist alliances. From a collective position it is then possible to tackle racist structures and institutional practices in social work agencies and, to some extent at least, in other social welfare and related agencies. Setting out one's own anti-racist stall without seeking to influence others is a very narrow strategy with limited effectiveness.

7. In similar vein, it must be recognised that anti-discriminatory practice is not only the responsibility of practitioners but also of managers and educators. Managers have a role to play in setting an appropriate agenda, supporting staff through the difficulties of establishing and maintaining anti-racist social work (Coulshed *et al.*, 2006) and so on. Similarly, social work educators have a crucial role to play in 'setting the context for change' (CD Project Steering Group, 1991) by helping workers and students to understand the nature of racist oppression and to begin to develop strategies for combating it. Practitioners, in turn, have a part to play in

supporting and encouraging such work on the part of managers and educators and to offer constructive criticism where appropriate.

8. As Ahmed (1991) argues, a strategy of 'permeation' is necessary. This means that issues of anti-racism should permeate policy, practice, management and training rather than be 'tagged on' as an additional consideration. Anti-racism should not be an optional extra but rather a fundamental dimension of our work. And this dimension needs to be linked to other important social divisions:

> The task for all of us is to ensure that anti-racist strategies are not seen in isolation from other disadvantages and oppressions. Anti-racism has to be class-conscious. It has to be gender-conscious . . . but race, gender and class have not often been theorised about. The issue for social work is how to bring it all together in theory and practice. (Ahmed, 1991, p. 180)

9. A central feature of anti-discriminatory practice in general and anti-racism in particular is that of *empowerment*. This involves seeking to maximise the power of clients and to give them as much control as possible over their circumstances. It is the opposite of creating dependency and subjecting clients to agency power. As we have seen, social work with black and ethnic minority clients is characterised by an over-emphasis on controlling at the expense of caring and supporting. Empowerment entails reversing that trend by using social work skills and resources in ways which support service users in overcoming racism (see Ahmad, 1990, pp. 46–50).

10. The position of black workers employed in predominantly white organisations needs to be recognised. One common response has been that of 'dumping' (Dominelli, 1989), that is, seeing anti-racism as the province of black workers. However, this can increase the sense of isolation and the pressure on black workers. Anti-racism must be a humanitarian endeavour in which black and white workers can work together to combat the oppression that black people – clients and colleagues – experience. Unless and until a supportive environment is created for black workers, the number of black social workers will remain low.

These ten points can, it is to be hoped, help people in social work to take their thinking and their practice forwards toward an anti-racist social work. They cannot, of course, provide formula answers, but that is no bad thing. Moving away from formulas and stereotypes towards a more critical and informed approach is a basic tenet of anti-discriminatory practice (Thompson, 2000a).

Anti-racist social work is a complex area but this can be no excuse for failing to get to grips with the issues. As David Divine (1990) so aptly put it:

> There must be an obligation on us all to support and help each other in a climate conducive to honest and humble exchange. There are no 'right on' answers and approaches. Once we acknowledge that fact, further progress can be made.
>
> (p. 14)

points to ponder

➤ Consider your own ethnicity. How would you describe yourself?
➤ How might your ethnic or racial background be significant in delivering social work services?
➤ What racial stereotypes are you aware of?
➤ How can you ensure that these do not influence your practice?
➤ How can you find out more about the ethnic diversity of the communities you (will) work in?

Guide to further learning

Ahmad and Atkin (1996) provide a good overview of community care issues in relation to race and ethnicity, while Ahmad (1993) concentrates on health issues.

Williams *et al.* (1998) is an informative set of readings with a European dimension. Kirton (2000) tackles the thorny issue of adoption, while Dwivedi and Varma (1996) tackle the broader question of children's needs. Alibhai-Brown (2001) provides an interesting discussion of 'mixed race' Britons.

Aluffi-Pentini and Lorenz (1996) offer a good blend of theory and practice in developing anti-racist ways of working with young people. Blakemore and Boneham (1993) address the race and ethnicity dimensions of working with older people, while Littlewood and Lipsedge (1997) concentrate on mental health issues. Stuart (1996) explores the intersection of disability issues with those of race and ethnicity.

Robinson (1995) explores the changes needed to psychology to make it compatible with the needs and circumstances of black people, while Lago and Thompson (1996) focus on counselling. Penketh (2000) is a helpful analysis of institutional racism, as is Marlow and Loveday (2000).

General texts on race and racism include Bowser (1995); Bulmer and Solomos (1999); Back and Solomos (2000); Lang (2000); Solomos (2003); and Pilkington (2003). Farrell and Watt (2001) present discussions about racism in Ireland. Malik (1996) is also a useful introduction to the complexities of this subject. Graham (2002) is an important text which explores social work issues from an African-centred perspective.

Thompson (2003b) examines issues of language and communication in relation to anti-racism.

Relevant websites include:

The Commission for Racial Equality   www.cre.org.uk

DIALOG   http://www.lg-employers.gov.uk/diversity/index.html

5 | Ageism and alienation

The terms 'sexism' and 'racism' have long been established in the English language and are not seen as technical terms or jargon. The term 'ageism', however, is much less well established and, although being used more and more in social work and related disciplines, it has only recently begun to enter the vocabulary of everyday speech. This would seem to be a reflection of the lack of awareness of ageism and the questions it raises, and also an indication of its relatively low status as an area of study. This very fact is itself characteristic of ageism – the marginalisation of issues relating to age, particularly the *problems* of old age.

Age is a social division; it is a dimension of the social structure on the basis of which power, privilege and opportunities tend to be allocated. Age is not just a simple matter of biological maturation – it is a highly significant social indicator. This is the case whatever our age – all ages are imbued with social significance – but as we shall see, old age has special consequences in terms of the attachment of meaning to life stages (Phillipson and Thompson, 1996). The focus in this chapter is therefore on the social position of older people and what implications this has for social work with this client group, although much of what is discussed here is also relevant to work with children and young people, as they too can experience ageism – discrimination on the grounds of age (see S. Thompson, 2005).

For a variety of reasons, including the effects of demographic changes now being felt, social work with older people is attracting far more attention than has ever been the case in the past. It is important, then, that due regard is given to questions of good practice in working with older people – that is, to the development of anti-ageist practice.

When we consider that social work with older people has considerable discriminatory potential, there is a serious danger that overworked staff will inadvertently increase the degree of oppression experienced by older people. This situation adds even greater weight to the argument that a clear understanding of ageism and the foundations of anti-ageist practice should be a high priority for workers in this field. This chapter attempts to begin that process of understanding.

What is ageism?

Hughes and Mtezuka (1992) describe ageism as: 'the social process through which negative images of and attitudes towards older people, based solely on the characteristics of old age itself, result in discrimination' (p. 220). The concept of ageism dates back to the 1960s and the work of Butler (Phillipson, 2000). Butler (1975) offered a definition of the term in which the three levels or dimensions of *P, C* and *S* are acknowledged:

> Ageism makes it easier to ignore the frequently poor social and economic plight of older people. We can avoid dealing with the reality that our productivity-minded society has little use for non-producers – in this case those who have reached an arbitrarily defined retirement age . . . Ageism is manifested in a wide range of phenomena, both on individual and institutional levels – stereotypes and myths, outright disdain and dislike, or simply subtle avoidance of contact; discriminatory practices in housing, employment and services of all kinds; epithets, cartoons and jokes.
> (p. 12)

Butler recognises the personal and institutional levels and relates the latter to structural issues such as productivity and the state-defined retirement age. The cultural level manifests itself in 'epithets, cartoons and jokes', as older people are frequently the objects of cruel humour – a reflection of their low status and the lack of respect accorded to them by dominant cultural values.

I shall focus later in this chapter on the structural dimension by considering the political economy approach of theorists such as Chris Phillipson. But for now the emphasis will be on the personal and cultural levels. In particular, I shall explore a number of common assumptions which both reflect and reinforce ageism. I shall expound each of these assumptions or 'equations' in turn:

Old equals useless This is the 'burden' model of old age. Older people are seen as 'past their best', no longer productive, no longer contributing to the economy and therefore a burden, a drain on the state's resources. This is often used as an excuse for not providing a service or for giving preferential treatment to younger people.

Old equals childlike Old age is often seen as a period of 'postadulthood' (Midwinter, 1990), as if having returned to a second childhood. Older people can find they are having decisions made for them (for example, by professionals or relatives) without consultation or their rights are being overlooked (Thompson, 1992b) or they are being patronised, for example, in the way they are referred to ('the old dear'). These are examples of what Hockey and James (1993) call 'infantilisation', a process parallel to the demeaning tendency to refer to adult women as 'girls'.

Old equals not like children Paradoxically, older people are not treated like children in terms of protection or provision of services. Social work with older people is often marginalised and treated as the 'poor relation' compared with more prestigious forms of practice such as child care (Thompson, 2002e).

Old equals ill As a general rule, it is true that the greater one's age, the higher the incidence of illness will be. However, this is a long way from the commonly held assumption that all or even most older people are ill. Some people even think of old age as an illness. But, in reality, the extent of illness and infirmity in old age is grossly exaggerated and misunderstood (Hughes, 1995).

Old equals not ill Once again we have a paradox. When older people are genuinely ill (that is, they are not simply the victims of an ageist assumption), they often meet resistance and their symptoms can easily be dismissed with a comment such as: 'What do you expect at your age?' This is reflected in health service priorities as, for example, when old age is seen as a contraindication for some forms of treatment (Sidell, 1995).

Old equals lonely Older people are often subjected to considerable pity as they are deemed to be 'lonely'. No doubt many older people are lonely, as indeed are many younger people. However, very many elderly people have a good social network and are not lonely. In addition, it is a mistake to equate being alone with being lonely. Whether someone is lonely or not needs to be assessed. To assume that an older person is lonely, without actually checking, is an ageist assumption.

Old equals asexual Sexuality in children tends to be discouraged and is seen as something 'reserved for adults'. However, following on from the second point above, it is significant that sexual activity amongst older people is often frowned upon or even seen as 'disgusting'. For example, an older man with a strong libido is described derogatively as a 'dirty old man' (de Beauvoir, 1977, p. 53) whereas his younger counterpart attracts more socially accept-able, albeit sexist, terms such as 'young buck'. Older people are thus denied their sexuality (Hughes, 1995).

Old equals unintelligent Older people are often perceived as being less intelligent than younger people. There is often an implicit assumption that intellectual capacities are lower, if not significantly lower, for those people who have reached old age. This can be accompanied by an assumption that confusion is a 'normal' part of the ageing process. Thus older people are expected to be slow on the uptake and unable to understand complex issues. This, in turn, can lead to workers talking to them in an oversimplified, thus patronising way.

Old equals poor It has long been recognised that class differences tend to be magnified in old age, and so poorer people may suffer considerable poverty when they reach old age (Phillipson, 1989). However, important though this is, we should not allow it to persuade us that old people, as a social group, are poor. Very many indeed are, but to begin one's assessment of an older person with the assumption that he or she is poor can lead to considerable prob-lems and could involve overlooking available solutions to present-ing problems.

Old equals inhuman There is a strong ideological tendency to dismiss older people, to deny them their humanity. I found a good example of this in an article in a newsletter of a local 'Alcohol Forum'. The author, a psychiatrist, is discussing safe limits for weekly alcohol consumption when he comments that: 'Safety limits are proposed in terms of alcohol units per week (10) but these limits are for males or females, not for the elderly'. Although the good intentions of the author are apparent elsewhere in the article, the common tendency to distinguish between 'ordinary people' (that is, males and females) and 'the elderly' is clearly in evidence.

This is not an exhaustive list and much more could be said on the topic. However, having gone some way towards clarifying what ageism is and what form it takes, let us now turn our attention to how these issues apply to social work.

The implications for social work

One manifestation of institutional ageism is the tendency for social work with older people to be seen as routine and uninteresting and more suited to unqualified workers and social work assistants than to qualified social workers. Indeed, some people argue, for this reason, that care management is not social work – see Thompson and Thompson (2005), for a view which strongly challenges this. For many staff, work with older people is seen as primarily matching service to need (and indeed the Griffiths Report and subsequent community care legislation tend to reinforce this – Kubisa, 1990).

It is relatively easy to focus on service provision without considering skills and methods of intervention. As I argued some time ago (Thompson, 1989), it is important to:

> ensure that social workers are allowed and encouraged to do social work with elderly people – to use social work methods. A truly anti-ageist practice would draw on a wide range of approaches and thus avoid making do with an almost mechanical matching of service to need.
> (p. ii)

The import of this comment has taken on an extra layer of significance in the era of care management (Thompson, 1995a).

---

practice focus 5.1

Chandra was a social worker in a mental health team. He worked with people from different age groups. However, he gradually came to specialise in working with older people. As he did so, he began to adapt more and more of his mental health knowledge, skills and methods of working to this older client group. He saw the development of this knowledge and skill base as particularly important, as he was aware of the danger of reducing work with older people to low levels of routine practice.

Froggatt (1990) examines the family dimension of social work practice with older people. She acknowledges that the complexities of what she calls 'later life families' have been paid scant attention and it is only in recent years that studies of 'intergenerational caring relationships' have appeared (p. 6).

Ageism would have us disregard the family context and concentrate on service provision. But, as Froggatt explains:

> Elderly people are almost always in some sense part of a family with kin-related and social support networks. Any change in the vulnerable elderly person's capacity to cope with daily living should be considered in relation to his/her place in the family network, and the capacity of that network to respond to the change.
> (p. 18)

Thus the familial context of social work with older people needs to be borne in mind.

Ageism has two sets of implications for social work assessment. The first relates to the points raised above. That is, assessment needs to address not only simple notions of need and service availability but also wider issues which form part of a comprehensive assessment. The second relates directly to ageism and can be subdivided into two parts. On the one hand, assessment should include consideration of the impact of ageism on older people's lives, including, as we shall see below, low self-esteem, feelings of being a nuisance and so on. On the other hand, care needs to be taken to ensure that ageist assumptions are not influencing the assessment work being undertaken. As with racism and sexism, if we are not actively 'swimming against the tide' of cultural and institutional ageism, we will be carried along with it, such is the strength of ageist ideology.

In similar vein, Jack (1995a) describes older people as being amongst the most disempowered of our citizens:

> Disempowered, that is, by poverty, poor housing and inadequate and frequently discriminatory health and social services. It is particularly important at this time to recognise the need for empowerment among older people because the so-called 'elderly' – a diverse population of ten million people between 60 and 100 plus – are increasingly being identified by cost-conscious governments, local authorities and service providers as a 'problem' due to their increasing numbers and, allegedly, greater consumption of health and

social services. This constitutes a very real threat to those arbitrarily assigned to this 'group' and all those claiming an interest in empowerment will therefore be concerned particularly with the plight of elderly people.
(p. 7)

These issues can therefore be seen as major factors that can affect our assessment of situations, in the sense that we may add to the disempowerment or contribute more positively to empowerment, depending on how aware we are of the operation of ageist processes and how prepared we are for dealing with them. Ageism therefore has major implications for assessment, and our awareness of ageism should flag up a number of dangers for us, such as assessment becoming nothing more than a test of eligibility for service (Milner and O'Byrne, 2002). Similarly, it is important that assessment should not be simply part of a brokerage role within the context of care management:

> Assessment is a process closely associated with care management and community care. However, it is important to note that it can also be used in a much broader sense. For example, the first stage in any problem-solving process is likely to be an assessment – a gathering of information and the development of an action plan . . . It extends far beyond the assessment of needs implicit in care management.
> This is an important point to make, as assessment is a process that all staff working with older people are likely to be involved with at one time or another.
> (Thompson, 1995a, p. 81)

To ignore the significance of assessment in working with older people can therefore be seen as an example of ageism in its own right.

But ageism also applies to other aspects of social work. One major aspect of this is the danger of what Fennell *et al.* (1988) call 'welfarism', the tendency to focus on the 'needs' of older people in welfare terms, to pay scant attention to their *strengths* and, in so doing, exaggerate the extent of the problems experienced in old age. This is applicable at two levels. In general terms, there is an often unspoken (C level) assumption that being old entails being in need of welfare services (Warnes, 1996) – but this needs to be balanced against the fact that only a relatively small proportion of people over retirement age receive social services assistance. More specifically, in relation to those older people who do become service users, welfarism can easily present them as a 'series of problems', rather than real people who have not only problems and needs but also strengths, assets and a positive contribution to make (Thompson and Bates, 1996).

One implication of this is that oppressive ageist practices can actually be perpetuated by the good intentions of workers and general public alike who see a 'welfarist' approach to older people as kind and humane. The influence of ageist ideology ensures that the demeaning and patronising nature of welfarism is rarely realised by those who hold such views. As with anti-racism, good intentions alone are not enough. Indeed, welfarism shows that unenlightened good intentions can unwittingly reflect and reinforce ageist stereotypes.

Taking these issues a step further, Walker (1987) suggests that the desire to achieve 'nursing' status can lead to residential care staff increasing the dependence of the elderly people in their care: 'A long history of research suggests that the interests of the staff of residential homes are likely to tend towards the creation of dependency rather than independence amongst elderly residents' (p. 52). The word 'dependency' is an important one, as it is instrumental in creating a negative image of older people and gives credence to notions of older people as a nuisance or a burden. It is therefore vitally important that social work staff do not use the term loosely or uncritically.

Dependency implies physical frailty, but Cameron *et al.* (1989) argue against the use of this misleading term 'frail elderly'. They point to the considerable inconsistency in the way the term is used and describe it as a 'service-led label' which excludes the client's own voice. Both terms, dependency and frailty, imply a medical model, one which focuses on physical capabilities and their decline or dysfunction. Such an approach runs the risk of oversimplifying the complex range of factors surrounding old age and reducing these to a medical or biological level. As Phillipson (1989) puts it:

old age is being represented as a cluster of physiological and biological problems – the construction of dependency through economic and social inequality usually being

ignored . . . terms such as 'frailty' and 'disability' are being
used to stigmatize particular groups of older people and are
being used to define service eligibility.
(p. 198)

He goes on to argue the case for moving away from dependency
towards 'interdependency'. This involves developing a partnership
between service providers and service users in relation to service
delivery and development. Where independence is either not feasi-
ble or not desirable, the alternative should not be dependency based
on the traditional paternalistic worker–client relationship. Rather,
it should be interdependency which:

provides recognition of the help older people need from us,
as well as the rewards to be gained from giving this help . . .
Most of all, the idea of mutuality between young and old,
worker and older person, might offer social work practice
the basis for a new vision of how work with older people
might be developed.
(Phillipson, 1989, p. 205)

The optimism inherent in this concept is to be welcomed, especially
in the context of a social work with older people which is often
dismissed as routine and uninteresting or reserved for unqualified
staff (Thompson, 1992b). Social work with older people is seen as
less prestigious than, say, childcare, and this in itself is a reflection
of ageism, based on the negative assumption that practice with
older people requires fewer skills and less application. Or, as
Preston-Shoot and Agass (1990) put it:

dominant images of people's worth are acted out in service
provision. Work with older people is seen as straightforward. It can wait. Child care is seen as complex and immedi-
ate. However, both require the same social work skills,
present the familiar social work dilemmas and require sensitive handling of separations, placements and culture.
(p. 10)

Ageism also manifests itself in terms of the social policy context
and legislative framework. For example, it has long been recognised
that older people's needs are covered by the same legislative and
policy umbrella as disabled or infirm people, thus indicating that

such people are considered a sufficiently homogeneous group to be catered for in this way – despite their varying needs and circumstances. Policy in relation to community care can also be seen to follow this pattern and reveal an assumption that there is no need for a clear policy in relation to older people as they can be 'tagged on' to other policies.

Similarly, Marshall (1990) argues that the absence of specific policy and legislation means that the protection afforded children is not available for older people as there are no equivalent statutory requirements.

There is another sense in which older people are not afforded the same protection as children. I am referring to the phenomenon of elder abuse which is receiving increasing attention (Bennett and Kingston, 1993; Biggs *et al.*, 1995; Eastman, 1994). As with child abuse, there is a problem in establishing a precise definition of what constitutes abuse or how the various forms should be categorised. However, this is not to deny the prevalence, significance or seriousness of such abuse. Older people can be physically or sexually abused, subjected to neglect (for those who are physically dependent on carers) and/or emotional abuse. These can be seen as a direct parallel with the abuse inflicted upon children.

However, there is an additional dimension as far as older people are concerned. Making decisions for children without consulting them may be considered by many as poor parenting, but this would rarely be seen as child abuse. But in the case of older people this can be seen as an infringement of civil liberties and, as such, a form of abuse. This denial of citizenship can be linked directly to ageism (Thompson, 1992b) and, more specifically, to the notion of 'infantilisation' – the tendency to treat older people as if they were children (Hockey and James,1993). Social workers need to be wary of colluding with this by falling into the trap of listening to the carer(s) without hearing the voice of the older person.

The Centre for Policy on Ageing guide, *Community Life,* stresses the notion of partnership, not only between agencies but also between service users and service providers. Part of such a partnership is the key role of consultation: 'The code emphasises the value of consultation at all times. At all points in the process, consumers and carers should be consulted and have some influence on the services provided for them' (CPA, 1990, p. 36). Where such consultation routinely takes place, the risk to older people can be significantly reduced as it makes elderly clients active participants rather than passive recipients. This helps to guard against the error of seeing carers as the 'parents' and thus in a position to make decisions on behalf of older people. It is only in a minority of situations (for example, where a carer holds Enduring Power of Attorney – see Thompson, 1995a, pp. 56–7) that rights are vested in a carer.

But perhaps the most frequently reported abuse situation is more overtly harmful than a denial of rights – that is, direct physical abuse and/or mental cruelty by over-stressed and under-supported carers (see Bennett *et al.,* 1997). Ageism entails devaluing and marginalising older people, dismissing their contribution and their needs and presenting them as a burden or nuisance. The ageism inherent in social and economic policy leaves many older people and their carers as a low priority in terms of service provision. All this combines to give rise to a number of situations in which the stresses and tensions are increasingly likely to lead to abuse. Ageism is therefore a significant factor.

A further implication of ageism for social work is the way the oppression experienced by older people can be internalised and manifest itself as low self-esteem. Marshall (1990) points out that, like racism and sexism, the stereotypes of ageism can be internalised by older people. Indeed, it is not surprising that a group of people who are constantly receiving strong negative messages should perceive themselves in strongly negative terms. This can have the effect of lowering morale and sapping confidence.

High self-esteem is premised on receiving positive messages, feeling valued and important but, as we have seen, ageism acts as significant barrier to receiving such positive signals. Social work staff need to be sensitive to these issues in order to:

(a) avoid reinforcing negative and demeaning images; and
(b) seek opportunities to give positive feedback and enhance self-esteem.

A major component of successfully achieving high self-esteem is that of maintaining a thread of meaning to one's life – having targets to aim for and goals to achieve. As Simone de Beauvoir puts it: 'There is only one solution if old age is not to be an absurd parody of our former life, and that is to go on pursuing ends that give our existence a meaning' (de Beauvoir, 1977, p. 601). She then goes on to give examples of some possibilities: 'devotion to individuals, to groups or to causes, social, political, intellectual or creative work' (ibid.). She argues that our lives have value if we attribute value to the lives of others – through love, friendship, compassion or even indignation. These are important lessons for social workers and social care workers. Ageism would have us focus on 'care' and dependency. Anti-ageist practice would have us look to activity, meaning, value and esteem. The task is not to 'look after' but to motivate, empower and promote self-esteem (Hughes, 1995; Thursz *et al.*, 1995).

Closely related to the notion of self-esteem is that of dignity. Dignity refers to the intrinsic worth of human beings and is therefore an important word in the anti-ageist vocabulary (Thompson, 1995a).

Set against this is the concept of 'risk', or more specifically protection from risk. Norman (1980) discusses a number of ways in which dignity and self-determination can be sacrificed in the name of protection from risk. In a later article she argues that 'an honest approach to the management of risk' should be part of a strategy in which improved professional practice can address issues of ageism (1987, p. 14).

Referring to the work of Brearley (1982), she comments on the need to understand risk as a matter of 'gambling', by weighing the dangers inherent in a particular situation against the potential benefits. She then goes on to clarify this by giving a concrete example:

> Does the physical safety of the move to live with a caring
> daughter or to residential care outweigh the psychological
> dangers of loss of independence? Does the danger to a
> daughter's health, earning power and family relationships
> outweigh the guilt and stress she feels in the present situa-
> tion?
> (p. 15)

The balance of risk is an important aspect of social work with older people and, from the perspective of anti-discriminatory practice, we must be wary of allowing ageist ideology to tilt the balance in favour of an over-cautious, perhaps somewhat paternalistic, approach.

practice focus 5.2

Mrs Linton lived alone and had no relatives in the area. Her neighbour, Mrs Jarvis, was becoming increasingly concerned about her and often contacted Social Services, the GP and the health visitor. However, Mrs Linton remained adamant that she did not need anyone's help and refused to receive services of any kind. At first, Mrs Jarvis felt that Mrs Linton should be forced to receive help for her own good. Eventually she came to accept that her elderly neighbour had the right to refuse services and, like many older people, chose to exercise that right. (Thompson, 1995a, p. 48)

Ageism manifests itself at all three levels, personal, cultural and structural, and so the implications for social work staff reach far and wide. The development of anti-ageist practice therefore presents a major challenge for all concerned. I shall outline some of the steps towards anti-ageist practice later in this chapter by way of conclusion. First, however, it is necessary to examine some of the arguments which have arisen in response to ageist ideology.

The anti-ageist response

In his classic text on the 'political economy' of old age, Phillipson (1982) makes the following important comment: 'I would argue that undue weight has been given to biological and psychological changes in old age (and the deterioration seen to accompany them), in contrast to the role played by the economic and political environment' (p. 2). He links negative attitudes towards older people to the structural requirements of the capitalist quest for profit. He argues that old age is seen as 'non-productive' and 'a period of social redundancy' (p. 7). But this is no coincidence – this negative and dismissive ideology is pervasive because it is linked inextricably with the economic requirements of the capitalist system.

Older people are seen as marginal to the labour market and are therefore assigned a lower status due to the emphasis on measuring social value in terms of one's contribution to the production of wealth. Old age therefore needs to be understood in economic and political terms. This structural approach was also evident in the works of Walker (1981, 1986, 1987) and, to a certain extent,

Townsend (1981, 1986), as well as various other writers who played a key role in establishing the discipline of critical gerontology (see the 'Guide to further learning' for details of works that have built on these foundations). This has proven to be an influential approach which has tended to counterbalance the traditional perspective on old age which sees this life stage as predominantly a medical problem as if old age were primarily a disease process (Hughes, 1995).

Indeed, 'medicalisation' can be seen as an aspect of ageism, part of the social construction of old age as a *problem*. This medical perspective has had a major impact on the theory and practice of welfare professionals, as Fennell *et al.* (1988) argue:

> By the 1950s, then, a body of knowledge was available to respond to the needs of an ageing population. Crucially, however, much of this knowledge was medically-inspired and orientated . . . But the influence of the medical perspective was adopted by other professions in the post-war period as they struggled to find an effective role with older people. Thus, for example, neither social work nor health visiting have built an independent knowledge base for work with this client group.
> (pp. 39–40)

Theorists who adopt a structural approach to old age are therefore keen to emphasise the social, political and economic influences on the situation of older people. That is, they see old age as a period of 'structured dependency' which is socially constructed rather than biologically determined.

Bytheway and Johnson (1990) also argue that the essence of ageism lies in adopting a biological interpretation of the ageing process: 'Ageism is a set of beliefs originating in the biological variations between people and relating to the ageing process' (p. 36). They then go on to present what they see as four central pillars of an anti-ageist response:

1. Abandon ageist language. We should avoid grouping people together according to their age. Age should only be referred to when necessary. (See also Chapter 2 above for a discussion of ageist language.)
2. Recognise age for what it is:

> What is required is an assertion of personhood, a
> continuing personal sense of social identity and a
> popular acceptance of the realities of ageing. If it is
> argued, for example, that life is a continuing process
> of development and 'becoming', then this implies
> that age does matter and is valued.
> (p. 137)

3. Avoid the restrictions of chronological age. How old a person
   is should not be used as a stipulation (for example, in determining eligibility for a service). Individuals or groups should
   not be excluded from jobs, services, participation and so on
   purely on the grounds of age.
4. Abandon the 'us–them' mentality. We are all subject to the
   ageing process. We should be aware of this and therefore
   avoid separating off 'the old': 'the most damaging thing we
   can do – contributing immensely to the power of ageism – is
   to seemingly deny that "we" who discuss these issues are
   somehow freed of the reality of the ageing experience'
   (p. 38).

In the same year that this article was published, the Church of
England also added its weight to the development of anti-ageism. A
report from the Board for Social Responsibility (1990), entitled
simply 'Ageing', draws attention to the: 'negative attitudes to
ageing that are widespread in industrialised societies' (p. 140).

The report links ageism to two major factors and these are:

● fear of death; and
● a materialistic culture which equates success with productivity
  and economic activity.

It is these issues, the report contends, which lead to stereotypical
negative attitudes towards older people and an undervaluing of
their positive contribution to society. The report argues that the
Church can play a more positive role in tackling ageism both within
its own institutional structures and practices and in wider society as
a whole. Also, in general social policy terms, a mixed economy of
welfare approach is recommended, based on the view that a combination of private, voluntary and state services can best meet the
needs of older people.

The role of the fear of death is one which also features in the work of de Beauvoir (1977). In particular she questions the notion of death being near for older people:

> The old man knows that he will die soon; the fatality is as present at seventy as it is at eighty, and the word 'soon' remains as vague at eighty as it did at seventy. It is not correct to speak of a relationship with death: the fact is that the old man, like other men, has a relationship with life and nothing else.
>
> (p. 492)

In short, old age has more to do with life than it has to do with death. And this 'affirmation' of life is a key part of the existentialist philosophy on which de Beauvoir's work is based. But it is perhaps the other strand of her thinking, her seminal role in the development of feminism, which should interest us more here. For what we need to recognise is that ageism does not operate in isolation. It intersects with other forms of discrimination such as sexism and racism. These combinations of oppression are significant for social work practice and so they are worthy of closer attention. A discussion of these areas forms the subject matter of the following section.

Multiple oppressions

For demographic reasons the world of older people is predominantly a female world (Arber and Ginn, 1995), as women far outnumber men in the later stages of life. The interrelationship of old age and gender therefore takes on a particular significance. Ginn and Arber (1995) explain this as follows:

> Gender and ageing are inextricably intertwined in social life; each can only be fully understood with reference to the other. As we age, we are influenced by the societal, cultural, economic and political context prevailing at different times in our life course. We are also profoundly influenced by our gender and by shifts in gender relations over the life course. Thus the connectedness of gender and ageing stems from both social change over time and from age-related life course events; social history and personal biography are interwoven over time. Yet ageing and gender have not been integrated in

sociological thought and have rarely been researched in
terms of their combined influence.
(p. 1)

It is not simply a mathematical matter of adding sexism to ageism.
The reality is much more complex than this. Older women will
have a long and cumulative experience of sexism and will also have
lived through a period of considerable change as far as social attitudes to women are concerned. The impact of sexism on older
women and the effects of the interaction of sexism and ageism
cannot therefore be routinely or straightforwardly predicted. These
are *empirical*, rather than theoretical, matters; that is, they cannot
be determined in advance, they need to be examined. There are,
however, broad principles and characteristics which can be
discerned.

Sontag (1978) described this combination of sexism and ageism
as the 'double standard of ageing', a double disadvantage of
discrimination. Victor (1987), in discussing these issues, argues
that:

> Growing older is less problematic for a man because masculin-
> ity is associated with qualities such as competence, autonomy
> and self control. These valued attributes withstand the ageing
> process much better than the qualities for which females are
> desired: beauty, physical attractiveness and childbearing . . .
> Later life is a time when men become grey-haired, distin-
> guished, wise and experienced whilst women are typified as
> worn out, menopausal, neurotic and unproductive.
> (p. 96)

These are significant issues in relation to self-esteem. Maintaining a
degree of dignity and self-worth can be seen to be more difficult for
older women due to the structural and ideological constraints, and
this, in turn, can lead to a sense of 'postadulthood' and infantilisation, as discussed earlier in this chapter.

Both these aspects, gender and age, also intersect with issues of
race and ethnicity. Fenton (1987) has pointed out that, due to the
earlier arrival in Britain of black men and their greater preponder-
ance amongst postwar immigrants (at the height of the labour
migration discussed in Chapter 4), there would be more black men
than black women in the elderly population during the 1990s.

The Report of the Board for Social Responsibility (1990) also argues that:

The special needs of elderly members of minority ethnic groups will become more important over the next few decades as the population ages and its profile becomes similar to that of the white population. One implication for policy making is the urgency of making sure that health and welfare services are sensitive to the needs of these groups. (p. 18)

And this sensitivity will also need to apply to the dimension of gender. Age, gender and race/ethnicity are fundamental aspects of our experience and social work and social care practice needs to have at least a basic understanding of these issues and how they interact in specific cases and particular contexts.

And, as if this were not complex enough, we must also take account of the socioeconomic dimension – that of class. As has been noted, class differences in early life tend to be amplified in old age, thus accounting in part for the higher incidence of poverty amongst elderly people (Walker, 1993; Marshall and Rowlings, 1998).

However, Norman (1985) made a major contribution in taking matters a step further when she introduced the concept of 'triple jeopardy'. Mays (1983) had earlier described the combination of racism and ageism ('double jeopardy') as: 'the product of the accumulated experiences and problems of a lifetime of membership of a minority group, as well as the current experience of problems associated with old age' (p. 73). Norman took both these sets of issues (racism and ageism) and sought to understand them in relation to class – the physical and economic disadvantages associated with low socioeconomic position. The marginalisation resulting from low income is reinforced and extended by the additional discriminatory impact of both racism and ageism.

This triple jeopardy is an important element in the social context of ethnic minority elders. It therefore needs to feature in social work assessments and interventions and, on a wider scale, policies and service plans. Oppression is both a social injustice and a barrier to self-realisation and, as such, the removal, reduction and prevention of oppression are valid and legitimate aims for social work. Where two or more such oppressions combine or intersect, their impact can be even more significant, the resulting disempowerment even more far reaching.

---

practice focus 5.3

Jackie was a care manager in a large urban authority, having recently moved from a rural area some distance away. She was finding it difficult to adjust to her new environment but was coping quite well. However, one case she was asked to deal with was quite unlike anything she had previously encountered. Mrs Singh was an 82-year-old woman whose origins lay in India. Since coming to Britain in the early 1950s she had lived in very poor housing with very limited income, in addition to which she had experienced racist taunts and abuse and physical violence at the hands of her late husband. Jackie felt quite overwhelmed by the sheer intensity of oppression Mrs Singh had encountered and for a little while she felt paralysed by it all, unable to respond. When she was able to respond and began to come to terms with the situation, she realised just how important it was to understand, and counter, the effects of discrimination in people's lives.

The point that this discussion reinforces is the need to adopt an holistic framework, an anti-discriminatory perspective which takes account of not only racism or sexism but also ageism and disablism (and indeed the other forms of discrimination which will be exemplified by the discussions in Chapter 7). But this holistic framework must be applicable to actual practice if it is to be of value. The final section of this chapter therefore addresses some of the key elements of putting such anti-discriminatory theory into practice.

Towards anti-ageist practice

Social work with older people has often been seen as low priority, relatively routine and undemanding work, although this view, in itself, is a reflection of ageist ideology and reveals a rather condescending (and misguided) attitude towards this area of work.

It is important to be clear about what the social work task entails and how it can be achieved within the context of anti-discriminatory practice. It is therefore necessary to consider the steps required to move towards an anti-ageist practice. Some of these are outlined here.

1. Ageist stereotypes can easily seduce us into making negative assumptions about older people and thus establishing a framework for discrimination and oppression. Anti-ageist practice is therefore premised on avoiding and challenging ageist assumptions and myths. This is particularly important in relation to the process of assessment. In fact, if we are not vigilant, assumptions can masquerade as assessment. The maxim should therefore be: *assess, don't assume*!

2. Much of the literature in relation to old age is from a medical perspective; old age is often presented as if it were a disease or pathological state. This has significant implications in terms of the construction of role expectations and attitudes. This, in turn, can have a major impact on self-image and thus on self-esteem. The ageism inherent in a medicalised approach to older people is a pitfall which social work must avoid. A key part of this is to cease using medical terminology in a social work context, for example, to speak of assessment and intervention rather than diagnosis and treatment.

3. Traditional social work is partly geared towards helping people 'adjust' to their personal and social circumstances. The problem with this is that it is: 'a "reductionist" approach insofar as it reduces a complex socio-psychological situation to a straightforward matter of pathology, of individual failing' (Thompson, 1991b, p. 16). Anti-ageist practice needs to transcend notions of 'adjustment' and focus instead on *empowerment* – the development of older people's personal power and seeking ways of increasing it, for example, through advocacy or access to resources.

4. Higgs (1997) discusses the welfare state's role in producing, or at least, reinforcing what can be described as 'structured dependency'. Social welfare practice can play a part in constructing or increasing dependency in older people. It is therefore essential, in moving towards anti-ageist practice, for social work to be active in avoiding dependency-creation. We should aim for 'interdependency' – the mutuality and human affirmation involved in helping each other. As Phillipson (1989) puts it:

Fostering the idea of interdependency needs, then, to become part of a new radical philosophy for work with older people. It provides recognition of the help older people need from us, as well as the rewards to be gained from giving this help. It also reminds us of the skills possessed by older people and the resources these might provide for activities and campaigns within the community.
(p. 205)

5. Ageism marginalises older people and casts them in secondary roles or presents them as useless and a burden to society. In view of this, we should not be surprised if many older people struggle to maintain a thread of meaning or sense of purpose to their lives and thus fall prey to low spirits or depression. In countering this, V. W. Marshall's notion of 'authorship' should be a useful part of the anti-ageist social worker's repertoire. It is a concept akin to empowerment – having a sense of being in control of one's life, and, as Marshall stresses, of one's death: 'if people want their lives to be meaningful stories with good endings, they also want to be the authors. This is the taking of responsibility for one's life as a whole, including its ending in death' (1986a, p. 142). Social work staff must not shy away from issues of death or dying for these are part of life, of meaning and of personal responsibility.

6. Ageism, as with other forms of oppression and discrimination, is both reflected in, and constructed by, language. Anti-ageist social work therefore needs to be sensitive to the role of language and thus avoid ageist and depersonalising terms such as 'the elderly'. We should always remember to add the word 'people', that is, 'elderly people', or better still 'older people'. The term 'elders' is also a positively valued one, especially as it has connotations of respect and dignity. Social work staff often use demeaning and perhaps patronising terms to refer to their older clients but may do so in good faith without realising their negative impact. Examples of this would be: 'old dears', 'my old darlings' and so on. What is needed, therefore, is a greater sensitivity to language so that it can become a tool of anti-ageism rather than a sign of unchallenged ageism.

7. The effectiveness and appropriateness of services offered and work undertaken will depend in large part on the quality of the assessment which establishes the framework for intervention. It is therefore important that such assessment should be *holistic* – taking account of a wide range of factors. The trap which lures many an unsuspecting worker is the routine matching of service to need. This is an 'off the peg' approach in which the complex process of assessment is reduced to checking eligibility for services available. This latter approach is too narrow and restrictive in its scope and has no impact on service development. It has no place in a genuinely anti-ageist practice.

8. Ageism has the effect of undermining a sense of dignity and the self-esteem which partly depends on it. Ageism marginalises, excludes and demoralises. A key task within a programme of developing anti-ageist practice must therefore be the promotion of dignity and the enhancement of self-esteem – a counterbalance to the prevalence of negative stereotypes. In effect, this is not a single task, but rather an aspect of all the tasks undertaken in work with older people – an essential dimension or underlying principle of all our dealings with older people.

9. One significant aspect of ageist ideology is the process of infantilisation – treating older people as if they were children. This manifests itself in relation to the question of taking risks. Social work has followed the medical profession in adopting a rather protective approach to this issue. As Norman (1987) puts it: 'we deny them, as we deny children, the right to take responsibility for their sexuality, their behaviour and their risk-taking' (p. 14). In recognising this we must also recognise that the more protective we become the more we challenge older people's rights to make their own decisions and be responsible for themselves. Anti-ageist practice needs to ensure that the protection offered is not at the expense of rights.

10. Anti-ageism is not a separate area of practice. It needs to be seen in relation to sexism (as the vast majority of older people are women) and racism (as the number of older black people is increasing significantly). These are fundamental aspects of human experience and need to be understood in

relation to each other. Anti-ageism needs to be part of the wider enterprise and challenge of anti-discriminatory practice. The lessons learned from anti-racism and anti-sexism must also be applied to anti-ageism. They are not in conflict or competition but, rather, part of the wider movement towards an emancipatory social work.

These are all important steps towards putting anti-ageism firmly on the social work agenda and, moreover, making it a reality in day-to-day practice.

---

points to ponder

➤ Consider your current age. What advantages and disadvantages does your age bestow upon you at the moment, given society's attitudes towards different people at different stages in the life course?
➤ What stereotypes of older people are you aware of?
➤ How can you ensure that these are not allowed to influence your practice?
➤ In what ways are older people treated like children and in what ways are they not?
➤ If you work with children and young people, which points made in this chapter also apply to them?

Guide to further learning

Sue Thompson's (2005) short text is an ideal introduction, while Marshall and Rowlings (1998) is a good introductory chapter to begin with. Thompson (1995a) and Hughes (1995) are both important texts in establishing the need for anti-ageism as a foundation of good practice. Similarly, Thursz et al. (1995) and Jack (1995b) are useful collections that focus on empowerment. Biggs (1993) and Biggs (1999) are both texts highly recommended for anyone who takes seriously the challenge of working with older people. Nolan et al. (2001) also offers some useful insights.

Sue Thompson (2002a) is very relevant to those working with older people in residential, day care and home care settings. Its main strength is that it addresses the issues from the point of view of the older person. Sue Thompson (2002b) addresses issues of loss and grief in old age.

Arber and Ginn (1995) and Bernard and Meade (1993) both provide important insights into gender and ageing. Blakemore and Boneham (1993) explore issues of race and ethnicity in old age. Sidell (1995) offers an insightful look at health issues in old age and Biggs *et al.* (1995) provide a useful introduction to the complex topic of elder abuse.

There are several good collections of readings on working with older people: Bond *et al.* (1993); Bland (1996); Jamieson *et al.* (1997). Hornstein (2001) provides an international perspective on age discrimination.

Phillipson (1982) and Fennell *et al.* (1988) are now both a little dated but are classic texts and are therefore well worth consulting.

Thompson and Thompson (2001) discuss moving away from traditional approaches to working with older people towards a model based on empowerment.

Relevant websites include:

Age Concern   www.ace.org.uk

Age Positive   www.agepositive.gov.uk

Seniors World   www.seniorsworld.co.uk/pensionersvoice

Better Government for Older People   www.bgop.org.uk

6 | Disability and social handicap

The field of social work with disabled people is a long-established one but it is only relatively recently that the basis of this work has been seriously questioned and challenged. The old assumptions and certainties are no longer intact and a very different approach to issues of disability is now firmly on the agenda.

The development of the Disabled People's Movement has introduced a new, politicised approach to meeting the needs of disabled people, an approach which is highly critical of traditional perspectives on this area of social work practice. This new approach is based on a social – rather than medical or psychological – model of disability and, as we shall see in more detail below, this entails quite a significant shift in how disability is to be perceived, understood and acted upon.

Social work with disabled people has never achieved a priority status and has, to a large extent, been marginalised as a minority special interest, often receiving minimal attention on professional qualifying courses. It has also often been subsumed within medical discourse and seen as a paramedical undertaking somewhat distanced from mainstream social work (parallel with health-related social work). It is thus given low status, low levels of funding and relatively little attention in terms of research and professional development.

This state of affairs can itself be seen as discriminatory and indicative of the marginalised and negatively valued position of disabled people and issues concerned with their well-being. This is illustrative of what has become known as *disablism,* systematic discrimination and prejudice against people with disabilities which produce a milieu of oppression and degradation.

What is disablism?

Disablism is a relatively new concept to be introduced into social work theory and practice. Like ageism, however, it is steadily gaining ground and achieving greater currency. This is important, as the issues cannot be confronted and problems resolved until they are firmly on the agenda. And to do this we need the vocabulary; we need to name the enemy we are fighting in order to recognise it and muster our resources against it.

Disablism is therefore an important term, even if the introduction of another 'ism' does seem trite and could lead some less sensitive people to dismiss it as an academic fad. Disablism refers to the combination of social forces, cultural values and personal prejudices which marginalises disabled people, portrays them in a negative light and thus oppresses them. This combination encapsulates a powerful ideology which has the effect of denying disabled people full participation in mainstream social life. As Oliver (1996) comments: 'Certainly it is true that disabled people have been systematically excluded from British society; they have been denied inclusion into their society because of the existence of disabling barriers' (p. 158). Such barriers are ideological as well as physical. Disablism therefore incorporates an undermining of citizenship, a point to which I shall return in more detail below.

Disablism shares many of the features of ageism: a tendency towards infantilisation, a patronising 'does she take sugar?' attitude, an assumption of illness and so on. Indeed Phillipson's (1982) analysis of the political economy of ageing also provides a framework for understanding the political economy of disability, as there are significant parallels.

This can be linked to PCS analysis as disablism can be seen to operate at all three levels:

P – Personal prejudice against disabled people is relatively commonplace and manifests itself in attitudes of revulsion, dismissiveness, and – paradoxically – also in misplaced charitable concern in which dignity and human rights are exchanged for patronage and good deeds. (This argument will be pursued more fully below.)

C – Cultural values reflect various responses to disability and disabled people, but they are primarily negative in their orientation. Dominant cultural norms are geared towards the able-bodied majority and popular notions present disabled people as either misfits or pathetic victims of personal tragedy. They are also subject to abusive and derogatory treatment in jokes and other forms of humour.

S – Disability is rarely recognised in sociology texts as a dimension of social stratification and yet it very clearly acts as a social division. This is manifested in the way public services and buildings are provided for the 'general public' but often without due regard for their appropriateness for disabled people, for example, in terms of access or other facilities. Thus, disabled people are structurally/ institutionally defined as a marginalised social group – that is, they are not seen as part of the 'general public'.

Oliver (1990) links disablism to the workings of capitalism, the role of wage labour and the pursuit of profit. These are structural factors which underpin the cultural and personal dimensions of disablism and the ideology which sustains them, as we shall see below in the section on the response of the Disabled People's Movement.

PCS analysis is therefore no less applicable to disablism than to the other forms of discrimination and oppression discussed in earlier chapters. One manifestation of disablism is to see disability as a personal tragedy and to focus on the individual level without considering the wider issues of how current social arrangements systematically marginalise and disempower disabled people. Marks (2000) comments as follows:

> *Disability* is a highly contested term. Medicine and its allied professions conceptualize disability as damage to a person's body or medical functioning requiring diagnosis, care or professional treatment. By contrast, the *social model* of disability argues that 'the problem' should not be located within an individual person, but rather in a 'disabling environment' which excludes and denigrates disabled people.
> (p. 93)

This passage introduces the notion of a social model of disability which is based on a fundamental distinction between impairment and disability. In the early stages of development of this model, the Union of the Physically Impaired Against Segregation (UPIAS, 1976) defined the two terms as follows:

> *Impairment*   lacking part or all of a limb, or having a defective limb, organ or mechanism of the body;
> *Disability*   the disadvantage or restriction of activity caused by a contemporary social organisation which takes no or little account of people who have physical impairments and

thus excludes them from the mainstream of social activities.
(pp. 3–4)

On this basis the Derbyshire Coalition of Disabled People, a key group in the development of the Disabled People's Movement in Britain, define disability in social rather than individual terms:

> We hold that disability is caused by segregative social arrangements which deny equality of opportunity for impaired people to participate in mainstream social activities. We are committed to the removal of all such barriers, whether physical, organisational or attitudinal and their replacement by arrangements which enable us to play a full part in the social, political and economic life of the county.
> (DCDP Equal Opportunities statement, 1986)

This raises a number of issues for social work staff – are they to be seen as part of the struggle to remove such barriers or are they themselves barriers and obstacles due to the tradition of individualism inherent in conventional approaches to disability? This is a question which will recur in some of the later discussions within this chapter.

To see disability as a matter of personal tragedy or pathology is, to use Ryan's (1971) concept, an example of 'blaming the victim' – that is, the wider social and political dimensions are ignored and the focus remains on a narrow, individualistic level. What is needed, therefore, is a social model of disability or, more specifically, a social oppression model, as this is consistent with the principles of anti-discriminatory practice. Such a model will be explored in more detail in the 'Disabled People's Movement' section below.

---

practice focus 6.1

Mary was a social worker who had recently joined a hospital-based team. When she made contact with Mrs Penhaligon to arrange a care package for her return home, she wanted to make sure that her needs were thoroughly assessed. However, Mrs Penhaligon found this intrusive and objected to what she saw as Mary's tendency to patronise her by overemphasising the difficulties she faced and underestimating her strengths and abilities. This situation began to teach Mary that disability was a much more complex issue than she had originally thought.

A social model of disability underpins the concept of *disablism*. Parallel with sexism, racism and ageism, as discussed in the preceding chapters, disablism can be seen as a form of discrimination against disabled people premised largely on the stereotypical view that such people are necessarily 'dependent'. A major contributor to this problem is a misguided emphasis on 'helping' people to become more 'independent' by providing care. This view of independence places power in the hands of the professional and can be seen to leave the disabled person more dependent rather than less. As Sapey (1998) argues:

> The alternative view of independence comes from the disabled people's movement and is concerned less with the ability of individuals to undertake tasks themselves than with their right to determine how, where and when these are done. The focus therefore shifts from the inadequacies of the individual to the barriers that confront people with impairments, both in the physical sense and in terms of constraints on autonomy.
> (p. 50)

The movement from an individual conception of disability to a social one has many implications for social work and it is to these that we now turn.

The implications for social work

Traditionally, social work with disabled people has a major practical emphasis with a focus on matching available services to assessed need. In this respect there is a strong parallel with traditional social work with older people, as discussed in the previous chapter. Oliver and Sapey (1999) are critical of such an approach, which fails to question what is meant by 'need' and also whether the services on offer are appropriate. They comment: 'If only social work with people with disabilities were as simple as this practical approach implies – the matching of resources to needs within a legal and statutory framework' (p. xiii). This in itself can be seen as indicative of disablism in so far as it fails to see disability as a social and political issue and reduces it to a matter of the welfare state providing services for 'dependent' people – thus socially constructing disability as a form of dependency. The 'practical' approach can therefore be understood as an additional form of social oppression that is instrumental in constructing an image of disabled people as helpless and not able to contribute to mainstream society.

This also has implications for those who care for disabled people, as it casts them in a role which can so easily reinforce notions of dependency and pathology. The dominant disablist ideology can have the effect of allowing and encouraging carers to contribute unwittingly to the oppression of the people they are, in most cases, genuinely trying to help.

What all this means is that social workers adopting an anti-discriminatory perspective cannot afford to settle for a 'practical' approach with an uncritical conception of need. Service delivery must therefore be based on a more sophisticated understanding of the notion of need and the related concept of *aiding*. What is often overlooked in relation to 'aids to daily living' is the degree of reliance on such aids by 'able-bodied' people. How many could lead 'normal' lives without everyday aids such as pens, cars, telephones, watches, cutlery, reading glasses, stairs and so on? There exists, for each of us, a 'structure of aiding', a set of practical and human support systems which enable us to pursue our day-to-day tasks and lifestyle. For a person with an impairment the structure of such aiding will be different from that of a person who does not have an impairment. However, this is a very different proposition from stating that disabled people need 'aid' (and, by implication, that non-disabled people do not).

The reality of the situation is that all people need some form of assistance or support to participate in mainstream social life. We all have our own requirements, some of which will be common to all, some of which are more individually tailored. However, the way in which such assistance is resourced is a significant issue. For example, government funding is provided in grants and services for individuals and groups, including business interests, and for the general public. That is, aiding is not only for those 'in need'. In fact, the majority of government funding is provided for groups other than people deemed to be 'in need' (spending on roads, defence, mainstream education and so on). It is therefore inappropriate, and indeed stigmatising, to see the needs of disabled people as 'special' as this draws an arbitrary line between those with an impairment and those without. To see aid as something disabled people need but which others do not is itself disabling and indeed disablist.

Traditional social work approaches to disability therefore run the risk of falling into this trap.

Oliver (1987) goes a step further by questioning the traditional helper–helped relationship (see also Finkelstein, 1981a, Davis, 1988):

> I would further criticise the 'professionalisation' of service for disabled people, on the assumption that the professionals know best what disabled people need and are in charge. The provision of services in such a way is at best patronising, and at worst further disabling, since disabled people may be pushed into becoming passive recipients of the kinds of services other people think they ought to have.
> (Oliver, 1987, p. 18)

What is needed, therefore, is a social work which focuses on partnership rather than paternalism and which sees disabled people not as dependent or childlike, but as an oppressed group who are denied the assistance they need, whilst assistance for other groups is more freely provided.

An example of this would be access to public buildings such as libraries. Steps, where needed, would be provided as a matter of course, whereas adding a ramp for wheelchair access to an existing building is likely to be regarded as a 'special' requirement and may therefore be denied on the grounds of cost. In this way disabled people may be excluded from libraries and other public buildings.

This has a major impact in terms of citizenship and rights. The citizenship of disabled people is undermined by the process illustrated in Figure 6.1, which also shows that it is not the impairment itself which is disabling but rather the social forces which exclude, marginalise and oppress – disability is the social response to the impairment. The handicap is therefore social rather than physical. This is captured well in Morris's brief but telling comment: 'it is not the inability to walk which disables someone but the steps into the building' (1991, p. 10, cited in Hughes, 1998, p. 77).

This places social workers in a pivotal position within the context of the 'care versus control' dilemma so characteristic of the profession and its undertakings. On the one hand, social work practice can reinforce the traditional individualist model:

> The individual model sees the problems that disabled people experience as being a direct consequence of their impair-

ment. The major task of the professional is therefore to adjust the individual to the particular disabling condition. There are two aspects of this: first there is physical readjustment through rehabilitation programmes designed to return the individual to as near normal a state as possible; and second, there is psychological adjustment which helps the individual to come to terms with physical limitations.
(Oliver and Sapey, 1999, p. 13)

The dangers of such a narrow, individualistic approach to social work have already been exemplified in earlier chapters. These include:

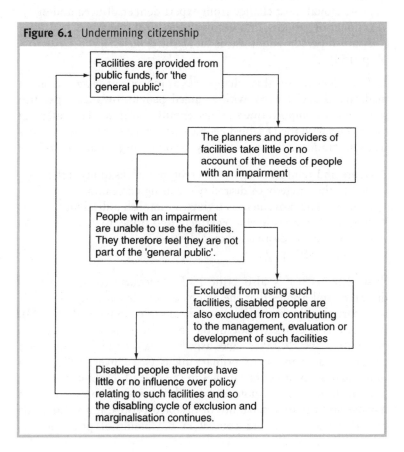

Figure 6.1 Undermining citizenship

Facilities are provided from public funds, for 'the general public'.

The planners and providers of facilities take little or no account of the needs of people with an impairment

People with an impairment are unable to use the facilities. They therefore feel they are not part of the 'general public'.

Excluded from using such facilities, disabled people are also excluded from contributing to the management, evaluation or development of such facilities

Disabled people therefore have little or no influence over policy relating to such facilities and so the disabling cycle of exclusion and marginalisation continues.

● A tendency to 'pathologise', to see the problem as being within the client/service user;
● A tendency to ignore wider cultural and structural factors; and
● Taken-for-granted discriminatory assumptions are not questioned.

In short, it reintroduces many of the weaknesses in theory and practice which radical social work sought to remove.

On the other hand, social work practice can confront, challenge and debunk the discriminatory and oppressive basis of the individualist model. Oliver and Sapey (1999) echo Finkelstein's (1981b) view that the real problem is:

> one of the need for a change in professional role – the professional must change from expert definer of need and/or rationer of services, and become a resource which the disabled person might use as he or she chooses.
> (p. 163)

A key element in this change is a movement away from a medicalised social work with disabled people towards a practice premised on empowerment. This entails social workers aligning themselves with the Disabled People's Movement and moving away from the traditional ethos of many disability organisations which:

> create and reinforce negative stereotypes of disability, referring to the 'tragedy of disability' or using demeaning imagery. The movement is trying to establish a disability culture to emphasise empowerment and pride, to create services run by disabled people themselves.
> (George, 1991, p. 21)

Brisenden (1986) is also critical of a medicalised approach to disability and argues that the emphasis on clinical diagnosis leads to a 'partial and inhibiting view of the disabled individual' (p. 173). Indeed, this is characteristic of the 'medical model' in general – a perspective which takes one aspect of a complex whole and presents it as a major or primary focus (see Oliver, 1990, for a fuller analysis of how this applies in the case of disability).

A medical model is not only unhelpful through presenting too narrow and negative a picture of disabled people, it also succeeds in relocating power and control in the hands of professionals, particularly medical professionals. This, in turn, plays a significant part in the social construction of dependency. Finkelstein (1991) also regrets the dominance of the medical model but sees it as part of a wider model which he terms the 'social death' model of disability, referring to the work of Miller and Gwynne (1972). These two researchers likened the institutionalisation of disabled people to a form of 'social death' but, sadly, their response to this was not to challenge this fundamentally but rather to make such a 'death' as humane and efficient as possible.

Finkelstein (1991) criticises Miller and Gwynne for adopting: 'the simplistic assumption that to be permanently disabled means that the individual is *intrinsically* non-equal to their peers (i.e. without help, a non-being)' (p. 26). Their model is a profoundly discriminatory one which banishes disabled people to a marginally less than human existence. As with the other forms of discrimination discussed in earlier chapters, the fact that the oppression experienced derives from misguided good intentions is of little comfort to those affected.

What emerges from these narrow perspectives is an image of disabled people as individuals for whom a 'cure or care' approach is appropriate. No account is taken of human rights, equality, independence or empowerment. These are all conveniently brushed to one side. It is clear, therefore, that an anti-discriminatory social work practice with disabled people must avoid the dangers of accepting a medical definition of disability or a conception of disabled people as 'socially dead'. The focus of practice must not be on the presumed inadequacies of disabled people but on the personal, cultural, structural and physical barriers to taking control of one's own life as far as possible – in short, a social work of empowerment. A significant aspect of this is a shift of focus from charity and compassion to advocacy and rights. As Oliver (1990) argues, social policies, including social work itself, should be geared towards alleviating oppression rather than 'compensating' disabled people for their 'tragedy'.

The question of the rights of disabled people is one which has received relatively little attention from social workers or indeed from the state. Barnes argues that there has been:

a further retreat from the notion of rights as a result of
policy makers' preference for voluntary rather than statutory

services. And while the introduction of the 1986 Disabled Persons (Services, Consultation and Representation) Act promised meaningful collaboration between service users and providers, there is widespread disregard for the law by local authorities.
(1991a)

One factor which can partly explain this disregard for the law and, by extension, the rights of disabled people, is the contradiction between the rights model implicit in this legislation and the medical model which can be seen to underpin the majority of policy and practice in social work agencies. Whilst a medicalised individualist view remains dominant, the emphasis will continue to be on 'adjustment' and treatment rather than empowerment, participation and rights.

This can be taken a step further by arguing that there is a need to change focus so that resources are diverted to dealing with the social causes of disability rather than seeking to deal with the effects. A movement away from a medical model to a social model is a key part of this. As Davis (1996) comments:

> For over four centuries in Britain, where disabled people have been among those singled out for legal treatment, we have been dealt with as a problem in need of special treatment and not as equal citizens with a right to full participation in the social mainstream. Countless millions of pounds have been and are spent on research into why we are the way we are, on attempts to cure us, or rehabilitate us, or conductively educate us, or in some other way make us approximate to able-bodiedness, or make us fit into a society designed to serve and perpetuate able-bodied interests. However, when (despite all this effort) we don't quite fit, or can't quite function, or we can't find jobs, millions more pounds are spent on social security, or welfare services, or heart-warming charitable endeavours designed to compensate us in some way for the personal tragedy that has befallen us.
> (p. 124)

The current emphasis on 'care management' as a key part of the development of community care also retains the influence of the

medical model – for example in the assumption that the professional experts know best what the needs of disabled people are.
Oliver (1996) is critical of the care management approach, which
often demonstrates a tendency to assume that the disabled person
cannot be his or her own care manager.

Anti-disablist practice therefore clearly entails dismantling the
traditional medicalised approach and constructing, in its place, a
social work practice premised on a social oppression model of
disability.

The development of the 'independent living' paradigm
(Campbell and Oliver, 1996) offers social workers a way forward
in tackling many of these issues. It focuses on achieving independence and achieving maximisation of one's potential. It mainly
manifests itself in the establishment of Centres for Independent
Living. Basically, such centres examine ways in which policies and
services can be changed or created to facilitate maximum independence.

Centres for Independent Living were introduced in the USA in
the early 1970s. In the mid 1980s a similar centre was established
in Britain, at Ripley in Derbyshire, but with a slightly different
focus. The Derbyshire centre is known as a Centre for *Integrated*
Living and constitutes a partnership between local disabled people
and the statutory service providers. At its inception the centre
aimed to provide a range of services:

1. Maintenance of and updating the Disabled Persons Register.
2. Setting up a county-wide care attendant register.
3. Housing services, from design to direct labour.
4. A co-ordinated, county-wide accessible transport service.
5. Mixed physical ability, commercially viable workshops.
6. Information, advice and associated support services.
7. Publicity and communications service.
8. Aids and equipment showroom and store.
9. 'Halfway House' rehabilitation service.
10. Peer counselling service. (DCDP, 1985)

This gives an outline of the thinking behind establishing the
centre and can act as a model for other areas to follow in seeking
an anti-discriminatory approach to social work with disabled
people.

practice focus 6.2

Following the reorganisation, a number of working parties were set up to consider the implications of the changes for particular client groups. Tom, the leader of the disability team, was quite insistent that a number of disabled people should be invited to contribute to the working party on disability services. At first he met some resistance from some of his more traditionally minded colleagues. However, he won the argument and the subsequent series of meetings was there-fore much more representative and much better informed.

Among the key elements of the CIL and other participatory approaches is a greater control by disabled people themselves over their lives and circumstances. But it must be recognised that poverty acts as a major limitation on such control. Without the financial wherewithal to build an independent lifestyle, people with an impairment will remain, to a certain extent at least, *dis*abled victims of a sociopolitical handicap rather than a physical one.

It is also important to recognise the twofold relationship between poverty and disability. On the one hand, disability consigns people with an impairment to a position of low income and, on the other hand, poverty can, in itself, be seen as a major cause of disability (Doyal, 1983; Oliver, 1990). See also Oliver (1996) for a discussion of disability and poverty. The links between disability and the economy will be discussed in the following section but the point to note at this stage is the significance of poverty as a restrictive factor in the lives of disabled people. This places issues of welfare rights advocacy on the social work agenda as well as steps towards improved employment opportunities.

Again the question of rights arises and this is indeed a major issue for anti-disablist social work – the development of an approach in which strategies of intervention address rights, inte-grated living and participation rather than simply adjustment or rehabilitation. This involves challenging discriminatory and oppressive structures, practices and attitudes both within and outside social work organisations.

The British Council of Organisations of Disabled People (BCODP) has been in the forefront of campaigning for anti-discrimination legislation (Barnes, 1991b; Bynoe *et al.*, 1991). Although the Disability Discrimination Act 1995 has gone some way towards tackling discrimination, it leaves many aspects of disablism untouched. As Chadwick (1996) argues, the legislation perpetuates an individualist model of disablement and fails to address the social basis of disability and the consequences of a society geared towards the able-bodied majority.

The anti-disablist response: the Disabled People's Movement

'The Disabled People's Movement' is a generic term used to describe the politicisation of disability issues and the constriction and consolidation of an approach which avoids, and indeed undermines, the traditional model of disability. The movement promotes, as we have seen, a model of disability as a form of social oppression rather than personal misfortune or 'tragedy'. It attempts to move away from forms of practice which:

● fail to acknowledge the significant physical and social barriers faced by disabled people;
● regard disabled people as 'sick' or necessarily in need of care and attention;
● reinforce unduly negative images and perceptions of disabled people;
● have a tendency to infantilise and patronise; and
● assume dependency rather than promote empowerment.

These points represent some of the various dimensions of oppression experienced by disabled people which are rarely, if ever, acknowledged by traditional approaches to disability.

The individualist approach which constructs disability as a matter of personal tragedy is a model the Disabled People's Movement seeks to replace with a more politically informed strategy for, as Oliver (1986) argues, the traditional approach leaves 'social and economic structures untouched' (p. 16). The types of changes needed are highlighted in the following passage from Hughes (1998):

If we were to adopt the view that disability is a form of social oppression, how might this be translated into policies? It would perhaps lead to social policies which focused on

disabled people as both the *collective* 'victim' and survivors of a prejudiced and discriminatory society rather than as *individual* victims of circumstance. Such social (rather than medical) policies would thus be geared to the alleviation of oppression rather than the compensation of individuals, and would lead to structural interventions such as the redistribution of resources, changing the physical environment, and equal rights policies.
(p. 77)

Finkelstein (1981b) links disability with social and political factors by tracing the historical development of the role of people with an impairment in the economy. Prior to the industrial revolution, such people were able to contribute to production in cottage and family-based industries as machines were relatively simple and easily adapted. Modern industrial methods, however, are less easily adapted, are located away from the home and involve a division of labour, thus excluding significant numbers of people with impairments from the labour market and consequently from the opportunity to be financially self-sufficient. Dependency is therefore caused not by the impairment itself but by the social arrangements which take no account of the needs of people with an impairment.

Oliver (1990) adopts a similar line of argument in linking the exclusion of disabled people to the workings of capital. He contends that there are both economic and ideological reasons for capitalist social relations to marginalise disabled people. Economically, they contribute to the 'reserve army of labour' in much the same way as women, ethnic minorities and older people. That is, disabled people provide the capitalist economy with a degree of flexibility in managing fluctuations in the demand for labour. Ideologically, the inferior position of disabled people serves 'as a warning to those unable or unwilling to work' (p. 70).

There are therefore structural reasons for the inequitable position of disabled people in western societies; it is no coincidence or historical accident – it is, in part at least, the outcome of historic material forces not unconnected with the nature of the capitalist economic system and the ideology of competitiveness and individualism which helps to sustain it. This ideology is instrumental in constructing disabled people in negative terms, as people with problems – or even as people who *are* problems. Thus, this dominant ideology of disability focuses specifically on the negative aspects of impairment and thereby presents a biased and unbalanced picture of disabled people. Indeed, it is a recurring theme in the literature on disablism that dominant ideologies of disability have a tendency to:

- stereotype disabled people as passive, dependent and in need of care (and sympathy);
- emphasise the negative effects of impairment; and
- treat disabled people as problems (rather than as people with problems caused by the social arrangements which undermine their autonomy and exclude them from mainstream society).

It is precisely this negative, demeaning and thus discriminatory, perspective on disability that the Disabled People's Movement is determined to fight and ultimately eliminate. The dehumanisation inherent in disablism is an important target for the attentions of those committed to achieving equality of opportunity and human rights.

Such dehumanisation manifests itself in the language used to describe, or refer to disabled people, as Brisenden (1986) indicates in the following passage:

> To begin with, we are not 'the disabled'. We are disabled people or even people with disabilities. It is important that we do not allow ourselves to be dismissed as if we all come under this one great metaphysical category 'the disabled'. The effect of this is a depersonalisation, a sweeping dismissal of our individuality, and a right to be seen as people with our own uniqueness rather than the anonymous constituents of a category or group. These words that lump us all together – 'the disabled', 'spina bifida', 'tetra-plegic', 'muscular dystrophy' – are nothing more than terminological rubbish bins into which all the important things such as people get thrown away.
> (p. 174)

This powerfully worded statement captures well the impact an ill-considered use of language can have on disabled people. A key factor in the struggle against disablism is therefore the development of a greater sensitivity to the discriminatory effects of language and the construction of a more appropriate vocabulary of empowerment (see also Slee, 1996).

Much work remains to be done before equality of opportunity can become a reality for disabled people. The 'charitable' approach which presents disabled people as objects of pity and sympathy has a long legacy, and so its influence and consequences will not wither away overnight. This is especially the case when we consider that this approach has not developed in isolation but is, rather, a reflection of the broader economic and political sphere which values people's contribution to society in terms of the part they play in the production process and the creation of wealth.

It is partly in recognition of these wider aspects that the Disabled People's Movement has sought to politicise disability issues by, for example, seeing them as a civil rights matter, a struggle for the replacement of charity with rights, rather than simply a call for more or better services. We are witnessing what de Jong (1979), referring to the work of Kuhn (1962), calls a 'paradigm shift'. What is called for is not a modification of the existing approach or 'paradigm' but rather a completely new paradigm which focuses not on individual tragedy or 'special' needs but more appropriately on the barriers to empowerment and self-realisation that a disabling society places before those citizens who have an impairment.

The Disabled People's Movement seeks to reconstruct the image of disabled people in the eyes of mainstream society. They seek to establish the recognition that *all* people require some form of aiding to live satisfactory day-to-day lives and we should not discriminate against people with an impairment simply because the aiding they require is different from the majority (that is, different *not* special). It is an arrogant and inaccurate assumption to see disabled people as those in need of aid as opposed to able-bodied people who are not.

This more radical approach casts down a considerable challenge to social workers, as the actions of social work staff cannot be neutral – they will either follow traditional lines and thus reinforce the oppression of disabled people or they will challenge traditional methods by contributing to the emancipation and empowerment of people with disabilities.

Multiple oppressions

So far in this chapter the emphasis has been specifically on the oppression inherent in the social response to disability. The aim of this section, then, is to widen the focus somewhat in order to consider how disablism intersects with other forms of discrimination and oppression. This is, of course, a complex and multifaceted area and so, once again, it must be recognised that the discussion here is exploratory and far from comprehensive.

Disablism has a particular link with ageism as the incidence of impairment is greater in the older age groups than in the population as a whole. This statistical point is often misconstrued, and it emerges as an aspect of ageist ideology: the false assumption that old age itself is a form of disability or impairment (see Chapter 5). However, what does in fact occur is that very many older people suffer the dual oppression of a combination of ageism and disablism; they are marginalised and negatively stereotyped on both counts. This can have the effect of amplifying the discriminatory impact of both forms of oppression. An example of this would be attitudes towards sexuality. As has been noted in Chapter 5, ageism constructs older people as asexual and thus presents sexual activity in old age as 'deviant'. A similar process occurs in relation to disabled people who are also assumed to be asexual. A disabled older person therefore faces an even greater attitudinal barrier to fulfilling sexual desire.

Many other examples could be given but I hope the point is clear that age and disability are not simply separate social forces – they converge and overlap in many significant ways which will have important implications for older disabled people. One result of this is that social workers who work with older people should be conscious not only of issues of ageism but also of disablism.

Gender also features as a significant dimension of the experience of disabled people. Lonsdale (1990) covers many aspects of the complex intertwining of gender and disability and she explores a number of important themes. One such theme is that of dependency:

> Dependency has particular implications for women because of the important part which gender plays in determining whether someone is expected or encouraged, or indeed is even allowed to be independent. Since women are encouraged to play a more dependent role in society than men, women with disabilities often have a particular struggle to achieve control over their own destinies, although they are

sometimes 'allowed' out of the passive and dependent female role.
(pp. 10–11)

Social expectations of dependency apply to women in general within the strictures of patriarchy, but for disabled women the additional stereotyped equation of disability with dependency further promotes an image of disabled women as people who need to be 'looked after'. It does not then take much imagination to see the impact of this as negative and limiting. Similarly, Lonsdale argues that women are 'invisible' in the majority of accounts of disability and so issues of gender and sexism are not paid adequate attention, even though far more women than men have disabilities.

---

practice focus 6.3

Paula was a student on placement at a disability resource centre where a range of advice, information and advocacy services was provided. Her main task was to interview people who sought a service and help to determine the most appropriate response to their request. In supervision Paula and her practice teacher discussed her work in some detail. From this it emerged that Paula was doing very well indeed in general terms. However, what also emerged was that she appeared to be operating within stereotypical expectations as far as gender was concerned. For example, in her dealings with men, Paula often addressed employment issues but rarely did so with the women who sought her help. In her anxiety to avoid relying on disablist assumptions she had neglected to take account of gender.

One account which does recognise the intersection of sexism and disablism is that of Oliver (1990). Drawing on the work of Brittan and Maynard (1984), he discusses the 'ideology of masculinity' and the limited responses to disablement available to men and women. That is, he recognises the way in which patriarchy seeks to predefine roles for both men and women and links this to specific issues of disability. Gender roles take on an extra significance from the standpoint of disability and place extra pressures and restrictions on disabled women in particular. He illustrates this by quoting Fine and Asch (1985):

Whereas disabled men are obliged to fight the social stigma of disability, they can aspire to fill socially powerful male roles. Disabled women do not have this option. Disabled women are perceived as inadequate for economically productive roles (traditionally considered appropriate for males) and for the nurturant, reproductive roles considered appropriate for females.

(p. 5)

Oliver describes this as a 'double disability' which compounds the oppression of the negative social response to impairment. Thus disabled women are seen as 'roleless' and 'lacking in opportunities for self affirmation' (Fine and Asch, 1985, p. 9). In short, sexism amplifies the negative effects of disablism.

Lonsdale (1991), however, offers some hope that the emergence of a new approach to disability can improve the situation for disabled women. She comments:

Women with disabilities, therefore, stand to gain considerably from a politics of disability that encourages assertiveness and independence and aims to put the control of social service provision back in the hands of the recipient.

(p. 15)

In addition, Morris (1993) points out that the intermeshing of gender and disability is not only applicable to women – it can also be potentially problematic for men:

We may want to identify the way that women experience particular disadvantages and powerlessness as a result of the structures of oppression associated with both gender and disability, but we should not lose sight of the fact that disabled men can also experience gender as an oppressive social construct.

(p. 92)

A social work of empowerment is also a relevant issue in considering how disability and race combine to provide another example of interlocking and mutually reinforcing oppressions. Mirza (1991) is critical of the lack of attention paid to the needs of ethnic minority communities in the National Health Service and Community Care Act 1990: 'Government failed to identify clearly the role of local authorities in ensuring that each aspect of their community care programme actively promoted equality or, at minimum, accounted for the impact of racial discrimination' (p. 123). As this is a major piece of legislation with regard to Social Services provision for disabled people, this criticism is a very telling one in relation to black people or people from ethnic minorities who are disabled and in need of services. It raises questions about the availability of ethnically sensitive service provision and perhaps identifies a barrier to the development of anti-racist practice.

In recent years there has been a notable, and very welcome, growth in literature addressing issues of anti-racist social work but sadly anti-racism in the context of social work with disabled people has yet to receive adequate attention. The dynamics of racism and disablism as a combination of oppressions remains a neglected area and one which clearly merits further research and the articulation of a coherent theory base. Stuart (1992) recognises the need for further work in this area and offers some useful pointers towards a more adequate theoretical understanding of the issues.

Oliver (1990) would also add gender as a further dimension of this under-researched area:

> In the absence of empirical data, there has also been little theorising on the effects of a combination of race, gender and disability on personal experience, though it has been suggested that concepts like 'multiple minority statuses' and 'multiple minority groups' might be a useful starting point for analysis (Deegan, 1985).
> (p. 175)

None the less, despite the relative lack of material to inform our understanding of such multiple oppressions, the significance of such combinations can be readily appreciated and their implications for practice can at least begin to be addressed.

Towards anti-disablist practice

This chapter has outlined the development of a new approach to social work with disabled people which is quite radically different from traditional perspectives. Much of the change has stemmed from disabled people who have sought to rework the helper–helped relationship. The movement remains a 'consumer-led' one, but this is not to say that social workers do not have a major contribution to make. The remainder of this chapter is therefore a set of suggestions for taking steps towards an anti-discriminatory social work with disabled people. These are by no means the only steps, but will, I hope, none the less help social workers to engage with the issues and determine, in more detail, the route they wish to follow.

1. Disabled people are people first. This may seem straightforward but it is something which is not always recognised in interactions between social workers and disabled clients. The history of social work intervention with disabled people is not a particularly happy one (Sapey and Hewitt, 1991; Morris, 1989). Much of the criticism has stemmed from the view that the focus tends to be on the disability rather than on the person (as per the medical model – see point 2 below). Anti-discriminatory practice must be based on seeing the person first, before the disability. As UPIAS (1980) put it: 'We look forward to the future – a world where physically-impaired people are truly people first, and last' (p. 46).
2. Social work with disabled people has for many years been dominated by the medical model. The social work task has been seen as a paramedical or ancillary task geared towards caregiving and rehabilitation. Preston-Shoot and Agass (1990) argue that a medicalised approach to social work has arisen due to the failure of social work to develop its own theory base. The more critical approach to disability developed by Oliver, Finkelstein and so on is now capable of creating that theory base so that the medical model is not needed to 'fill the gap'. Treating disabled people as if they were ill or necessarily in need of medical supervision is dehumanising and oppressive. Anti-discriminatory practice must therefore aim for a 'demedicalisation' of social work.
3. Traditional social work with disabled people is premised on an individual model of personal tragedy and efforts are geared towards the individual for his or her lack of functional ability. However, this has now been challenged by a social oppression model of disability which emphasises the personal, cultural, structural and environmental barriers which prevent disabled people from participating fully in mainstream social,

political and economic life. In fact, the individual model is seen as a further barrier to self-realisation as it translates issues of human rights into matters of care and rehabilitation. Anti-discriminatory practice must therefore be based on a social, rather than an individual model of disability.

4. Following on from this, it needs to be recognised that the service disabled people's organisations are looking for is one based on rights rather than compassion. As Sapey and Hewitt (1991) put it:

> If we see disabled people as people in need rather than people whose rights to resources are being denied or rationed, then the concept of need can also become disabling. While it is necessary to review the language of legislation, it is more important to ensure that it is interpreted in a manner that will afford disabled people their rights.
> (pp. 42–3)

They go on to argue that there is a social work role in helping disabled people to assert their own choices and thus move to a less dependent role. This can be a key part in the development of anti-disablist practice.

5. The dominance of disablist ideology which constructs disabled people as passive and pitiful victims of personal tragedy is reflected in, and reinforced by, the language used to refer to disabled people. It is therefore important to ensure that discriminatory and dehumanising language is avoided and discouraged. Depersonalising terms such as 'the disabled', 'the handicapped' or 'spastic' not only contribute to the oppression of disabled people but also legitimate such oppression by making it seem natural, 'normal' and a straightforward part of everyday life. A more sensitive and positive use of language is therefore called for.

6. Part of the discriminatory ideology of disablism is the tendency to see disabled people as those in need of aid as opposed to 'normal' people who do not need such aid. This is an oppressive and divisive myth which isolates disabled people from the mainstream of society. By disguising the assistance all people rely on and the public resources which finance much of such assistance, the type of aiding required

by people with an impairment appears to be 'special' and costly – and is therefore vulnerable to cutbacks and rationing and seen as a privilege rather than a right. It therefore needs to be remembered that *aiding is for all* and therefore the needs of people with an impairment are different rather than a 'special case'. Social workers can play a part in drawing attention to this and thus contribute to 'destigmatising' disability.

7. Given that aiding is for all, we are all 'dependent' to some extent on assistance. The fact that such a reliance is exaggerated and overemphasised in the stereotype of disability is a further dimension of disablist ideology. It is therefore important that social work intervention has the effect of promoting independence as far as possible. There is a danger that an uncritical social work practice informed by received ideas will assume dependency to be the norm and thus run the risk of creating such dependency by establishing a 'self-fulfilling prophecy'. What is needed therefore is a practice based on partnership rather than paternalism.

8. A focus on independence is precisely the strategy of Centres for Integrated Living (CILs). These centres involve putting power and control into the hands of disabled people themselves. This is, of course, entirely consistent with anti-disablism and a movement to be supported and encouraged. The development of anti-discriminatory practice will therefore be hindered by a traditional approach which sees the social work task in predominantly casework terms and shies away from community involvement or wider-scale initiatives. CILs should not be seen as developments ripe for professional colonisation, but nor should they be seen as a separate venture largely unconnected with the aims, values and interests of social workers.

9. The casework approach has also tended to produce an emphasis on practical tasks, a very pragmatic sorting out services and benefits approach. It is no doubt partly due to this that social work with disabled people has tended to be seen as a lower status branch of social work, often consigned to unqualified staff. Social work with disabled people is a professional endeavour which requires commitment and a range of skills, including assessment, negotiation, advocacy,

counselling and so on. Helping to overcome oppression is a skilled and demanding task and should not be viewed as a subordinate, lower status aspect of social work – as that would itself be a disablist assumption to make.

10. Perhaps the central concept in the development of anti-disablist practice is that of *empowerment*. Traditional approaches to disability continued to disempower people with an impairment, to deprive them of aspects of control over their own lives. They are disenfranchised by marginalisation, isolation and dehumanisation – at a personal level through prejudice and misdirected pity; at a cultural level through negative stereotypes and values; at a structural level through a society dominated by capitalist notions of 'survival of the fittest' and charity for those who are 'handicapped' from competing. Empowerment amounts to working alongside disabled people to help overcome and challenge the oppression they experience. This involves counselling geared towards confidence-boosting and similar measures on the one hand, and advocacy and the promotion of citizenship on the other.

Social work has never been a static entity and is therefore no stranger to change and innovation. However, it must be recognised that the changes required to develop anti-disablist social work practice are, in many ways, major and radical. This does not mean it cannot be done; indeed it is already underway in some areas. But this is clearly a major challenge for social work and one to which I very much hope we are able to rise.

points to ponder

> Do you have a disability or do you know someone who has a disability?
> If so, can you see how social attitudes and expectations affect the experience of disability?
> What stereotypes of disabled people can you identify?
> How can you ensure that you do not allow these to affect your practice?
> How can social workers be involved in empowering disabled people rather than making them dependent?

Guide to further learning

Sapey (1998) is a useful introductory chapter to begin with. Oliver and Sapey (1999) is an updated version of a classic text which has had a profound influence on social work thinking. Other important works involving leading thinker and activist, Mike Oliver, include: Oliver (1990); Oliver (1991); Oliver (1996); Campbell and Oliver (1996) and Swain *et al.* (1993).

Barton (1996) is an important text that provides a sociological perspective on disability. Lonsdale (1991) links disability issues with questions relating to gender. Hales (1996) provides an informative and insightful set of readings on the theme of 'towards an enabling society'. Marks (1999) provides considerable food for thought.

Sapey (2002) and Sapey (2004) are two important contributions to our understanding of the relationship between disability and loss. Clements and Read (2003) provide a helpful guide to the implications of the Human Rights Act 1998 for disabled people.

The journal *Disability and Society* is a regular source of relevant articles.

Relevant websites include:

    The Disability Rights Commission   www.drc.gb.org

    The Rowan Organisation   www.therowan.org

    The British Council of Disabled People   www.bcodp.org.uk

7 | Diversity and oppression

Each of the preceding four chapters has concentrated on a major area of discrimination and oppression – gender, race, age and disability. However, it would be a mistake to assume that these are the only sources of oppression with which anti-discriminatory practice needs to concern itself.

There are many other diverse forms and sources of oppression which have an impact on social work and attention needs to be drawn to the wide range of issues not already incorporated in the four main areas covered so far. Arguably, each of the topics discussed in this chapter could justify a full chapter of its own. The fact that they 'share' a chapter is in no way an indication that they are unimportant or less relevant to social work. It is simply a matter of limitations on space – a text which did justice to such a range of topics would be vast indeed. The emphasis, then, is not on each area as a discrete aspect of discrimination in its own right, but rather as part of a broader pattern representing the diversity of forms of oppression.

This chapter can therefore expect only to scratch the surface of these various areas. None the less, this is an important part of the process of developing anti-discriminatory practice, as the first part of this process must be to recognise the existence of the form of oppression in question and thus begin to place it on the agenda. By raising some of the issues here, I hope to contribute to raising levels of consciousness and thereby provide leads for interested readers to follow up and perhaps use as the basis of discussion and further learning.

Before proceeding to consider each of these various sources of oppression, and thus widening out the analysis so far presented, I shall first outline some aspects of oppression which will help to cast light on the discussions that follow. This will set the scene for exploring the discrimination and oppression associated with sexual identity; religion; language, nation and region; mental health problems; and mental impairment.

Aspects of oppression

In Chapter 2 oppression was defined as, amongst other things, 'the negative and demeaning exercise of power'. Similarly, the Webster's *Third New International Dictionary* uses the phrase 'unjust or cruel exercise of authority or power' in its definition of oppression. Power and oppression are therefore closely linked.

In order to understand oppression as a dimension of the lives of social work clients (and potential clients), it is therefore necessary to be clear about the part played by power and how it operates. This is particularly important, as power is a unifying theme across the various subsections of this chapter – it is a concept which can be seen to apply in each of the topics covered. It links together what may otherwise appear a relatively unrelated series of issues. Hugman (1991) argues that: 'power is not an isolated element of social life, but one which interweaves occupational and organisational structures with the actions of professionals, individually and collectively' (p. 38).

Where social workers, and indeed other human services professionals, come into contact with clients, power is always on the agenda; it is: 'an integral aspect of the daily working lives of professionals' (Hugman, 1991, p. 1). This has very much been the case in the preceding four chapters in terms of the power of men in relation to women, white people in relation to black, young in relation to old, and able-bodied in relation to disabled. In addition, we must recognise the power of social workers in terms of:

- knowledge and expertise;
- access to resources;
- statutory powers; and
- influence over individuals, agencies and so on.

Power is an aspect of the relationship between social workers and their clients – in addition to the social divisions which go to make up the social structure. This raises two sets of potential problems:

1. The social worker's power can be used in an oppressive way – that is, it can be abused (Thompson, 1991b);
2. The social worker may not be sufficiently sensitive to issues of power/powerlessness and oppression as they relate to clients in terms of their social location – gender, race, age and so on.

Emancipatory forms of practice therefore need to be very sensitive to issues of power, and not simply in relation to the four main areas of discrimination discussed so far. Power is a general feature of social work and is also specifically relevant to the other forms of discrimination outlined in this chapter.

Oppression is also significant in relation to identity. The traditional view of identity as a narrow, psychological issue is increasingly being challenged as sociological and political aspects of identity are receiving greater attention. And oppression is an important factor in understanding this wider view of identity formation. Woodward (1997) challenges the narrowness of conventional views of identity when she argues that:

> identities are forged through the marking of difference. This marking of difference takes place both through the *symbolic* systems of representation, and through forms of *social* exclusion. Identity, then, is not the opposite of, but *depends on,* difference. In social relations, these forms of symbolic and social difference are established, at least in part, through the operation of what are called classificatory systems. A classificatory system applies a principle of difference to a population in such a way as to be able to divide them and all their characteristics into at least two, opposing groups – us/them (e.g. Serb/Croat); self/other.
> (p. 29)

It follows, then, that it is important for social work education and practice (particularly in relation to assessment, for example) to take on board this broader conception of identity. An individual's identity will owe much to his or her social location and thus possible or actual experiences of discrimination and oppression.

Social workers have often been criticised for taking too narrow and individualistic an approach, and thus failing to appreciate wider social patterns (Mills, 1970). For example, Dale and Foster (1986) are critical of psychodynamic approaches that do not recognise: 'that the problems faced by their individual female clients might have been more related to their positions in society than to their individual psyches' (p. 96, quoted in Rojek *et al.*, 1989, p. 2). Social workers who seek to develop anti-discriminatory practice need not only to move beyond the individual level to understand the social, but also to appreciate how the social has a major impact on the personal and subjective. Who I am is not just a matter of my unique and personal life-world, it is also a matter of my *social location* and to what extent and in what ways I may experience oppression.

The various forms of oppression – be it sexism, racism, disablism and so on, or, as we shall see below, heterosexism, sectarianism or internal colonialism and so on – can be seen to have an impact on identity in terms of:

- alienation, isolation, marginalisation;
- economic position and life-chances;
- confidence and self-esteem; and
- social expectations, career opportunities and so on.

The links between identity and oppression are significant, although an analysis which does justice to these issues is far beyond the scope of a more generalised, introductory text such as this. The basic linkages should none the less be borne in mind when considering the various sources of oppression discussed below.

The final aspect of oppression I wish to consider here is that of its complex, multifaceted nature. This is to revisit and reaffirm the point made in Chapter 2 that there can be no simple or crude model of oppression and especially no spurious 'hierarchy of oppressions'. As we have noted, oppression is a dimension, or outcome, of a power relationship, specifically a relationship premised on discrimination. Such relationships are, of course, diverse and many-sided, forming an intricate web of social patterns and interactions. To reduce this to a simplistic, uni-dimensional model of oppression as the evil or unenlightened behaviour and attitudes of certain social groups (men, white people and so on) is a form of crude 'reductionism'. It reduces a complex, empirically variable situation to the status of a monolithic, undifferentiated concept (Sibeon, 1991a; 1996; Thompson, 2000a). This is a point to which I shall return below.

The complexity and variability are reflected in the diversity of sources of oppression outlined below and are also captured in this comment from Hudson (1989): 'The dynamics and effects of oppression are like a kaleidoscope where the configurations of, and relationships between, different forms of oppression are constantly moving and changing' (p. 93).

Having re-examined, and extended to some degree, our understanding of oppression, let us now move on and address, in turn, a number of additional sources of oppression, beginning with discrimination against gay men, lesbians and bisexuals.

Sexual identity

The 1980s and 1990s saw an increased awareness of issues of sexual identity and the discriminatory and negative treatment of homosexuals. Such discrimination has increasingly been recognised as unjust and, in some areas, has been included in equal opportunities policies (Blakemore and Drake, 1996). Field (1995) captures the nature and extent of such oppression in the following passage:

> The rise of ultra-right fascist organisations, unchecked by states or governments, is precipitating an atmosphere of terror amongst gays and black people. Violent homophobic attacks are on the increase. Lesbians and gays are still losing custody of their children because their sexuality is regarded as making them 'unfit' parents. Many public housing tenants lose their homes when their partners die because their relationships are still not recognised. Despite softly-softly guidelines, gay people are systematically harassed and entrapped by police. Homosexual men – and occasionally women – continue to be arrested, convicted and imprisoned for consensual sexual relationships. Homophobic ideas and attitudes, both blatant and subtle, continue to pour into people's homes and heads via the mass media.
> (pp. 1–2)

The heightened awareness of such issues has been recognised in the coining of a new term in the anti-discriminatory vocabulary – 'heterosexism', which can be explained in the following terms:

> *Heterosexism* reflects the dominance of the world-view in which heterosexuality is used as the standard against which all people are measured; everyone is assumed to be heterosexual unless proven otherwise, and anyone not fitting into this pattern is considered to be abnormal, sick, morally corrupt and inferior. The assumption of heterosexuality and its superiority is perpetuated through its institutionalization within laws, media, religions and language, which either actively discriminate against non-heterosexuals or else render

them invisible through silence. Just as the concepts of racism and sexism have helped us to understand the oppression of black people and women, so the concept of heterosexism has assisted us in theorizing lesbian and gay oppression.
(Wise, 2000, p. 154)

As Wise implies, there are strong parallels between heterosexism and other forms of discrimination (not least the applicability of PCS analysis). For example, there is a reliance on biological (or pseudo-biological) explanations of why homosexuality is not 'natural' and is therefore 'deviant' and to be discouraged. However, to argue that one form of sexuality is natural while another is not is a matter of ideological construction rather than biological explanation. It amounts, as Hocquenghem (1978) points out, to arguing that: 'Some of us are part of nature, and some not' (p. 48). The oppressive implications of this assumption are, of course, vast and so it is not too difficult to appreciate the negative impact of this aspect of heterosexism.

A further parallel is the alienation, marginalisation and destructive humour to which gay men, lesbians and bisexuals are subjected. A very negative and discriminatory attitude is even witnessed within the so-called caring professions. For example, Munro and McCulloch (1969), in a text written for social workers, comment that: 'Most lesbians are content to keep their homosexual inclinations hidden from general view and it is only the most psychopathic among them who make a show of their abnormality' (p. 157, quoted in Hart, 1980, pp. 46–7). This comment was made many years ago but we should not be complacent in assuming that the problems no longer apply.

One of the factors which can be seen to underlie heterosexism is a degree of paranoia, a fear that an acceptance of homosexuality will undermine family values to the extent that the social and moral order will be seriously weakened. Brown (1998a) uses the term 'homophobia' to refer to the fear and hatred of homosexuality. Homophobia is therefore a key aspect of heterosexism.

Haselden (1991) discusses a similar theme and comments on the impact of AIDS on the gay community. He argues that the determination of gay people to be sexually active regardless of AIDS is seen as self-destructive and self-indulgent. He then goes on to link this with the impression this gives to heterosexuals and the impact it has on them:

> At our most self-indulgent we show the futility of individual existence and inspire the hatred of a wider community, we remind people of their own mortality, we become perpetually discontent and rummage through the world looking for some purpose or meaning to our lives.
> (p. 20)

These comments add to Hocquenghem's view that: 'The problem is not so much homosexual desire as the fear of homosexuality' (1978, p. 35). Such fear and paranoia can lead to people having to conceal their sexual identity and make a secret of their personal, intimate relationships or even deny them for fear of reprisal, ridicule or some other form of social sanction. For example, Webb (1989b) refers to a member of the Proud Old Lesbians group in London who allows her home help to assume she is heterosexual in order to avoid hostility.

Heterosexism can be seen as particularly problematic for older people or disabled people as it is often assumed that they have no sexuality. The notion of homosexuality being applicable in the case of older or disabled people is therefore doubly oppressive for those prejudiced enough to subscribe to heterosexism – and therefore doubly oppressive for those so affected by this form of discrimination.

Discrimination against gay men, lesbians and bisexuals can be seen to have two major sets of implications, one in relation to staff/service providers and the other in relation to clients/service users.

One common assumption which can have a profoundly discriminatory effect on staff is the false notion that homosexuals are a threat to children. It is commonly assumed by many people that homosexuals regard children as valid objects of sexual desire. This is reflected in, for example, the French use of the term *pédéraste,* which literally means 'lover of children', to refer to homosexuals in general – and this is even confirmed in the dictionary definition (*Le Petit Robert*). It is therefore important that such discriminatory assumptions at the cultural level are not allowed to influence our thoughts and actions at the personal level. The risk any individual poses to children is something that needs to be assessed very carefully in each case and is not something that should be distorted by inaccurate and discriminatory generalisations or stereotypes.

The irrational view of homosexuality as a threat is indicative of the paranoia which both reflects and reinforces heterosexist ideology. This ideology is also apparent in some social work dealings with clients. As Webb (1989b) puts it: 'All the while social workers, home helps and so on at best assume clients are heterosexual and at worst make homophobic comments' (p. 21). An insensitive, ill-informed social work practice can therefore not only fail to play a part in tackling the oppression of heterosexism but can actually contribute significantly to such oppression.

---

practice focus 7.1

Len was an experienced social worker in an emergency duty team. One night he was called out to deal with a situation in which Mrs Todd, an elderly woman, was in need of urgent support. As a result of this referral, Len contacted Mrs Todd's son, Alan. Alan expressed a willingness to care for his mother but explained that this might cause friction as he had had little contact with her since he 'came out' and she told him he was no longer her son. The realisation that Alan was gay had a profound effect on Len – it generated very strong negative feelings in him. Some days later Len reflected on the situation and his feelings, and felt very guilty about his negative reaction. He began to realise just how deeply ingrained discriminatory feelings and prejudices can be.

The development of anti-discriminatory practice must therefore be based on a greater understanding of homosexuality and heterosexism. This is particularly the case in relation to child care in Britain, at least, where the Children Act 1989 expects the self-esteem needs of gay young people to be addressed. Sone (1991) explains it as follows:

> [Social services] departments must come out of the closet and place the needs of lesbian and gay young people firmly on the agenda. The potential for this revolution can be found in The Children Act. The guidance on family placements states that when leaving care 'the needs and concerns of gay young men must be recognised and approached sympathetically'.
> (p. 12)

It is to be hoped, of course, that anti-discriminatory practice will amount to more than a sympathetic approach, as this has patronising and tokenistic connotations. However, as part of a broader-based commitment to fighting oppression, this is a worthwhile start.

Heterosexism is a deeply ingrained set of ideas and practices both within and outside social work. It is a significant and widespread form of oppression which merits inclusion on the anti-discriminatory practice agenda. It is beyond the scope of this book to present a full picture of what would be required to develop an adequate basis for anti-heterosexist practice. However, the following points can take us some distance in that direction:

● Identity is an important concept in social work and so the tendency to neglect issues of *sexual* identity must be resisted.
● The 'heterosexual assumption' is something to be avoided. That is, we should not automatically assume that a person is heterosexual. This has the effect of presenting homosexuality as deficient rather than different.
● Harassment policies, where they exist, should address harassment on the grounds of sexual identity (Thompson, 2000b).
● A person's sexual identity should not be seen as a significant factor in terms of risk assessment, eligibility for services and so on.
● Training in relation to sexuality and sexual identity should be recognised as a mainstream issue and not marginalised as an issue for specialist workers (HIV counsellors, for example).

Religion

Religion is, of course, a major social institution which has profound effects on social organisation, politics, the economy, cultural norms and, not least, personal beliefs and values. The potency of religion is therefore immense.

The term 'religion' is frequently used in the singular as if it were a single, unified concept or force. However, we should not allow this to distract us from recognising the plurality of religion, the fact that we live in a multi-faith society. There exist a multiplicity of religions and, within the major religions, a number of 'subdivisions' or variations as, for example, in the Islamic faith. Such religious diversity is often closely linked with ethnic or racial groupings, although not exclusively so. Indeed, a sensitivity to, and awareness of, religious values and practices is a significant component of ethnically sensitive practice as discussed in Chapter 4.

Religion is significant in relation to all three levels of PCS analysis:

P – one's religious beliefs (or lack of them) can be a fundamental part of one's identity and be a major guide to action on the basis of moral principles or required practices (for example, rituals).
C – shared cultural norms and values can owe much to religion and can be enshrined in the particular religion's system of symbolic representations of reality.
S – stratification systems can be based on religion (for example, caste) and, indeed, the links between religion and wider sociopolitical factors have been extensively explored (for example, Weber's study *The Protestant Ethic and the Spirit of Capitalism,* first published in 1904).

Religion can play a central part in the lives of social work clients at a number of levels and therefore needs to be taken into account in social work assessment, intervention, evaluation and policy planning.

Having clarified, to some extent, the need to take account of religious factors, let us now turn our attention to a particular dimension of religion and its relationship with discrimination and oppression. The issue I am referring to is that of sectarianism and I shall be using the example of Northern Ireland, drawing on the work of Brewer (1991). Brewer defines sectarianism as:

> actions, attitudes and practices determined by beliefs about religious difference, which results in them being invoked as the boundary marker to represent social stratification and conflict.
> (p. 101)

It is important to note that religion is not seen as the primary social difference, but rather as indicative of other social or political differences. Brewer refers to a number of studies which: 'highlight the importance of religion as a social marker through which conflict is articulated rather than as a source of conflict in its own right' (p. 101). Such conflicts include socioeconomic inequality between Protestants and Catholics and different political objectives (political union with the UK versus unity with the Republic of Ireland).

In many ways, sectarianism can be seen to parallel racism, and Brewer lists eight such parallels before going on to emphasise two of the main differences:

1. Sectarianism is based on discrimination relating to *stereotypical* assumptions (that is, generalisations about behaviour) whereas racism hinges on *phenotypical* assumptions (that is, generalisations about physical appearance).
2. It is possible to disguise, conceal or change one's religion and/or behaviour whereas physical differences such as skin colour cannot be changed.

None the less, Brewer argues that some principles apply to both anti-racism and anti-sectarianism (and, indeed, perhaps more widely to anti-discriminatory practice in general). These are:

● equal treatment for people;
● protection from derogatory stereotypes, myths and abuse;
● protection of religious and cultural diversity; and
● equality of opportunity to society's rewards.

An understanding of sectarianism is clearly important for social workers in Northern Ireland and Brewer's paper is helpful in drawing out some of the practice implications. However, we should note that, whilst Northern Ireland is a good example of sectarianism, the concept is, of course, far more widely applicable on a national and international basis than simply within the province.

Of course, sectarianism is not the only example of the interaction of religion and oppression or discrimination. Religion is a highly significant dimension of our existence at a number of levels and a wide variety of examples could be given of problems arising from conflicting religious ideologies. Space does not permit a detailed analysis of these, but it is certainly worth exploring one particular area – the contradiction between some religious beliefs and some aspects of anti-discriminatory practice.

One example of this is the restriction on women and the concomitant inequalities enshrined in some religious doctrines. Similarly, Connolly (1991) discusses what she sees as dangerous aspects of religious fundamentalism. For example, she expresses concern about the creation of racially segregated schools and, later in the same article, she comments on: 'the further growth of religious bigotry, and racist bigotry sheltering under the name of religion' (p. 76). As with sectarianism, the issue here is not so much religion itself, but rather the social and political implications of certain aspects of certain religions.

This is a vast and complex area and I have only barely begun to scratch the surface in my treatment of the issues here. Much work remains to be done before our understanding of these matters even begins to approach a level of adequacy (although Moss, 2005, is a good step in the right direction). It is important that social workers acknowledge the complexity and vastness of this dimension of social interaction and thus recognise the need to seek advice and guidance in dealing with such issues. It is not possible for social workers to be 'experts' in this area, given our current level of knowledge. None the less, this should not be used as an excuse for failing to address such issues to the best of our abilities. It is through making such attempts that much of the necessary learning will take place. While it would be unrealistic to expect social work staff to have the necessary knowledge of the variety of religions they are likely to encounter, it is quite realistic to expect the appropriate literature to be consulted as and when required (see, for example, Collins *et al.*, 1993; Green, 1991, 1993).

Language, nation and region

As with our discussion of religion above, the issues of language and nation – and, to a lesser extent, region – are very relevant to the subject matter of Chapter 4 in relation to ethnicity and racism. There are, of course, close links between factors associated with one's language, national or regional identity and ethnic groupings.

A key unifying concept in this area is that of *culture* – what can be defined at its simplest as shared ways of seeing, thinking and doing. Cultural values and norms differ across regions and nations, and also within or across linguistic groups. Indeed, language is a central part of culture. As Carter and Aitchison (1986) comment:

> The character and vitality of a culture is to a large extent
> language-dependent. Language helps to preserve traditions,

shapes modes of perception, and profoundly influences
patterns of social intercourse and behaviour.
(p. 1)

They go on to quote Mandelbaum (1949, p. 162): 'No two
languages are ever sufficiently similar to be considered as representing the same social reality' (ibid.).

On this basis, the language or languages one speaks (and, by
implication, through which one conducts one's own social interactions) have a profound impact on the way in which we experience
our existence – the medium through which we make sense of our
world and construct our reality.

This will be very significant where the social worker is from a
different linguistic background from the client or group with which
he or she is working. This may be where languages of ethnic minority groups are involved, for example, Urdu or Gujerati, and the
appropriate use of an interpreter is likely to be needed. The legislative base also requires practitioners to demonstrate some degree of
linguistic sensitivity, for example in terms of the Children Act 1989
or the requirement, under the Mental Health Act 1983, to interview
'in an appropriate manner', although it must be acknowledged that
such issues may frequently be neglected (Morris and Williams,
1994).

Making sure that members of ethnic minorities have the opportunity to communicate their needs, wishes and feelings is, of course,
part and parcel of anti-racist practice. However, there are other
cross-linguistic situations which are not so readily associated with
racism – although *ethnocentrism* does tend to feature. I am referring to bilingual nations such as Canada and Wales. As Drakeford
and Morris (1998) point out: 'Almost every state in Europe is at
least bilingual, in the sense of having more than one indigenous
language, as well as languages spoken by migrants from other
places' (p. 93). To take Wales as an example, there are over half a
million people within the principality who speak the Welsh
language (2001 census figures). Most of these people also speak
English but it should be noted that, for very many, English is a
'second language'. For dealing with sensitive matters, perhaps of an
emotional nature, communicating in one's first language is very
much to be preferred.

---

practice focus 7.2

Ceri was a social worker in a family placement team. She regularly
used Welsh as a means of communication with clients and colleagues,
including foster carers. She often felt uncomfortable about placing
Welsh-speaking children with foster carers who spoke only English but
a shortage of foster carers often meant that choices were not available. However, the matter was particularly significant in the case of
one eight-year-old girl who, when placed with English-speaking foster
carers, began to disclose incidents of sexual abuse that had occurred
when she had stayed with her aunt and uncle. However, she very
quickly 'clammed up', and it was only when Ceri visited her and
communicated in Welsh that she felt able to discuss some very painful
and distressing experiences.

This point was largely recognised by the former governing body for
social work education, CCETSW, who developed a policy on the
Welsh language:

> CCETSW has a responsibility to establish and maintain stan-
> dards of education and training and to promote good and
> effective practice. In Wales with its bilingual system of
> education this reasonably requires CCETSW to ensure that
> Welsh medium education and training is available and that
> English medium education and training is culturally and
> linguistically sensitive.
> (CCETSW, 1991a, p. 48)

The policy went on to recognise that a client has the basic right to
choose the language of interaction with the social work agency. It
is important, therefore, to ensure that linguistic issues are
addressed, particularly in bilingual communities. Failure to do so
could act as an extra layer of oppression by forcing Welsh speakers
(or indeed speakers of any non-dominant language – the issue is not
confined to Wales) to communicate from a position of relative
weakness. Furthermore, Bellin (1994) also argues that it is necessary, in working with bilingual individuals, families and communities, to give due regard to *both* languages:

> Social work practice needs to recognize that the bilingual
> Welsh-speaker is just as much an integrated whole person as

a monolingual. This means that it is an unacceptable short-cut to rely on just one language for intervention or rendering of service.
(p. 116)

To take no account of a client's first language can be seen as devaluing that language and indeed the culture of which it forms part and the personal identity of the client(s) concerned. This is an example of 'ethnocentrism', the tendency to take one's own cultural or ethnic standpoint for granted without reference to other perspectives, thus imposing one's own definitions as the 'norm'.

One notable manifestation of ethnocentrism in this context is to equate 'British' with 'English', as if Wales and Scotland were simply regions of England. This is captured in Morgan's (1982) comment in which he refers to: 'that notorious entry in *the Encyclopaedia Britannica* – in which were encapsulated all the humiliation and patronising indifference which helped to launch the modern nationalist movement in the principality – "for Wales, see England" ' (p. 3). There are clear implications here for anti-discriminatory social work practice. Social workers need to be sensitive to the culture and values of not only black and ethnic minority communities, but also national, regional and linguistic groups. To ignore these factors is to ignore major aspects of the client's experience, values and social location and thus fall foul of ethnocentrism.

The concept of ethnocentrism is a useful one in so far as it takes us beyond the individual level of personal prejudice and emphasises the role of culture and thus the social dimension. However, this in itself has limitations as it takes no account of the structural level. One approach to these issues which does have a structural basis is that of Hechter (1975) who introduced the concept of 'internal colonialism'. Nairn (1986) describes it in the following terms:

British capitalist development produced a set of of 'internal colonies' in its Celtic fringe, for basically the same reasons as it created external colonisation all over the globe. It is the contradictory nature of capitalist growth to do so.
(p. 199)

Harris (1991), in a paper discussing anti-racist social work, draws parallels between the oppression of black people and the historic treatment of the Welsh. He comments:

Language is the main medium by means of which culture is transmitted. It is also the mechanism which enables the functions of conceiving, defining, refining and articulating ideas. Therefore if cultural hegemony is the objective, it is not surprising that bilingualism could not be tolerated either, as in the case of the Welsh the possession of that ability would have placed them in an advantageous position. The Welsh would have enjoyed the flexibility and facility of operating within and between two language mediums, while still retaining their cultural autonomy. In contrast the English ruling class would have been constrained, since being monolingual, they would have been unable to enter directly into the consciousness of the Welsh. Colonised people and immigrants are often encouraged by means of bribes or coercion to adopt the language of their oppressors.
(pp. 138–9)

A key term here is 'cultural hegemony'. Anti-discriminatory social work should play no part in the maintenance of such dominance with its implied oppression of cultural or linguistic minorities.

The example given here has been that of Wales, but the same issues can be seen to apply to a wider range of peoples in a wide variety of places in which social work is practised. Negative and derogatory stereotypes of Irish people is an example which springs readily to mind.

There is therefore a need for social workers to give due consideration to the issues of national, regional and linguistic identity as they apply in the locality in which they work. Without this there is a danger that an insensitive social work practice can contribute further to the oppression of 'cultural hegemony' rather than play a part in reducing the alienation and disempowerment it engenders.

Mental health problems

Of course, anti-discriminatory practice is not to be restricted to a particular client group or groups, but there are specific issues which arise in relation to each such group. For example, people who are defined as 'mentally ill' face areas of discrimination and oppression specifically as a result of being so labelled.

People who are deemed to be mentally disordered often

encounter a negative response, even to the point of outright hostility, from the community at large. However, it is often the case that the response of professionals can also be experienced as oppressive. This is due, in no small part, to the tendency to view issues of mental disorder in terms of a medical model, that is to adopt a 'medicalised' approach. Such an approach has been criticised by many (for example, Laing, 1965; Heather, 1975; Ingleby 1981a; Thompson, 1991a; see also *Promoting Equality*) for its narrow and distorted perspective which presents moral, social and political matters as medical problems and therefore clearly located within the domain of the medical profession. Busfield (1986) describes Szasz's views on this issue in the following terms:

> The notion of mental illness is, Szasz claims, but a metaphor for what should, more accurately, be called 'problems in living', for except for the organic mental illnesses (those with identifiable physical causes) which would be better thought of as brain diseases, what is termed mental illness mystifies what is in fact a moral judgement, for the term illness suggests a scientific and objective assessment of sickness based on identifiable physical pathology. On the contrary it is a moral judgement and should be recognized as such.
> (p. 86)

Translating moral issues into medical ones has two implications which are particularly relevant to anti-discriminatory practice:

1. *Power*   The 'medicalisation' of mental disorder gives considerable power to members of the medical profession and the administrative, technical and professional structures of which they form a part.
2. *Stereotypes*   The classification system inherent in the medical model can be seen to have the effect of producing stereotypes of people said to be suffering from 'mental illness'. It concentrates on generalities at the expense of specifics.

These are both key aspects of the process of discrimination and the oppression that results. We therefore need to look carefully at their impact on service users and systems of service delivery.

The power of the medical profession to define and control deviance is a long-established one which is not commonly challenged within welfare practice on a day-to-day basis. This power base and its influence on social work thinking and practice can act as a significant obstruction to the development of a social work of empowerment. This applies in a number of ways, for example:

1. As Conrad (1981) points out: 'medicalised definitions of deviance *remove responsibility* for behaviour from the individual' (p. 119). People diagnosed as mentally ill are disempowered and stigmatised by the application of such a label as their actions are deemed to be beyond their control. This then legitimises the use of external controls (medication, detention in hospital).
2. Banton *et al.* (1985) argue that medical discourse produces a cleavage between the individual's experience of pain or distress and the wider social context which underpins it. Thus the emphasis is on 'treating' individuals rather than tackling the underlying sources of distress:

> Thus medicine is consumed instead of action being taken; questions surrounding the massive incidence of stress and disturbance in society are transformed into arguments over the adequacy of resources for 'treatment'.
> (p. 36)

This is a further example of 'blaming the victim' by reducing a complex web of social, moral, political and economic factors to a simple pathology 'within' the individual.

These two examples relate both to power and to the individual, but in different ways. In the first, the personal power of the individual is denied and, in the second, the effects of wider power structures are translated into individual pathology. In both cases the individual is disempowered.

Similar issues apply to the process of stereotyping. Medicine claims to be an objective science and therefore seeks to establish clear and explicit diagnostic categories. And, of course, when categories are being applied to people, the danger of stereotyping is one to be wary of.

This applies particularly to the diagnostic label of 'schizophrenia' which is a much disputed concept. It has been criticised by many as a vague 'catch-all' which covers a broad range of problems (see, for example, Boyle, 1990). This lack of rigour is captured by the statistic that a person is two to three times more likely to be diagnosed as schizophrenic in the United States of America than in Britain (Miles, 1987).

Applying labels to people on the basis of a dubious scientific objectivity is a process which has distinctly oppressive connotations. There is a clear danger of setting up stereotypical expectations which have profoundly negative and discriminatory implications.

It is evident, therefore, that an uncritical approach to mental health social work which adopts the tenets of the medical model is not conducive to anti-discriminatory practice. What is called for is an approach which is more attuned to the cultural and structural levels and does not stop short at the individual level.

The cultural level is important in terms of shared meanings and values – the context in which the supposedly 'schizophrenic' behaviour can be rendered intelligible (Laing and Esterson, 1970). That is, we cannot assume, as conventional psychiatry does, that 'mad' behaviour is meaningless and without foundation. An anti-discriminatory approach would be less dismissive and would be more attuned to Laing's:

> long struggle to show that those labelled 'schizophrenic' are coherent in their agony – that their turns of phrase, silences, behaviour and hallucinations make a certain sense, given some dispassionate knowledge of the relationships within which they are located.
> (Ticktin, 1989, p. 4)

The structural level is also very relevant. Consider, for example, the links between gender and mental health (Brown and Harris, 1978) or race and mental health (Littlewood and Lipsedge, 1997). But even beyond this, the medical model can itself be seen as a generalised vehicle of oppression. As White (1988) comments:

> I see madness as a political/biological revolt against repressive normality, a system of fear and conformity where people are afraid to think and behave differently. Psychiatry is a way of terrorising people back into a normality where they won't revolt against an oppressive system of social and economic relationships.
> (p. 22)

Clearly, this view raises a number of issues which merit much more attention than I am able to devote to them here. None the less, I hope my main point is clear, namely that the medical model with its individualist focus has a discriminatory and oppressive impact and is therefore not an adequate basis for an emancipatory social work practice.

---

practice focus 7.3

Stella was a social worker in a community-based multidisciplinary mental health team and had over 20 years' experience as a practitioner. She had sometimes had disagreements with psychiatrists but had never had reason to question the medical dominance of mental health issues. However, when Stuart joined the team on placement, he brought with him a lot of ideas about oppressive practice, the need for rights to be promoted and the need for user participation in service planning, delivery and evaluation. Stella was forced to reconsider her views. At first she saw Stuart as an idealistic student who did not understand the realities of practice. However, the more she got to know him, the more she respected him, and the more she began to take seriously the problems and limitations of an uncritical acceptance of the medical model of mental health issues. Stella and Stuart were therefore able to learn a lot from each other.

Mental impairment

For many years issues of mental disorder and mental impairment were dealt with together in policy and legislation under the generic title of 'Mental Health'. Now, however, they are increasingly being treated as separate entities, although some degree of overlap still remains.

One significant difference between the two sets of issues is, of course, that the biological basis of mental health problems is disputed whilst the physiological basis of mental impairment is widely accepted. However, the fact that there is a physiological dimension should not be used as a basis for justifying a medically orientated approach to this area of practice. Oliver's (1990) critique of the medicalisation of disability can also be seen to apply to mental impairment, as the marginalisation and dehumanisation inherent in disablism are also applicable to people who have a mental impairment (for example, Down's Syndrome). Many of the points raised in Chapter 6 are therefore also very relevant here for it can equally be argued that any 'functional disability' engendered by the impairment is amplified and magnified by the social response which attaches negative stereotypes and marginalises yet another group of citizens from the mainstream of social life. People with a mental impairment can therefore be seen to face both disablism generally and, to some degree, discrimination specifically related to issues of learning disability and its confusion with mental 'illness'.

The social response has gone through various stages over the years, forming four distinct models of mental impairment:

The threat to society model This was a dominant view at the beginning of the twentieth century and was influenced by the eugenics movement who saw mentally impaired people as 'morally defective' and thus a threat to the social order. Thankfully, this view is no longer dominant but is, none the less, still evident in the attitudes of some people.

The medical model The development of the National Health Service in Britain in the 1940s played a key part in helping the medical profession establish a dominant position and redefine the 'problem' as a medical one, thus requiring the development of a new medical specialism.

The subnormality model In this model the focus is on educational achievement and the perceived limitations engendered by mental impairment. A key aspect of this model is the measurement of intelligence by means of IQ tests. As IQ is measured in relation to chronological age one implication of this model is that people with a mental impairment are seen as perpetual children. They are *sub*normal.

The special needs model The focus here is on 'learning difficulties' and attempts are made to achieve the integration of people with a mental impairment into ordinary life as far as possible. However, the emphasis is on *special* needs and this, in itself, establishes barriers to full integration, especially as the focus remains on the individual and his or her perceived inadequacies rather than on social organisation.

Although there is a broad chronological development through from models 1 to 4, this can be misleading, as elements of earlier models persist and influence later models. However, what all these models have in common is a tendency to marginalise and disempower, to a greater or lesser extent, people with a mental impairment in much the same way as disablism does. Indeed, the discussion in Chapter 6, of the 'structure of aiding', is equally applicable in this context. We can question the appropriateness of providing services on an individualistic basis without taking account of the commonalities, of the status of people with a mental impairment as members of a disadvantaged social group whose rights can be affected by negative, demeaning and patronising social attitudes. What is needed, from an anti-discriminatory point of view, is an approach which:

> stresses the humanity of those affected and their right to a place in society and a fair share of resources, using a logic similar to that used to argue against racial and sexual prejudice.
> (Clements, 1987, p. 3)

The concept of 'normalisation' (Wolfensberger, 1972) has been very influential in seeking to reintegrate people with learning difficulties into mainstream society. However, the fact that attempts to 'normalise' are directed predominantly at those people excluded, rather than the processes, structures or ideologies which promote such exclusion in the first place, suggests a strong element of blaming the victim.

A further criticism of normalisation arises in relation to its conception of just what is normal. This is particularly the case in relation to members of ethnic minority communities. For example, Baxter *et al.* (1990) are critical of the tests used in assessment procedures:

> Such tests are based on the assumption that individuals will identify with images based on white middle-class lifestyles and experiences. Racial stereotyping, inappropriate cultural approaches and language or communication difficulties further decrease the value of traditional assessments for black and ethnic minority children.
> (p. 23)

Despite these problems, there does appear to be a growing movement away from a paternalistic 'looking after these poor people' approach towards a genuine aim of empowerment and maximum independence or, to use Phillipson's (1989) term, 'interdependence'.

Once again, this brief analysis most certainly does not do justice to the complexity of the issues, but I hope it has none the less succeeded in its more modest aim of raising awareness of some of the elements involved in developing a truly anti-discriminatory practice.

Of course, with each of the topics discussed in this chapter, we have been able only to skim the surface of each of the areas concerned. And, it should also be recognised, we have by no means explored the full range of possible forms of discrimination. Consider, for example, that it can be shown that people who are dying are often discriminated against (Bevan, 1998), and indeed this is not the only group of people who face discrimination without receiving the same attention or recognition as others.

The aim has been one of flagging up a range of issues which merit further study, debate and development as part of the struggle to achieve a social work practice and theory base premised on principles of challenging discrimination and reducing or removing oppression – in short, principles of *emancipatory* practice.

Diversity and multiple oppressions

One of the clear implications of this chapter is that people are different, in the sense that the population in general and social work's clientele in particular are characterised by immense diversity. Furthermore, what this chapter has also shown is that where there is difference, there is the potential for unfair discrimination. Anti-discriminatory practice is, or should be, more than simply tackling those well-publicised areas of discrimination and oppression that attract considerable attention – it should encompass *all* forms of discrimination that can be seen to lead to disadvantage, disempowerment and oppression.

While the managing diversity approach (Kandola and Fullerton, 1998) can be criticised for being too individualistic and paying inadequate attention to cultural and structural levels of discrimination, one of its strong points is that it acknowledges:

● the significance of diversity and the need to affirm and value it;

● that differences between people can and should be seen as assets to be appreciated rather than problems to be solved; and
● that difference can so easily lead to unfair discrimination.

Race, ethnicity, gender, class, sexual identity, age, language, disability, religion and so on are just some of the dimensions of diversity and therefore just some of the ways in which difference can so easily be translated into discrimination and oppression as a result of the various power-related processes that have been discussed in previous chapters. However, these are not only dimensions of diversity in a sociological sense, they are also dimensions of experience in a psychological sense. That is, each sociologically defined area of discrimination can be analysed and explored as a discrete aspect of the social world. However, to each individual person, these are not discrete areas, they are very real dimensions of experience, part and parcel of our lived experience (*le vécu*) and have to be understood as such. That is, the reality for each person is a combination of perhaps several of these different areas, rather than simply discrete, unconnected areas to be considered.

This means in effect that we must consider each situation in its own right, rather than apply general principles in a reductionist and dogmatic way. We must not make assumptions about 'men' or 'black people' or 'disabled people' or 'Welsh speakers', but rather consider each unique individual *in the context of* what we know of these broad categories and their sociological significance – to link the social level of context to the personal level of unique individual experience (Thompson, 2000c), rather than fall into one of the two disastrous but none the less common traps of either (i) treating unique individuals as if they were simply social categories; or (ii) failing to recognise that individuals are unique partly because of the diversity of the social context that plays a part in shaping all of our experiences.

points to ponder

➤ In what ways do social workers have power?
➤ Can you think of ways in which such power could be abused?
➤ How can you ensure that your practice does not involve the abuse or misuse of power? →

> →
> ➤ Can you identify any other possible areas of discrimination and
>   oppression that have not featured in this or the previous chapters?
> ➤ What do these areas have in common?

Guide to further learning

Power in relation to anti-discriminatory practice is discussed in
Thompson (2003a), while the power of language receives extensive
treatment in Thompson (2003b). Hugman (1991) is a well-established and helpful text addressing power issues in the caring professions.

The importance of identity is very helpfully explored in
Woodward (1997). Fook (2002) is also helpful in this regard.
Westwood (2002) is a very helpful sociological account of power.

Sexual identity now has a growing literature base. General or
theoretical texts include Fuss (1991); Duberman *et al.* (1991);
Bristow and Wilson (1993); and Blasius and Phelan (1997) while
Davies and Neal (1996) address issues relating to 'gay affirmative'
counselling and therapy. Social work issues are covered in Brown
(1998a, b).

Religion in relation to social work is discussed in Patel *et al.*
(1998) and Moss (2005). Issues relating to the Welsh language
(with implications for other linguistic groups) are discussed in
Huws Williams *et al.* (1994). Mental health problems have a wide
literature base but a good starting point is Heller *et al.* (1996). See
Thompson (2003a) for a critical perspective on the medical model
of mental health problems and Laurance (2003) for an interesting
critical view of the mental health system from a journalist's
perspective. Mental impairment has a less well-developed literature
base in relation to discrimination but a useful starting point is
Stanton (1998).

Relevant websites include:

Stonewall   www.stonewall.org.uk

MIND The National Association for Mental Health
www.mind.org

The British Institute for Learning Disabilities
www.bild.org.uk

People First   www.peoplefirst.org.uk

The Welsh Language Society   http://cymdeithas.com/english/

8 | Conclusion

Establishing a basis of equality and social justice in service provision is no easy matter. The situation is made extremely complex by virtue of the number of forms of discrimination, the subtle and intricate ways they manifest themselves and the vested power interests which act as obstacles to change. Consequently, there can be no simple formula solutions which give a clear and straightforward path to follow.

The full development of anti-discriminatory practice must be a longer-term aim if more than lip service is to be achieved. This does not mean that significant improvements and advances cannot be made in the short term. Indeed, the establishment of a strong edifice of anti-discriminatory policy and practice in the long term will depend on the firm foundations to be laid in the short term. The success of such a venture must depend ultimately on collective action and commitment. But each individual has a part to play in the major change from traditional approaches to social work to a form of practice based on principles of emancipatory practice – countering the various forms and processes of discrimination and the oppression they produce.

This book is intended as a guide for those who wish to play their part in this major change. But it must be recognised that it is only a guide; in itself it cannot produce emancipatory practice. It can only make a contribution by:

- helping to develop the necessary knowledge base;
- stimulating debate, discussion and further study of the relevant issues;
- motivating readers to develop the skills, values and attitudes needed;
- encouraging the creation of support groups and a collective approach; and
- acting as an introduction, and bridge, to other more specialist texts on the subject.

To facilitate meeting these aims it would be helpful to restate some of the main themes of the book, by way of a concluding summary, and to examine some of the issues affecting the way forward.

The main themes

There have been a number of recurring themes and it is perhaps worth commenting on seven of these in particular:

Power

Social work is a *political* activity; that is, it operates within the context of sets of power relations – the power of law and the state, the power inherent in social divisions such as class, race and gender, and the microlevel power of personal interactions. Indeed, power can be seen to operate at all three levels, personal, cultural and structural (Thompson, 2003a). Also, many of the problems social workers tackle have their roots in the abuse of power – child abuse, for example.

Diversity

We live and work in a society characterised by considerable diversity. *Difference* is therefore a key issue. It is important that we recognise the dangers of (perceptions of) difference becoming the basis of unfair discrimination and thus oppression. Diversity and difference can be seen as assets to be valued and celebrated – sources of stimulation and enrichment, rather than problems to be solved.

PCS analysis

Traditional social work relates primarily to the level of the individual, with only limited recognition of the level of culture, values and shared meanings. Anti-discriminatory practice, by contrast, takes a much wider view – indeed an holistic perspective – which takes account of all *three* levels – P, C and S – and the interactions between them. It is not sufficient to address only the P level (many traditional forms of practice) or only the structural (the less sophisticated versions of radical social work) – an analysis that does justice to the complexities of social work must have a broader focus, encompassing a range of issues at all three levels.

Ideology

An ideology is a set of ideas which both reflects and reinforces a set of power relations with which it is associated. For example, patriarchal ideology both reflects the powerful position of men in relation to women and, by promoting sexism, reinforces that power. Ideology acts as the 'glue' which binds together the three levels of PCS analysis and, as such, has considerable discriminatory potential.

Oppression

Certain actions, attitudes and structures have the effect of oppressing particular individuals and groups – specifically those 'out groups' which are discriminated against within the social structure. Often the oppression is unintended on the part of individuals, but none the less deeply ingrained in cultural patterns and institutional structures. Unfair discrimination is the primary source of oppression.

Empowerment

Traditional approaches to social work take little or no account of the oppression inherent in certain aspects of social organisation. They therefore see the social work task as one of *adjustment* to the 'natural order of things' rather than a contribution to the political struggle against oppression. Thus, the focus in anti-discriminatory practice is on *empowerment* rather than adjustment. As Mullaly (1993) comments:

> Empowerment is not a technique but a goal and a process. As a goal, it will not be reached overnight, just as the oppressive conditions within our current social order did not suddenly appear. As a process it is ongoing. The major premise underpinning empowerment is that people are not objects to be exploited, to be controlled, or to be oppressed. People are subjects with inherent dignity and worth that should not be conditional on race, gender, class or any other inherent characteristic. All people should have reasonable opportunities and choices over their life situations and their social environments. Empowerment is a goal and a process for overcoming oppression.
> (pp. 162–3)

No middle road

Social work practice cannot avoid the question of discrimination and oppression. The actions of social workers and the policies of their agencies will have the effect of either (a) challenging and undermining, on a minor scale at least, the discrimination to which clients are subject or (b) tacitly condoning and thus reinforcing such discrimination. There can be no middle road.

There are, of course, many other themes and issues which have arisen but it is to be hoped that the seven outlined above encapsulate the main thrust of the philosophy of emancipatory practice expounded here. But how can these themes be integrated into day-to-day practice? How can they become an established part of social work? These are some of the issues I now wish to explore, in outline at least, and to focus on some of the dangers and obstacles which can stand in the way of developing a firm foundation of anti-discriminatory practice.

The way forward

Chapters 3 to 6 each ended with some guidance and suggestions concerning the implementation of principles of anti-discriminatory practice in relation to the particular area of discrimination being discussed. It is to be hoped that these points raised with regard to specific issues will encourage and stimulate practice developments in the fields of work concerned. However, we should supplement these specific aspects by considering more general suggestions concerning the translation of critical emancipatory theory into the reality of practice.

Again I must be very selective as there is so much that can be said about these issues, so many debates yet to be worked through. I shall therefore restrict myself to fourteen particular comments, broken down into seven positive steps I feel need to be taken, and seven dangers to be avoided.

Positive steps

1. Much of the discrimination inherent in social work can be seen to be unintentional – due to a lack of awareness rather than deliberate attempts to oppress. For this reason, *awareness train-*

ing has a major part to play. By bringing workers together in a training context, instances and issues of discrimination can be identified and levels of awareness can thus be raised. Greater awareness at the *P* level can begin to undermine, to some limited degree at least, discriminatory culture and ideology at the *C* level. Awareness training therefore begins the process of challenging and confronting discrimination. It also acts as a foundation for other forms and levels of training.

2. The diversity approach is still in a relatively underdeveloped state, but we can none the less see the benefits of valuing diversity, of taking a broad-based, positive approach to tackling discrimination. The main advantage of the diversity approach is that it helps us to avoid the culture of defensiveness that has grown up around efforts to tackle discrimination and oppression.

3. Awareness training provides a consciousness-raising role for individuals but its value can be multiplied by raised collective awareness and subsequent *collective action*. Examples of groups set up with this aim include: women's groups, race and culture groups, disability forums, equal opportunities monitoring groups. Recent years have seen a significant growth in the number and influence of such groups. A collective response to examples of discrimination can have a much more potent effect than an individual response. In addition, each individual can act with greater confidence in the knowledge that there exists the backing of others within a collective anti-discriminatory project.

4. Sibeon (1991b) comments on anti-intellectual tendencies in social work which devalue theory and advocate a 'common sense' approach to social work (see also Jones, 1996). This is a particularly dangerous approach as far as anti-discriminatory practice is concerned. 'Common sense' amounts, in fact, to a mixture of dominant ideologies – sexist, racist and so on. It is a collection of taken-for-granted assumptions which are likely to be discriminatory and oppressive in their content and impact (Thompson, 2000a). It is therefore essential that practice should be based on a clear and explicit theory base in order to be able to swim against the tide of dominant discriminatory assumptions. Anti-discriminatory social work therefore needs to be based on *integrating theory and practice*.

5. In order to develop emancipatory forms of practice we need to ensure that the issues and principles are seen as central – they are not an optional extra to be tagged on the end if time and resources permit. Equality and social justice should be central features of all social work theory, policy and practice. They need to be on the agenda for every service planning group, every working party, every course curriculum, every team philosophy and so on. Treating the subject as a separate, discrete area runs the risk of allowing it to become marginalised – a specialist subject for those who are interested, but not a mainstream issue. This is unacceptable, for, as we have seen, *good practice must be anti-discriminatory practice.*

6. Perhaps the most fundamental step towards anti-discriminatory practice that we can take is to become, and remain, *open and critical in relation to our own practice* (whether as direct practitioners, supervisors or educators). We need constantly to re-evaluate our practice and examine it in relation to our aims of challenging discrimination and thereby making a contribution to removing, reducing or alleviating oppression. The prefix 'anti' in anti-discriminatory practice is very significant; it denotes fighting against a powerful and established ideology. If we become complacent by failing to check that we are carrying through an emancipatory stance, discriminatory ideologies can subtly re-establish themselves in our thoughts and actions.

7. We can also promote anti-discriminatory practice by ensuring, as far as possible, that our actions are consistent with the principles of good practice more broadly. That is, if we wish to be well-equipped to tackle discrimination and oppression, we need to ensure that we are not allowing other factors to undermine the quality and effectiveness of our work. We therefore need to make sure that our practice is critically reflective, systematic and well-informed (see Thompson, 2005, for a discussion of these issues).

Dangers

1. Anti-discriminatory practice challenges people's values and their taken-for-granted assumptions in constructing their own sense of reality. Such a challenge can prove very threatening and destabilising. If not handled sensitively, exposure to anti-

discriminatory ideas and values can prove so alien and threat-ening as to arouse considerable resistance and barriers to change. Too strong and insistent an approach is likely to be counterproductive and raise obstacles rather than awareness; indeed, it could be argued that an insensitive and overzealous approach to 'converting' others is not only a disservice to emancipatory practice but also a form of oppression in itself. If we are to avoid contributing to a culture of defensiveness, our focus needs to be on educating and convincing, not bullying.

2. The whole area of oppression and anti-discrimination is a complex and intricate field of study with many contentious and problematic aspects. It is a *political* matter and therefore subject to competing values and interpretations. Consequently there can be no simple 'formula' solutions or easy answers. There are two interrelated dangers which arise from this: firstly, *reductionism,* the process of reducing a multifaceted, multilevel set of issues to a simple, single-level entity (for exam-ple, reducing PCS to personal prejudice); and, secondly, *dogma-tism,* translating an open and dynamic theoretical system into a closed and static belief system or dogma.

3. Anti-discriminatory practice is indeed a complex area with many dimensions, such as race, gender, age and so on. One primary dimension which has received relatively little attention in this book is that of class. However, it has featured less here as it is more firmly established as a relevant factor in social work (due in no small part to the influence of the radical social work movement) and *not* because it is less important. A clear danger, therefore, is to fail to take account of the class dimen-sion – the socioeconomic circumstances which (a) underpin and magnify other forms of oppression and (b) act as a major source of oppression in their own right. The danger, therefore, is one of going from a situation (for example, in the 1970s) where class was seen as the primary, if not only, dimension of oppression to a situation in which it is barely considered (Jordan, 2000).

4. Class is part of the political underpinnings of anti-discrimina-tory practice and is also a key element in marxist theory which, in turn, is a central feature of radical social work. The influ-ence of marxism has declined in recent years to be replaced, to a certain extent, by a New Right philosophy which seeks to

'roll back the state' by lessening the state's role in welfare provision. The resulting privatisation of welfare and its reliance on the profit motive are unlikely to provide fertile soil for the development of emancipatory forms of practice. Although the crude marxism of the 'Case Con' radicalism of the 1960s offered a far from adequate basis for social work, the rejection of a socialist political philosophy seriously weakens the scope for developing anti-discriminatory practice.

5. A further danger to be identified is that of 'colluding with the rhetoric'. What this means is that some people may use the right language and may make the right gestures but without any underlying commitment to the values and principles of anti-discriminatory practice. They are just 'going through the motions', perhaps to avoid being branded as racist, sexist or whatever, or perhaps through confusion, ignorance, or insecurity about how to practise in a genuinely anti-discriminatory way. This is a particularly worrying state of affairs as it gives the impression that equality and social justice are being pursued when, in fact, inequalities are being maintained, condoned and reinforced.

6. A very significant danger is that of complacency. For example, I have encountered people who reject anti-discriminatory practice as being based on an exaggeration of the nature and extent of discrimination. We live in a mature democracy, they argue, and so discrimination cannot be as much of an issue as some people make out. This is a very naïve view which fails to take account of the extensive research base and the equally important base of the day-to-day experiences of social workers and clients. A variation on the complacency theme is the idea that, because we now have an extensive body of anti-discrimination legislation, the problems are of a fairly minor nature or extent. As we have seen, although the law can be very helpful, it has serious limitations when it comes to the complexities of discrimination and oppression.

7. Although not a widespread problem, the danger of competitiveness is still one worthy of mention. It is unfortunately the case that some people see adopting a social justice perspective not so much as a foundation of good practice or a moral-political imperative, but rather as a means to an end – to achieve promotion, obtain academic brownie points or whatever. While

I have no objection to people having personal ambitions, it is sad that some people use an apparent commitment to justice and humanitarian values primarily for their own personal ends.

There are, of course, many other dangers and many other positive steps, although I am not able to pursue these here (see Thompson 2003a for further analysis of these issues). The points raised are intended not as a comprehensive overview, but rather as a set of pointers to guide and inform further discussion and action.

Social work is traditionally seen as operating on a knife edge of care and control. The discussions in this book, and more widely within the anti-discriminatory movement, not only recognise the significance of this knife edge but also relate it to another 'knife edge' situation. I am referring to the thin line between oppression and empowerment. That line also cuts through the centre of social work: the actions of social workers (and their agencies) are crucial in determining whether oppression is increased and strengthened or, alternatively, challenged and undermined through the process of empowerment.

Anti-discriminatory practice seeks to ensure that empowerment is to the fore in order to ensure that social work is a progressive force for social change and amelioration rather than a repressive arm of an uncaring state bureaucracy. The challenge is a major one, but the rewards for success are high, as indeed are the costs of failure.

Bibliography

Abercrombie, N. and Warde, A., with Deem, R., Penna, S., Soothill, K., Urry, J., Sayer, A. and Walby, S. (2000) *Contemporary British Society*, 3rd edn, London, Polity.

Acharyya, S. (1996) 'Practising Cultural Psychiatry: The Doctor's Dilemma', in Heller *et al.* (1996).

Adams, R. (2002) *Social Work and Empowerment*, 3rd edn, London, Macmillan Press – now Palgrave Macmillan.

Adams, R. (2003) *Empowerment and Social Work*, 3rd edn, Basingstoke, Palgrave Macmillan.

Adams, R., Dominelli, L. and Payne, M. (eds) (2002) *Social Work: Themes, Issues and Critical Debates*, 2nd edn, Basingstoke, Palgrave Macmillan.

Ahmad, B. (1990) *Black Perspectives in Social Work*, Birmingham, Venture Press.

Ahmad, W. I. U. (ed.) (1993) *'Race' and Health in Contemporary Britain*, Birmingham, Open University Press.

Ahmad, W. I. U. and Atkin, K. (eds) (1996) *'Race' and Community Care*, Buckingham, Open University Press.

Ahmed, S. (1987) 'Racism in Social Work Assessment,' in BASW Social Work and Racism Group (1987).

Ahmed, S. (1991) 'Developing Anti-Racist Social Work Education Practice', in CD Project Steering Group (1991).

Alibhai-Brown, Y. (2001) *Mixed Feelings: The Complex Lives of Mixed-Race Britons*, London, The Women's Press.

Allen, I. (1990) *Care Managers and Care Management*, London, Policy Studies Institute/Joseph Rowntree Memorial Trust.

Allen, S. (1987) 'Gender, Race and Class in the 1980s', in Husband (1987).

Alibhai-Brown, Y. (2001) *Mixed Feelings: The Complex Lives of Mixed-Race Britons*, London, The Women's Press.

Aluffi-Pentini, A. and Lorenz, W. (eds) (1996) *Anti-Racist Work with Young People: European Experiences and Approaches*, Lyme Regis, Russell House Publishing.

Amos, V., Lewis, G., Mama, A. and Parmar, P. (1984) 'Many Voices, One Chant: Black Feminist Perspectives', *Feminist Review*, 17.

Anderson, J. and Ricci, M. (eds) (1990) *Society and Social Science: A Reader*, Milton Keynes, Open University Press.

Arber, S. and Ginn. J. (1991) *Gender and Later Life: A Sociological Analysis of Resources and Constraints*, London, Sage.

Arber, S. and Ginn, J. (eds) (1995) *Connecting Gender and Ageing: A Sociological Approach*, Buckingham, Open University Press.

Atkin, K. and Rollings, J. (1996) 'Looking After Their Own? Family Caregiving Among Asian and Afro-Caribbean Communities', in Ahmad and Atkin (1996).

Back, L. and Solomos, J. (eds) (2000) *Theories of Race and Racism: A Reader*, London, Routledge.

Bailey, R. and Brake, N. (eds) (1975) *Radical Social Work*, London, Edward Arnold.

Banton, R., Clifford, P., Frosh, S., Lousada, J. and Rosenthall, J. (1985) *The Politics of Mental Health*, London, Macmillan Press – now Palgrave Macmillan.

Barn, R. (1993) *Black Children in the Public Care System*, London, Batsford.

Barnes, C. (1991a) *Institutional Discrimination Against Disabled People: A Case for Legislation*, British Council of Organisations of Disabled People.

Barnes, C. (1991b) *Disabled People in Britain and Discrimination: A Case for Anti-Discrimination Legislation*, London, Hurst and Co. in association with BCODP.

Barton, L. (ed.) (1996) *Disability and Society: Emerging Issues and Insights*, London, Longman.

Baxter, C., Poonia, K., Ward, L. and Nadirshaw, J. (1990) *Double Discrimination*, London, King's Fund Centre.

Bayne-Smith, M. (ed.) (1996) *Race, Health and Gender*, London, Sage.

Beauvoir, S. de (1972) *The Second Sex*, Harmondsworth, Penguin.

Beauvoir, S. de (1977) *Old Age*, Harmondsworth, Penguin.

Bell, V. (1993) *Interrogating Incest: Feminism, Foucault and the Law*, London, Routledge.

Bellin, W. (1994) 'Caring Professions and Welsh-speakers: A Perspective from Language and Social Psychology', in Huws Williams *et al.* (1994).

Bennett, G. and Kingston, P. (1993) *Elder Abuse: Concepts, Theories and Interventions*, London, Chapman & Hall.

Bennett, G., Kingston, P. and Penhale, B. (1997) *The Dimensions of Elder Abuse: Perspectives for Practitioners*, London, Macmillan Press – now Palgrave Macmillan.

Berger, P. L. (1966) *Invitation to Sociology*, Harmondsworth, Penguin.

Berger, P. L. and Luckmann, T. (1967) *The Social Construction of Reality*, Harmondsworth, Penguin.

Bernard, M. and Meade, K. (eds) (1993) *Women Come of Age*, London, Edward Arnold.

Bevan, D. (1998) 'Death, Dying and Inequality', *Care: The Journal of Practice and Development* 7(1).

Bevan, D. (2002) 'Poverty and Deprivation', in Thompson (2002d).

Bhat A., Carr-Hill, R. and Ohri, S. (eds) (1988) *Britain's Black Population: A New Perspective*, Aldershot, Gower.

Bhavanani, K. and Coulson, M. (1986) 'Transforming Socialist Feminism: the Challenge of Racism', *Feminist Review*, 2.

Biggs, S. (1993) *Understanding Ageing*, Buckingham, Open University Press.

Biggs, S. (1999) *The Mature Imagination: Dynamics of Identity and Beyond*, Buckingham, Open University Press.

Biggs, S., Phillipson, C. and Kingston, P. (1995) *Elder Abuse in Perspective*, Buckingham, Open University Press.

Blackburn, D. G. (2000) 'Why Race is Not a Biological Concept', in Lang (2000).

Blakemore, K. and Boneham, M. (1993) *Age, Race and Ethnicity*, Buckingham, Open University Press.

Blakemore, K. and Drake, R. (1996) *Understanding Equal Opportunity Policies*, London, Prentice-Hall/Harvester Wheatsheaf.

Bland, R. (ed.) (1996) *Developing Services for Older People and Their Families*, London, Jessica Kingsley Publishers.

Blasius, M. and Phelan, S. (eds) (1997) *We Are Everywhere: A Historical Sourcebook of Gay and Lesbian Politics*, London, Routledge.

Board for Social Responsibility (1990) *Ageing*, London, Church House Publishing.

Bocock, R. and Thompson, K. (eds) (1992) *Social and Cultural Forms of Modernity*, Cambridge, Polity Press.

Bond, J. and Coleman, P. (eds) (1990) *Ageing in Society*, London, Sage.

Bond, J., Coleman, P. and Peace, S. (eds) (1993) *Ageing in Society*, 2nd edn, London, Sage.

Bottomore, T. B. and Rubel, M. (eds) (1963) *Selected Writings in Sociology and Social Philosophy*, Harmondsworth, Penguin.

Bowser, B. P. (ed.) (1995) *Racism and Anti-Racism in World Perspective*, London, Sage.

Boyle, M. (1990) *Schizophrenia: A Scientific Delusion?*, London, Routledge.

Brake, M. and Bailey, R. (eds) (1980) *Radical Social Work and Practice*, London, Edward Arnold.

Braye, S. and Preston-Shoot, M. (1995) *Empowering Practice in Social Care*, Buckingham, Open University Press.

Brearley, C. P. (1982) *Risk and Ageing*, London, Routledge & Kegan Paul.

Brechin, A., Liddiard, P. and Swain, J. (eds) (1981) *Handicap in a Social World*, London, Open University/Hodder and Stoughton.

Brewer, J. D. (1991) 'The Parallels Between Sectarianism and Racism: the Northern Ireland Experience', in CCETSW (1991b).

Brisenden, S. (1986) 'Independent Living and the Medical Model of Disability', *Disability, Handicap and Society*, 1 (2).

Bristow, J. and Wilson, A. R. (eds) (1993) *Activating Theory: Lesbian, Gay, Bisexual Politics*, London, Lawrence & Wishart.

Brittan, A. and Maynard, M. (1984) *Sexism, Racism and Oppression*, Oxford, Blackwell.

Brook, E. and Davis, A. (eds) (1985) *Women, The Family and Social Work*, London, Tavistock.

Brown, G. W. and Harris, T. (1978) *The Social Origins of Depression*, London, Tavistock.

Brown, H. C. (1998a) 'Lesbians and Gay Men: Social Work and Discrimination', in Lešnik (1998).

Brown, H. C. (1998b) *Social Work and Sexuality: Working with Lesbians and Gay Men*, London, Macmillan Press – now Palgrave Macmillan.

Browne, D. (1996) 'The Black Experience of Mental Health Law', in Heller *et al.* (1996).

Bryan, B., Dadzie, S. and Scafe, S. (1985) *The Heart of the Race*, London, Virago.

Bryson, V. (1999) *Feminist Debates: Issues of Theory and Political Practice*, London, Macmillan Press – now Palgrave Macmillan.

Bullock, A. and Stallybrass, O. (1977) *Dictionary of Modern Thought*, London, Fontana.

Bulmer, M. and Solomos, J. (eds) (1999) *Racism*, Oxford, Oxford University Press.

Burke, A. (1984) 'Racism and Mental Illness', *International Journal of Social Psychiatry*, 29 (1).

Burke, A. (1986) 'Social Work and Intervention in West Indian Psychiatric Disorder', in Coombe and Little (1986).

Burke, B. and Harrison, P. (2000) 'Race and Racism in Social Work', in Davies (2000).

Burr, V. (2003) *Social Constructionism*, 2nd edn, London, Routledge.

Burstyn, V. and Smith, D. E. (eds) (1985) *Women, Class, Family and the State*, Toronto, Garamond Press.

Busfield, J. (1986) *Managing Madness: Changing Ideas and Practice*, London, Hutchinson.

Busfield, J. (1996) *Women, Men and Madness: Understanding Gender and Mental Disorder*, London, Macmillan Press – now Palgrave Macmillan.

Butler, R. N. (1975) *Why Survive? Being Old in America*, New York, Harper and Row.

Bynoe, I., Oliver, M. and Barnes, C. (1991) *Equal Rights For Disabled People: The Case for a New Law*, London, Institute for Public Policy Research.

Bytheway, W.R. and Johnson, J. (1990) 'On Defining Ageism', *Critical Social Policy*, 29.

Cameron, E., Badger, F. and Evers, H. (1989) 'How the Services Categorise', *Community Care*, 25 May.

Campbell, J. and Oliver, M. (1996) *Disability Politics: Understanding Our Past, Changing Our Future*, London, Routledge.

Carlen, P. and Worrall, A. (eds) (1987) *Gender, Crime and Justice*, Milton Keynes, Open University Press.

Carter, H. and Aitchison, J. (1986) 'Language Areas and Language Change in Wales: 1961–1991', in Hume and Pryce (1986).

Carter, P., Jeffs, T. and Smith, M. (1989) *Yearbook of Social Work and Social Welfare* 1, Milton Keynes, Open University Press.

Carver, V. and Liddiard, P. (eds) (1978) *An Ageing Population*, Sevenoaks, Hodder and Stoughton.

Cavanagh, K. and Cree, V. E. (eds) (1996) *Working with Men*, London, Routledge.

CCETSW (1989) 'Requirements and Regulations for the Diploma in Social Work', CCETSW Paper 30, London, Central Council for Education and Training in Social Work.

CCETSW (1991a) 'Rules and Requirements for the Diploma in Social Work', CCETSW Paper 30, 2nd edn, London, CCETSW.

CCETSW (1991b) *One Small Step Towards Racial Justice*, London, CCETSW.

CCETSW (1995) *Assuring Quality in the Diploma in Social Work I: Rules and Regulations for the DipSW*, London, CCETSW.

CD Project Steering Group (eds) (1991) *Setting the Context for Change*, London, CCETSW.

Chadwick, A. (1996) 'Knowledge, Power and the Disability Discrimination Bill', *Disability and Society*, 11(1).

Chakrabarti, M. (1990) 'Racial Prejudice' Open University, Workbook 6, Part 1 of K254, *Working with Children and Young People*.

Cheetham, J. (ed.) (1981) *Social and Community Work in a Multi-Racial Society*, London, Harper & Row.

Christie, A. (ed.) (2001) *Men and Social Work: Theories and Practices*, Basingstoke, Palgrave Macmillan.

Clarke, J. and Cochrane, A. (1998) 'The Social Construction of Social Problems', in Saraga (1998).

Clements, J. (1987) *Severe Learning Disability and Psychological Handicap*, Chichester, Wiley.

Clements, L. and Read, J. (2003) *Disabled People and European Human Rights*, Bristol, Policy Press.

Coates, D. (1990) 'Traditions of Thought and the Rise of Social Science in the United Kingdom', in Anderson and Ricci (1990).

Cohen, M.B. and Mullender, A. (eds) (2002) *Gender and Groupwork*, London, Routledge.

Colgan, F. and Ledwith, S. (1996) 'Women as Organisational Change Agents', in Ledwith and Colgan (1996).

Collins, D., Tank, M. and Basith, A. (1993) *Customs of Minority Ethnic Religions*, Aldershot, Arena.

Connell, R.W. (2002) *Gender*, Cambridge, Polity.

Connolly, C. (1991) 'Washing our Linen: One Year of Women Against Fundamentalism', *Feminist Review*, 37.

Conrad, P. (1981) 'On the Medicalisation of Deviance and Social Control', in Ingleby (1981b).

Coombe, V. and Little, A. (eds) (1986) *Race and Social Work*, London, Tavistock.

Cooper, D. (ed.) (1968) *The Dialectics of Liberation*, Harmondsworth, Penguin.

Corby, B. (1989) 'Alternative Theory Bases in Child Abuse' in Stainton Rogers *et al.* (1989).

Corrigan, P. (ed.) (1980) *Capitalism, State Formation and Marxist Theory*, London, Quartet.

Corrigan, P. and Leonard, P. (1978) *Social Work Practice Under Capitalism: A Marxist Approach*, London, Macmillan Press – now Palgrave Macmillan.

Coulshed, V. and Mullender, A. with Jones, D. and Thompson, N. (2006) *Management in Social Work*, 3rd edn, Basingstoke, Palgrave Macmillan.

CPA (1990) *Community Life: A Code of Practice for Community Care*, London, Centre for Policy on Ageing.

Cranny-Francis, A, Waring, W., Stavropoulos, P. and Kirkby, J. (2003) *Gender Studies: Terms and Debates*, Basingstoke, Palgrave Macmillan.

Crompton, I. and Thompson, N. (2000) *The Human Rights Act 1998: A Training Resource Pack*, Wrexham, Learning Curve Publishing.

Crompton, R. (1993) *Class and Stratification*, Cambridge, Polity Press.

Crowley, H. (1992) 'Women and the Domestic Sphere', in Bocock and Thompson (1992).

Culley, L. and Dyson, S. (eds) (2001) *Ethnicity and Nursing Practice*, Basingstoke, Palgrave Macmillan.

Dale, J. and Foster, P. (1986) *Feminism and The Welfare State*, London, Routledge & Kegan Paul.

Dallos, R. and McLaughlin, E. (eds) (1993) *Social Problems and the Family*, London, Sage.

Dallos, R. and Sapsford, R. (1997) 'Patterns of Diversity and Lived Realities', in Muncie *et al.* (1997).

Dalrymple, J. and Burke, B. (1995) *Anti-Oppressive Practice, Social Care and the Law*, Buckingham, Open University Press.

Davies, D. and Neal, C. (eds) (1996) *Pink Therapy: A Guide for Counsellors and Therapists Working with Lesbian, Gay and Bisexual Clients*, Buckingham, Open University Press.

Davies, M. (ed.) (2000) *The Blackwell Encyclopaedia of Social Work*, Oxford, Blackwell.

Davies, M. (ed.) (2002) *The Blackwell Companion to Social Work*, 2nd edn, Oxford, Blackwell.

Davis, K. (1988) 'Issues in Disability: Integrated Living', Open University, Unit 19 of D211 *Social Problems and Social Welfare*.

Davis, K. (1996) 'Disability and Legislation: Rights and Equality', in Hales (1996).

DCDP (1985) 'Development of the Derbyshire Centre for Integrated Living', Chesterfield, Derbyshire Coalition of Disabled People.

Deegan, M. (1985) 'Multiple Minority Groups: A Case Study of Physically Disabled Women', in Deegan and Brooks (1985).

Deegan, M. and Brooks, N. (eds) (1985) *Women and Disability: The Double Handicap*, New Brunswick, Transaction Books.

Denney, D. (1983) 'Some Dominant Perspectives in the Literature Relating to Multi-Racial Social Work', *British Journal of Social Work*, 13.

Devine, F. (1997) *Social Class in America and Britain*, Edinburgh, Edinburgh University Press.

Divine, D. (1990) 'Sharing the Struggle', *Social Work Today*, 22 November.

Dobelniece, S. (1998) 'Poverty and Deprivation', in Lešnik (1998).

Dominelli, L. (1989) 'An Uncaring Profession? An Examination of Racism in Social Work', *New Community*, 15 (3).

Dominelli, L. and McLeod, E. (1989) *Feminist Social Work*, London, Macmillan Press – now Palgrave Macmillan.

Donnison, D. (1998) *Policies for a Just Society*, London, Macmillan Press – now Palgrave Macmillan.

Doyal, L. (1983) 'The Crippling Effects of Underdevelopment', in Shirley (1983).

Drakeford, M. and Morris, S. (1998) 'Social Work with Linguistic Minorities', in Williams *et al.* (1998).

Duberman, M. B., Vicinus, M. and Chauncey, G. (eds) (1991) *Hidden From History: Reclaiming the Gay and Lesbian Past*, Harmondsworth, Penguin.

Durkheim, E. (1952) *Suicide*, London, Routledge & Kegan Paul.

Dwivedi, K. N. and Varma, V. P. (eds) (1996) *Meeting the Needs of Ethnic Minority Children*, London, Jessica Kingsley Publishers.

Eastman, M. (ed.) (1994) *Old Age Abuse: A New Perspective*, 2nd edn, London, Chapman & Hall.

Elliot, F. R. (1996) *Gender, Family and Society*, London, Macmillan Press – now Palgrave Macmillan.

Engels, F. (1976) *The Origin of the Family, Private Property and the State*, London, Lawrence and Wishart (originally published 1844).

EOC (1982) 'Caring for the Elderly and Handicapped: Community Care Policies and Women's Lives,' Manchester, Equal Opportunities Commission.

Farrell, F. and Watt, P. (eds) (2001) *Responding to Racism in Ireland*, Dublin, Veritas.

Fawcett, B., Featherstone, B., Fook, J. and Rossiter, A. (eds) (2000) *Practice and Research in Social Work: Postmodern Feminist Perspectives*, London, Routledge.

Featherstone, B. (2004) *Family Life and Family Support: A Feminist Analysis*, Basingstoke, Palgrave Macmillan.

Featherstone, M. and Hepworth, M. (1990) 'Images of Ageing', in Bond and Coleman (1990).

Fennell, G., Phillipson, C. and Evers, H. (1988) *The Sociology of Old Age*, Milton Keynes, Open University Press.

Fenton, S. (1987) *Ageing Minorities: Black People as They Grow Old in Britain*, London, Commission for Racial Equality.

Fernando, S. (1989) *Race and Culture in Psychiatry*, London, Tavistock/ Routledge.

Ferns, P. (1987) 'The Dangerous Delusion', *Community Care*, 8 January.

Field, N. (1995) *Over the Rainbow: Money, Class and Homophobia*, London, Pluto.

Finch, J. (1984) 'Community Care: Developing Non-Sexist Alternatives', *Critical Social Policy*, 9.

Finch, J. and Groves, D. (eds) (1983) *A Labour of Love*, London, Routledge & Kegan Paul.

Fine, M. and Asch, A. (1985) 'Disabled Women: Sexism without the Pedestal', in Deegan and Brooks (1985).

Finkelstein, V. (1981a) 'Disability and the Helper/Helped Relationship', in Brechin *et al.* (1981).

Finkelstein, V. (1981b) 'Disability and Professional Attitudes', Sevenoaks, NAIDEX Convention.

Finkelstein, V. (1991) 'Disability: An Administrative Challenge?' in Oliver, M. (1991).

Fischer, A. (ed.) *Gender and Emotion: Social Psychological Perspectives*, Cambridge, Cambridge University Press.

Fisher, M. (1994) 'Man-Made Care: Community Care and the Older Male', *British Journal of Social Work*, 24(5) 659–80.

Fook, J. (2002) *Social Work: Critical Theory and Practice*, London, Sage.

Foster-Carter, O. (1987) 'Ethnicity: The Fourth Burden of Black Women – Political Action', *Critical Social Policy*, 20.

Foucault, M. (1977) *Discipline and Punish: The Birth of the Prison*, London, Allen Lane.

Foucault, M. (1979) *The History of Sexuality. Volume 1; An Introduction*, London, Allen Lane.

Francis, E. (1991a) 'Racism and Mental Health: Some Concerns for Social Work', in CD Project Steering Group (1991).

Freire, P. (1972) *Pedagogy of the Oppressed*, Harmondsworth, Penguin.

Friedan, B. (1963) *The Feminine Mystique*, London, Gollancz.

Froggatt, A. (1990) *Family Work with Elderly People*, London, Macmillan Press – now Palgrave Macmillan.

Fuss, D. (1991) *Inside/Out: Lesbian Theories, Gay Theories*, London, Routledge.

George, M. (1991) 'Do It Yourself', *Community Care*, 9 May.

Giddens, A. (1971) *Capitalism and Modern Social Theory*, Cambridge, Cambridge University Press.

Giddens, A. (2001) *Sociology*, 4th edn, Cambridge, Polity Press.

Ginn, J. and Arber, S. (1995) ' "Only Connect": Gender Relations and Ageing', in Arber and Ginn (1995).

Gittins, D. (1985) *The Family in Question* (2nd edn, 1993), London, Macmillan Press – now Palgrave Macmillan.

Glendinning, C. (1987) 'Impoverishing Women', in Walker and Walker (1987).

Graham, M. (2002) *Social Work and African-centred Worldviews*, Birmingham, Venture Press.

Green, J. (1991) *Death with Dignity: Meeting the Needs of Patients in a Multi-Cultural Society*, London, Macmillan Press – now Palgrave Macmillan.

Green, J. (1993) *Death with Dignity: Volume II*, London, Macmillan Press – now Palgrave Macmillan.

Grimwood, C. and Popplestone, R. (1993) *Women, Management and Care*, London, Macmillan Press – now Palgrave Macmillan.

Gruber, C. and Stefanov, H. (eds) (2002) *Gender in Social Work: Promoting Equality*, Lyme Regis, Russell House Publishing.

Gurnah, A. (1984) 'The Politics of Racism Awareness Training', *Critical Social Policy*, 11.

Hales, G. (ed.) (1996) *Beyond Disability: Towards an Enabling Society*, London, Sage.

Hallett, C. (1996) *Women and Social Policy*, 2nd edn, London, Prentice-Hall/Harvester Wheatsheaf.

Halmos, P. (1965) *The Faith of the Counsellors*, London, Constable.

Hanmer, J. and Statham, D. (1988) *Women and Social Work* (1999, 2nd edn), London, Macmillan Press – now Palgrave Macmillan.

Harris, V. (1991) 'Values of Social Work in the Context of British Society in Conflict with Anti-Racism', in CD Project Steering Group (1991).

Hart, J. (1980) 'It's Just a Stage We're Going Through: the Sexual Politics of Casework', in Brake and Bailey (1980).

Haselden, R. (1991) 'Gay Abandon', *The Guardian*, 7 September.

Hearn, J. (1982) 'Radical Social Work – Contradictions, Limitations and Political Possibilities', *Critical Social Policy*, 4.

Heather, N. (1975) *Radical Perspectives in Psychology*, London, Methuen.

Hechter, M. (1975) *Internal Colonialism: the Celtic Fringe in British National Development 1536–1966*, London, Routledge & Kegan Paul.

Heller, T., Reynolds, J., Gomm, R., Muston, R. and Pattison, S. (eds) (1996) *Mental Health Matters: A Reader*, London, Macmillan Press – now Palgrave Macmillan.

Henley, A. (1986) 'The Asian Community in Britain', in Coombe and Little (1986).

Heraud, B. (1970) *Sociology and Social Work*, Oxford, Pergamon.

Higgs, P. (1997) 'Citizenship Theory and Old Age: From Social Rights to Surveillance', in Jamieson *et al.* (1997).

Hockey, J. and James, A. (1993) *Growing Up and Growing Old: Ageing and Dependency in the Life Course*, London, Sage.

Hocquenghem, G. (1978) *Homosexual Desire*, London, Allison & Busby.

hooks, b. (1982) *Ain't I a Woman: Black Women and Feminism*, London, Pluto.

hooks, b. (1986) 'Sisterhood: Political Solidarity Between Women', *Feminist Review*, 23.

Hornstein, Z. (ed.) (2001) *Outlawing Age Discrimination: Foreign Lessons, UK Choices*, Bristol, Policy Press.

Hudson, A. (1989) 'Changing Perspectives: Feminism, Gender and Social Work', in Langan and Lee (1989).

Hughes, B. (1995) *Older People and Community Care: Critical Theory and Practice*, Buckingham, Open University Press.

Hughes, B. and Mtezuka, E. M. (1992) 'Social Work and Older Women', in Langan and Day (1992).

Hughes, G. (1998) 'A Suitable Case for Treatment', in Saraga (1998).

Hugman, R. (1991) *Power in Caring Professions*, London, Macmillan Press – now Palgrave Macmillan.

Hugman, R. (1994) *Ageing and the Care of Older People in Europe*, London, Macmillan Press – now Palgrave Macmillan.

Hume, I. and Pryce, W. T. R. (eds) (1986) *The Welsh and Their Country*, Llandysul, Dyfed, Gomer.

Humphries, B. (ed.) (1996) *Critical Perspectives on Empowerment*, Birmingham, Venture Press.

Husband, C. (1986) 'Racism, Prejudice and Social Policy', in Coombe and Little (1986).

Husband, C. (ed.) (1987) *'Race' in Britain: Continuity and Change*, 2nd edn, London, Hutchinson.

Hutchinson-Reis, M. (1989) ' "And for those of us who are black?", Black Politics in Social Work', in Langan and Lee (1989).

Huws Williams, R., Williams, H. and Davies, E. (eds) (1994) *Gwaith Cymdeithasol a'r Iaith Gymraeg/Social Work and the Welsh Language*, Cardiff, University of Wales Press.

Ingleby, D. (1981a) 'Understanding "Mental Illness" ', in Ingleby (1981b).

Ingleby, D. (1981b) *Critical Psychiatry: The Politics of Mental Health*, Harmondsworth, Penguin.

Jack, R. (1995a) 'Introduction', in Jack (1995b).

Jack, R. (ed.) (1995b) *Empowerment in Community Care*, London, Chapman & Hall.

Jackson, S. and Jones, J. (eds) (1998) *Contemporary Feminist Theories*, Edinburgh, Edinburgh University Press.

Jaggar, A. and Rothenberg, P. (eds) (1993) *Feminist Frameworks: Alternative Theoretical Accounts of the Relations Between Women and Men*, New York, McGraw-Hill.

Jamieson, A., Harper, S. and Victor, C. (eds) (1997) *Critical Approaches to Ageing and Later Life*, Buckingham, Open University Press.

Jansz, J. (2000) 'Masculine Identity and Restrictive Emotionality', in Fischer (2000).

Jones, C. (1996) 'Anti-Intellectualism and the Peculiarities of British Social Work Education', in Parton (1996).

Jones, C. (2002) 'Social Work and Society', in Adams *et al.* (2002).

Jones, C. and Novak T. (1980) 'The State and Social Policy', in Corrigan (1980).

Jones, C. and Novak, T. (1999) *Poverty, Welfare and the Disciplinary State*, London, Routledge.

Jong, G. de (1979) 'The Movement For Independent Living', in Brechin *et al.* (1981).

Jordan, B. (1990) *Social Work in an Unjust Society*, Hemel Hempstead, Harvester Wheatsheaf.

Jordan, B. (2000) *Social Work and the Third Way*, London, Sage.

Kandola, R. and Fullerton, J. (1998) *Diversity in Action: Managing the Mosaic*, 2nd edn, London, Chartered Institute of Personnel and Development.

Katz, J. (1978) *White Awareness*, University of Oklahoma Press.

King, D. (1993) 'Multiple Jeopardy: The Context of a Black Feminist Ideology', in Jaggar and Rothenberg (1993).

Kirton, D. (2000) *Race, Ethnicity and Adoption*, Buckingham, Open University Press.

Kubisa, T. (1990) 'Care Manager: Rhetoric or Reality', in Allen (1990).

Kuhn, T. (1962) *The Structure of Scientific Revolutions*, Chicago, University of Chicago Press.

Laing, R. D. (1965) *The Divided Self*, Harmondsworth, Penguin.

Laing, R. D. (1967) *The Politics of Experience and the Bird of Paradise*, Harmondsworth, Penguin.

Laing, R. D. and Cooper, D. (1971) *Reason and Violence*, London, Tavistock.

Laing, R. D. and Esterson, A. (1970) *Sanity, Madness and the Family*, Harmondsworth, Penguin.

Lago, C. with Thompson, J. (1996) *Race, Culture and Counselling*, Buckingham, Open University Press.

Lang, B. (ed.) (2000) *Race and Racism in Theory and Practice*, Oxford, Rowman and Littlefield.

Langan, M. (2002) 'Radical Social Work', in Adams *et al.* (2002).

Langan, M. and Day, L. (eds) (1992) *Women, Oppression and Social Work: Issues in Anti-discriminatory Practice*, London, Routledge.

Langan, M. and Lee, P. (eds) (1989) *Radical Social Work Today*, London, Unwin Hyman.

Laurance, J. (2003) *Pure Madness: How Fear Drives the Mental Health System*, London, Routledge.

Ledwith, S. and Colgan, F. (eds) (1996) *Women in Organisations: Challenging Gender Politics*, London, Macmillan Press – now Palgrave Macmillan.

Lees, S. (1997) *Ruling Passions: Sexual Violence, Reputation and the Law*, Buckingham, Open University Press.

Lentell, H. C. (1988) 'An Introduction to the Family', Unit 6 of the Open University Course, D211 *Social Problems and Social Welfare*.

Leonard, P. (1966) *Sociology in Social Work*, London, Routledge & Kegan Paul.

Leonard, P. (1989) Foreword to Dominelli and McLeod (1989).

Lešnik, B. (ed.) (1998) *Countering Discrimination in Social Work*, Aldershot, Arena.

Lister, R. (1997) *Citizenship: Feminist Perspectives*, London, Macmillan Press – now Palgrave Macmillan.

Littlewood, R. and Lipsedge, M. (1997) *Aliens and Alienists: Ethnic Minorities and Psychiatry*, 3rd edn, London, Routledge.

Loney, M., Bocock, R., Clarke, J., Cochrane, A., Graham, P. and Wilson, M. (eds) (1991) *The State or the Market*, 2nd edn, London, Sage.

Lonsdale, S. (1990) *Women and Disability*, London, Macmillan Press – now Palgrave Macmillan.

Lonsdale, S. (1991) 'Out of Sight, Out of Mind', *Community Care*, 9 May.

Luthra, M. (1997) *Britain's Black Population: Social Change, Public Policy and Agenda*, Aldershot, Arena.

MacLeod, M. and Saraga, E. (1988) 'Challenging the Orthodoxy: Towards a Feminist Theory and Practice', *Feminist Review*, 28.

Macpherson, W. (1999) *The Stephen Lawrence Inquiry: Report of an Inquest*, London, The Stationery Office.

Malik, K. (1996) *The Meaning of Race*, London, Macmillan Press – now Palgrave Macmillan.

Mama, A. (1989a) 'Violence Against Black Women: Gender, Race and State Responses', *Feminist Review*, 23.

Mama, A. (1989b) *The Hidden Struggle*, London, LRHRU/Runnymede Trust.

Mama, A. (1991) 'Race, Gender and Citizenship', Paper presented at the Critical Social Policy 'Citizenship and Welfare' conference, London.

Mandelbaum, D. G. (ed.) (1949) *Selected Writings of Edward Sapir: A Study in Phonetic Symbolism*, Berkeley, CA, University of California.

Manning, N. and Page, N. (eds) (1992) *Social Policy Review*, London, Social Policy Association.

Marks, D. (1999) *Disability: Controversial Debates and Psychosocial Perspectives*, London, Routledge.

Marks, D. (2000) 'Disability', in Davies (2000).

Marlow, A. and Loveday, B. (eds) (2000) *After Macpherson: Policing After the Stephen Lawrence Inquiry*, Lyme Regis, Russell House Publishing.

Marshall, M. (1990) *Social Work with Old People*, 2nd edn, London, Macmillan Press – now Palgrave Macmillan.

Marshall, M. and Rowlings, C. (1998) 'Facing Our Futures: Discrimination in Later Life', in Lešnik (1998).

Marshall, V. W. (1986a) 'A Sociological Perspective on Aging and Dying', in Marshall (1986b).

Marshall, V. W. (1986b) *Later Life: The Social Psychology of Aging*, London, Sage.

May, M., Page, R. and Brunsdon, E. (eds) (2001) *Understanding Social Problems: Issues in Social Policy*, Oxford, Blackwell.

Mays, N. (1983) 'Elderly South Asians in Britain: A Survey of Relevant Literature and Themes for Future Research', *Ageing and Society*, 3 (1).

McLellan, D. (1995) *Ideology*, 2nd edn, Buckingham, Open University Press.

Midwinter, E. (1990) 'An Ageing World: The Equivocal Response', *Ageing and Society*, 10.

Miles, A. (1987) *The Mentally Ill in Contemporary Society*, Oxford, Basil Blackwell.

Miles, R. (1989) *Racism*, London, Routledge.

Miles, R. and Solomos, J. (1987) 'Migration and the State in Britain: A Historical Overview', in Husband (1987).

Miller, E. J. and Gwynne, G. V. (1972) *A Life Apart*, London, Tavistock.

Millett, K. (1971) *Sexual Politics*, London, Rupert Hart-Davis.

Mills, C. W. (1970) *The Sociological Imagination*, Harmondsworth, Penguin.

Milner, J. and O'Byrne, P. (2002) *Assessment in Social Work* (2nd edn), Basingstoke, Palgrave Macmillan.

Mirza, K. (1991) 'Waiting for Guidance', in CCETSW (1991b).

Morgan, K. O. (1982) *Rebirth of a Nation: Wales 1880–1980*, Oxford University Press/University of Wales Press.

Morris, D. and Williams, G. (1994) 'Language and Social Work Practice: The Welsh Case', in Huws Williams *et al.* (1994).

Morris, J. (1989) 'Women Confronting Disability', *Community Care*, 29 June.

Morris, J. (1991) *Pride Against Prejudice*, London, Women's Press.

Morris, J. (1993) 'Gender and Disability', in Swain *et al.* (1993).

Moss, B. (2005) *Religion and Spirituality*, Lyme Regis, Russell House Publishing.

Muldoon, J. (2000) 'Race or Culture: Medieval Notions of Difference', in Lang (2000).

Mullaly, R. (1993) *Structural Social Work: Ideology, Theory and Practice*, Toronto, McClelland and Stewart.

Mullender, A. (1996) *Rethinking Domestic Violence*, London, Routledge.

Mullender, A. (1997) 'Gender', in Davies (1997).

Muncie, J., Wetherell, M., Langan, M., Dallos, R. and Cochrane, A. (eds) (1997) *Understanding the Family*, 2nd edn, London, Sage.

Munro, A. and McCulloch, W. (1969) *Psychiatry for Social Workers*, Oxford, Pergamon Press.

Nairn, T. (1986) 'Culture and Politics in Wales', in Hume and Pryce (1986).

Nelson, A. (1990) 'Equal Opportunities: Dilemmas, Contradictions, White Men and Class', *Critical Social Policy*, 28.

Nolan, M., Davies, S. and Grant, G. (eds) (2001) *Working with Older People: Key Issues in Policy and Practice*, Buckingham, Open University Press.

Norman, A. (1980) *Rights and Risk*, London, Centre for Policy on Ageing.

Norman, A. (1985) *Triple Jeopardy: Growing Old in a Second Homeland*, London, Centre for Policy on Ageing.

Norman, A. (1987) 'Overcoming an Old Prejudice', *Community Care*, 29 January.

O'Brien, M. (1990) 'The Place of Men in Gender-Sensitive Therapy', in Perelberg and Miller (1990).

Office for National Statistics (2003) *Social Trends 33*, Basingstoke, Palgrave Macmillan.

Office for National Statistics (2005) *Social Trends 35*, Basingstoke, Palgrave Macmillan.

Oliver, M. (1986) 'Social Policy and Disability: Some Theoretical Issues', *Disability, Handicap and Society*, 1 (1).

Oliver, M. (1987) 'From Strength to Strength', *Community Care*, 19 February.

Oliver, M. (1989a) 'The Social Model of Disability', in Carter *et al.* (1989).

Oliver, M. (1989b) 'Social Work with Disabled People', *Social Work Today*, 6 April.

Oliver, M. (1990) *The Politics of Disablement*, London, Macmillan Press – now Palgrave Macmillan.

Oliver, M. (ed.) (1991) *Social Work, Disabled People and Disabling Environments*, London, Jessica Kingsley.

Oliver, M. (1996) *Understanding Disability: From Theory to Practice*, London, Macmillan Press – now Palgrave Macmillan.

Oliver, M. and Sapey, B. (1999) *Social Work with Disabled People*, 2nd edn, London, Macmillan Press – now Palgrave Macmillan.

Ong, B. N. (1985) 'The Paradox of "Wonderful Children": The Case of Child Abuse', *Early Childhood Development and Care*, 21.

Pannick, D. (1985) *Sex Discrimination Law*, Oxford, Clarendon Press.

Parton, C. and Parton, N. (1989) 'Women, the Family and Child Protection', *Critical Social Policy*, 24.

Parton, N. (ed.) (1996) *Social Theory, Social Change and Social Work*, London, Routledge.

Parton, N. and O'Byrne, P. (2000) *Constructive Social Work: Towards a New Practice*, London, Macmillan Press – now Palgrave Macmillan.

Pascall, G. (1986) *Social Policy: A Feminist Analysis*, London, Tavistock.

Pascall, G. (1997) *Social Policy: A New Feminist Analysis*, London, Routledge.

Patel, N., Naik, D. and Humphries, B. (eds) (1998) *Visions of Reality: Religion and Ethnicity in Social Work*, London, CCETSW.

Payne, G. (2000) *Social Divisions*, London, Macmillan Press – now Palgrave Macmillan.

Pearson, G. (1975) *The Deviant Imagination*, London, Macmillan Press – now Palgrave Macmillan.

Penketh, L. (2000) *Tackling Institutional Racism*, Bristol, The Policy Press.

Perelberg, R.J. and Miller, A.C. (eds) (1990) *Gender and Power in Families*, London, Tavistock/Routledge.

Phillipson, C. (1982) *Capitalism and the Construction of Old Age*, London, Macmillan Press – now Palgrave Macmillan.

Phillipson, C. (1989) 'Challenging Dependency: Towards a New Social Work with Older People' in Langan and Lee (1989).

Phillipson, C. (2000) 'Ageism', in Davies (2000).

Phillipson, C., Bernard, M. and Strang, P. (eds) (1986) *Dependency and Interdependency in Later Life*, London, Croom Helm.

Phillipson, C. and Thompson, N. (1996) 'The Social Construction of Old Age: New Perspectives on the Theory and Practice of Social Work with Older People', in Bland (1996).

Phillipson, C. and Walker, A. (1986) *Ageing and Social Policy: A Critical Assessment*, Aldershot, Gower.

Pickering, M. (2001) *Stereotyping: The Politics of Representation*, Basingstoke, Palgrave Macmillan.

Pilkington, A. (2003) *Racial Disadvantage and Ethnic Diversity in Britain*, Basingstoke, Palgrave Macmillan.

Pizzey, E., Shackleton, J. R. and Unwin, P. (2000) *Women or Men – Who are the Victims?*, London, Civitas.

Polenberg, R. (1980) *One Nation Divisible*, Harmondsworth, Penguin.

Preston-Shoot, M. and Agass, D. (1990) *Making Sense of Social Work: Psychodynamics, Systems and Practice*, London, Macmillan Press – now Palgrave Macmillan.

Preston-Shoot, M. (1998) *Acting Fairly: Working Within the Law to Promote Equal Opportunities in Education and Training*, London, CCETSW.

Pritchard, C. and Taylor, R. (1978) *Social Work: Reform or Revolution?* London, Routledge & Kegan Paul.

Radford, L. (2001) 'Domestic Violence', in May *et al.* (2001).

Ramazanoglu, C. (1989) *Feminism and the Contradictions of Oppression*, London, Routledge.

Rex, J. (1986) *Race and Ethnicity*, Milton Keynes, Open University Press.

Richardson, D. and Robinson, V. (eds) (1993) *Introducing Women's Studies* (1997 2nd edn), London, Macmillan Press – now Palgrave Macmillan.

Riches, G. (2002) 'Gender', in Thompson (2002d).

Roberts, K. (2001) *Class in Modern Britain*, Basingstoke, Palgrave Macmillan.

Robinson, L. (1995) *Psychology for Social Workers: Black Perspectives*, London, Routledge.

Rojek, C., Peacock, G. and Collins, S. (1988) *Social Work and Received Ideas*, London, Routledge.

Rojek, C., Peacock, G. and Collins, S. (eds) (1989) *The Haunt of Misery: Critical Essays in Social Work and Helping*, London, Routledge.

Rooney, B. (1980) 'Active Mistakes – A Grass Roots Report', *Multi-Racial Social Work*, 1.

Rooney, B. (1987) *Racism and Resistance to Change*, Liverpool, Merseyside Area Profile Group.

Rowbotham, S. (1973) *Woman's Consciousness, Man's World*, Harmondsworth, Penguin.

Roys, P. (1988) 'Social Services', in Bhat *et al.* (1988).

Rush, F. (1981) *The Best Kept Secret*, Englewood Cliffs, CA, Prentice-Hall.

Ryan, W. (1971) *Blaming the Victim: Ideology Serves the Establishment*, London, Pantheon.

Sapey, B. (1998) 'Social Work and Independent Living', in Lešnik (1998).

Sapey, B. (2002) 'Disability', in Thompson (2002d).

Sapey, B. (2004) 'Impairment, Disability and Loss: Reassessing the Rejection of Loss', *Illness, Crisis and Loss*, 12(1).

Sapey, B. and Hewitt, N. (1991) 'The Changing Context of Social Work Practice', in Oliver (1991).

Saraga, E. (1993) 'The Abuse of Children', in Dallos and McLaughlin (1993).

Saraga, E. (ed.) (1998) *Embodying the Social: Constructions of Difference*, London, Routledge.

Sartre, J-P. (1976) *Critique of Dialectical Reason*, London, Verso.

Segal, L. (1999) *Why Feminism?*, Cambridge, Polity.

Shah, N. (1989) 'It's Up to You, Sisters: Black Women and Radical Social Work', in Langan and Lee (1989).

Shirley, O. (ed.) (1983) *A Cry for Health: Poverty and Disability in the Third World*, Frome, Third World Group and ARHTAG.

Sibeon, R. (1991a) 'Emancipatory Theories, Policies and Practices in a Welfare Profession: An Anti-Reductionist Perspective on Social Work Politics', Paper presented at the British Sociological Association Annual Conference, Manchester.

Sibeon, R. (1991b) *Towards a New Sociology of Social Work*, Aldershot, Avebury.

Sibeon, R. (1996) *Contemporary Sociology and Policy Analysis: The New Sociology of Public Policy*, Eastham, Tudor Business Press.

Sidell, M. (1995) *Health in Old Age: Myth, Mystery and Management*, Buckingham, Open University Press.

Simpkin, M. (1989) 'Radical Social Work: Lessons for the 1990s', in Carter *et al.* (1989).

Sivanandan, A. (1991) 'Black Struggles Against Racism', in CD Project Steering Group (1991).

Skellington, R. (1996) *'Race' in Britain Today*, 2nd edn, London, Sage.

Slee, R. (1996) 'Clauses of Conditionality: The "Reasonable" Accommodation of Language', in Barton (1996).

Smith, D. (1995) *Criminology for Social Workers*, London, Macmillan Press – now Palgrave Macmillan.

Social Services Inspectorate (1991) *Women in Social Services: A Neglected Resource*, London, HMSO.

Solomos, J. (1989) *Race and Racism in Contemporary Britain* (2003, 3rd edn), London, Macmillan Press – now Palgrave Macmillan.

Solomos, J. (2003) *Race and Racism in Contemporary Britain*, 3rd edn, Basingstoke, Palgrave Macmillan.

Sone, A. (1991) 'Outward Bound', *Community Care*, 8 August.

Sontag, S. (1978) 'The Double Standard of Ageing', in Carver and Liddiard (1978).

Soydan, H. and Williams, C. (1998) 'Exploring Concepts', in Williams *et al.* (1998).

Spicker, P. (2001) 'Income and Wealth', in May *et al.* (2001).

Stainton Rogers, W., Hevey, D. and Ash, E. (eds) (1989) *Child Abuse and Neglect: Facing the Challenge*, London, Batsford.

Stanton, T. (1998) 'Intellectual Disability, Oppression and Difference', in Lešnik (1998).

Stepney, P. and Ford, D. (eds) (2000) *Social Work Models, Methods and Theories: A Framework for Practice*, Lyme Regis, Russell House Publishing.

Storkey, E. (1991) 'Race, Ethnicity and Gender', Open University, Unit 8 of D103 *Society and Social Science*.

Stuart, O. (1992) 'Double Oppression: An Appropriate Starting Point?' *Disability, Handicap and Society*, 7 (2).

Stuart, O. (1996) ' "Yes, We Mean Black Disabled People Too": Thoughts on Community Care and Disabled People from Black and Minority Ethnic Communities', in Ahmad and Atkin (1996).

Sullivan, M. (1987) *Sociology and Social Welfare*, London, Allen & Unwin.

Swain, J., Finkelstein, V., French, S. and Oliver, M. (eds) (1993) *Disabling Barriers – Enabling Environments*, London, Sage.

Taylor, C. and White, S. (2000) *Practising Reflexivity in Health and Welfare: Making Knowledge*, Buckingham, Open University Press.

Thompson, N. (1989) 'Understanding Their Past and Family Lives', *Community Care*, 25 May.

Thompson, N. (1991a) 'The Legacy of Laing: A Critique of the Medical Model in Social Work and Social Care', *Social Science Teacher*, 20 (2).

Thompson, N. (1991b) *Crisis Intervention Revisited*, Birmingham, Pepar.

Thompson, N. (1992a) *Existentialism and Social Work*, Aldershot, Avebury.

Thompson, N. (1992b) 'Age and Citizenship', *Elders: Care and Practice*, 1 (1).

Thompson, N. (1995a) *Age and Dignity: Working with Older People*, Aldershot, Arena.

Thompson, N. (1995b) 'Men and Anti-Sexism', *British Journal of Social Work*, 25 (4).

Thompson, N. (1997) 'Children, Death and Ageism', *Child and Family Social Work*, 2 (1).

Thompson, N. (1998a) 'Towards a Theory of Emancipatory Practice', in Lešnik (1998).

Thompson, N. (1998b) 'Beyond Orthodoxy', *Care: the Journal of Practice and Development*, 7(1).

Thompson, N. (2000a) *Theory and Practice in Human Services*, Buckingham, Open University Press.

Thompson, N. (2000b) *Tackling Bullying and Harassment in the Workplace*, Birmingham, Pepar.

Thompson, N. (2000c) 'Existentialist Practice', in Stepney and Ford (2000).

Thompson, N. (2002a) *People Skills*, 2nd edn, Basingstoke, Palgrave Macmillan.

Thompson, N. (2002b) *Social Work with Children, Young People and Their Families*, Lyme Regis, Russell House Publishing.

Thompson, N. (2002c) 'Anti-Discriminatory Practice', in Davies (2002).

Thompson, N. (ed.) (2002d) *Loss and Grief: A Guide for Human Services Practitioners*, Basingstoke, Palgrave Macmillan.

Thompson, N. (2002e) 'Social Work with Adults', in Adams *et al.* (2002).

Thompson, N. (2003a) *Promoting Equality: Challenging Discrimination and Oppression*, 2nd edn, Basingstoke, Palgrave Macmillan.

Thompson, N. (2003b) *Communication and Language: A Handbook of Theory and Practice*, Basingstoke, Palgrave Macmillan.

Thompson, N. (2005) *Understanding Social Work: Preparing for Practice*, 2nd edn, Basingstoke, Palgrave Macmillan.

Thompson, N. and Bates, J. (1996) *Learning from Other Disciplines: Lessons from Nurse Education and Management Theory*, Norwich, University of East Anglia Social Work Monographs.

Thompson, N., Osada, M. and Anderson, B. (1994a) *Practice Teaching in Social Work*, 2nd edn, Birmingham, Pepar.

Thompson, N., Murphy, M. and Stradling, S. (1994b) *Dealing with Stress*, London, Macmillan Press – now Palgrave Macmillan.

Thompson, N. and Thompson, S. (2001) 'Empowering Older People: Beyond the care Model', *Journal of Social Work* 1(1).

Thompson, N. and Thompson, S. (2005) *Community Care*, Lyme Regis, Russell House Publishing.

Thompson, S. (2002a) *From Where I'm Sitting*, Lyme Regis, Russell House Publishing.

Thompson, S. (2002b) 'Old Age', in Thompson (2002d).

Thompson, S. (2005) *Age Discrimination*, Lyme Regis, Russell House Publishing.

Thursz, D., Nusberg, C. and Prather, J. (eds) (1995) *Empowering Older People: An International Approach*, London, Cassell.

Ticktin, S. (1989) 'Obituary: R.D. Laing', *Asylum*, 4 (1).

Tomlinson, D. and Trew, W. (eds) (2002) *Equalising Opportunities, Minimising Oppression: A Critical Review of Anti-Discriminatory Policies in Health and Social Welfare*, London, Routledge.

Townsend, P. (1981) 'The Structured Dependency of the Elderly: A Creation of Social Policy in the Twentieth Century', *Ageing and Society*, 1 (1).

Townsend, P. (1986) 'Ageism and Social Policy', in Phillipson and Walker (1986).

Ungerson, C. (ed.) (1985) *Women and Social Policy*, London, Macmillan Press – now Palgrave Macmillan.

United Nations (1996) *Platform for Action and the Being Declaration*, New York, United Nations.

UPIAS (1976) *Fundamental Principles of Disability*, London, Union of the Physically Impaired Against Segregation.

UPIAS (1980) 'Disability Challenged', *The Bulletin on Social Policy*, 10.

Victor, C. (1987) *Old Age in Modern Society*, London, Croom Helm.

Vince, R. (1996) *Managing Change: Reflections on Equality and Management Learning*, Bristol, The Policy Press.

Wadham, J. and Mountfield, H. (1999) *Blackstone's Guide to the Human Rights Act 1998*, London, Blackstone Press.

Walby, S. (1990) *Theorizing Patriarchy*, Oxford, Basil Blackwell.

Walker, A. (1981) 'Towards a Political Economy of Old Age', *Ageing and Society*, 1 (1).

Walker, A. (1986) 'The Politics of Ageing in Britain', in Phillipson *et al.* (1986).

Walker, A. (1987, 1991) 'The Social Construction of Dependency in Old Age', in Loney *et al.* (1991).

Walker, A. (1993) 'Poverty and Inequality in Old Age', in Bond *et al.* (1993).

Walker, A. and Walker, C. (eds) (1987) *The Growing Divide*, London, CPAG.

Warnes, A. (1996) 'The Demography of Old Age: Panic Versus Reality', in Bland (1996).

Watson, J. and Woolf, M. (2003) *Human Rights Act Toolkit*, London, Legal Action Group.

Watters, C. (1996) 'Representations and Realities: Black People, Community Care and Mental Illness', in Ahmad and Atkin (1996).

Waugh, P. (1998) 'Postmodernism and Feminism', in Jackson and Jones (1998).

Webb, S. (1989a) 'Dispelling the Myths of Disability with Awareness', *Social Work Today*, 6 April.

Webb, S. (1989b) 'Old Lesbians: Out and Proud', *Social Work Today*, 4 April.

Weber, M. (1930) *The Protestant Ethic and the Spirit of Capitalism*, London, George Allen & Unwin.

Weber, M. (1947) *The Theory of Social and Economic Organization*, New York, Free Press.

Weeks, J. (1986) *Sexuality*, London, Tavistock.

Westwood, S. (2002) *Power and the Social*, London, Routledge.

White, D. (1988) 'Madness and Psychiatry', *Asylum*, 3 (2).

White, J. (1997) 'Family Therapy', in Davies (1997).

Whitehouse, P. (1986) 'Race and the Criminal Justice System', in Coombe and Little (1986).

Whyte, A. (1989) 'The Long Route to Hospital', *Community Care*, 23 September.

Williams, C., Soydan, H. and Johnson, M. R. D. (eds) (1998) *Social Work and Minorities: European Perspectives*, London, Routledge.

Williams. F. (1987) 'Racism and the Discipline of Social Policy: A Critique of Welfare Theory', *Critical Social Policy*, 20.

Williams, F. (1989) *Social Policy: A Critical Introduction*, London, Polity.

Williams, F. (1991) 'Citizenship, Social Policy and Theory', Paper presented at the Critical Social Policy 'Citizenship and Welfare' conference, London.

Williams, F. (1992) 'Somewhere Over the Rainbow: Universality and Diversity in Social Policy', in Manning and Page (1992).

Williams, J. E. (2000) 'Race and Class: Why All the Confusion?', in Lang (2000).

Wilson, F.M. (2003) *Organizational Behaviour and Gender*, 2nd edn, Aldershot, Ashgate.

Wise, S. (2000) 'Heterosexism', in Davies (2000).

Wolfensberger, W. (1972) *The Principle of Normalization in Human Services*, Toronto, National Institute on Mental Retardation.

Woodward, K. (ed.) (1997) *Identity and Difference*, London, Sage.

Woolfe, S. and Malahleka, B. (1990) 'The Obstacle Race: The Findings of the BASW Report on an Action Research Project into Ethnically Sensitive Social Work', Birmingham, BASW.

World Health Organisation (1980) *International Classification of Impairments, Disabilities and Handicaps: A Manual Relating to the Consequences of Disease*, Geneva, World Health Organisation.

Zacune, C. (1991) 'Alternative Families for Black Children and Social Work Practice', Occasional Paper No. 1, University of Keele.

Index

Abercrombie *et al.* 46, 48, 49
ABSWAP 9
Acharyya, S. 81
Adams, R. 20
Advocacy 117
Ageism 13, 18, 25, 34, 40, 45, 46, 98,
    99, 101–4, 106, 108–20, 122, 123,
    126, 139
Ahmad, B. 19, 80–2, 85, 93–5
Ahmad, W. I. U. 82, 96
Ahmad and Atkin 96
Ahmed, S. 77, 83, 88, 95
AIDS 153
Alienation 69, 98, 151, 153
Alhibai-Brown, Y. 96
Allen, S. 91
Aluffi-Pentini and Lorenz 96
Amos *et al.* 91
Arber and Ginn 19, 45, 71, 113, 121
Assertiveness 23
Assimilation 5, 87, 89
Atkin and Rollings 76

Back and Solomos 97
Bailey and Brake 6, 14
Banton *et al.* 165
Barn, R. 81
Barnes, C. 131, 135
Barton, L. 147
Baxter *et al.* 169
Bayne-Smith, M. 45
Beauvoir, S. de 48, 101, 108, 109, 113
Bell, V. 70
Bellin, W. 161
Bennett and Kingston 107
Bennett *et al.* 108
Berger, P. L. 4, 22, 28, 70
Berger and Luckmann 31, 35
Bernard and Meade 71, 121
Bevan, D. 46, 170
Bhavanani and Coulson 91
Biggs, S. 120, 121
Biggs *et al.* 107

Biological imperative 51
Blackburn, D. G. 24
Blakemore and Boneham, 19, 97, 121
Blakemore and Drake 19, 152
Blaming the victim 125, 165
Bland, R. 121
Blasius and Phelan 172
Board for Social Responsibility 112, 115
Bond *et al.* 121
Bottomore and Rubel 34
Bowser, B. P. 19
Boyle, M. 165
Brake and Bailey 6
Braye and Preston-Shoot 20
Brearley, C. P. 109
Brewer, J. D. 157, 158
Brisenden, S. 130, 137
Bristow and Wilson 172
British Council of Organisations of
    Disabled People (BCODP) 134
British Sociological Association (BSA) 37,
    45
Brittan and Maynard 140
Brook and Davis 8
Brown and Harris 55, 166
Brown, H. C. 153, 172
Browne, D. 80
Bryan *et al.* 92
Bryson, V. 54, 65, 71, 75, 91
Bullock and Stallybrass 49
Bulmer and Solomos 97
Burke, A. 81
Burke and Harrison 73
Burr, V. 23
Busfield, J. 19, 54, 164
Butler, R. N. 99
Bynoe *et al.* 135
Bytheway and Johnson 111

Cameron *et al.* 105
Campbell and Oliver 133, 147
Capitalism 6, 8, 14, 29, 34, 64, 65, 90,
    91, 110, 157

Care management 102, 104, 132, 133
Carlen and Worrall 53
Carter and Aitchison 89
Carter *et al.* 8
Cavanagh and Cree 19, 71
CCETSW 1, 10, 19, 161
CD Project Steering Group 19, 94
Centre for Policy on Ageing (CPA) 107
Centres for Integrated Living (CILs) 133, 134, 145
Chadwick, A. 175
Chakrabarti, M. 74
Cheetham, J. 84
Child abuse/protection 107
Christie, A. 71
Citizenship 15, 40, 71, 107, 122, 123, 128, 146
Clarke and Cochrane 43
Class 5, 8, 9, 14–16, 22, 23, 25, 29, 34, 43, 44, 46, 48, 64, 65, 83, 90–2, 95, 101, 115, 171, 174, 179
Clements, J. 169
Clements and Read 147
Coates, D. 62
Cohen and Mullender 71
Collectivism 8
Colgan *et al.* 60
Collins *et al.* 159
Community care 58, 68, 96, 104, 107
Connell, R.W. 71
Connolly, C. 158
Conrad, P. 165
Consciousness-raising 3, 69, 177
Cooper, D. 3
Corby, B. 57
Corrigan and Leonard 6
Coulshed *et al.* 59, 60, 94
CPA 107
Cranny-Francis *et al.* 71
Creed 1, 22
Crompton, R. 46
Crompton and Thompson 12, 19
Crowley, H. 63
Cultural deficit 73, 93
Cultural difference 73, 86, 93
Cultural level 27–9, 31, 33, 36, 38, 41, 42, 49, 55, 67, 75, 122, 123, 157, 166, 174, 177

Dale and Foster 150
Dallos and Sapsford 59
Dalrymple and Burke 20
Davies and Neal 172
Davis, K. 38, 128, 132
Debunking 4, 69
Deegan, M. 142

Dehumanisation 8, 14, 25, 38, 66, 137, 139, 140, 141, 144, 151, 168
Denney, D. 92
Dependency 25, 69, 95, 109, 117, 126, 131, 135–7, 139, 140, 145
Depression 54, 55, 81, 118
Deprivation 23
Derbyshire Coalition of Disabled People (DCDP) 125, 133
Devine, F. 46
Diploma in Social Work (DipSW) 1
Disabled People's Movement 25, 122, 124–6, 130, 135, 137, 138
Disablism 25, 26, 34, 45, 116, 122–4, 126, 127, 135, 137, 139–41, 144, 151, 168
Discourse 165
Diversity 2, 11, 13, 41, 46, 84, 86, 148, 158, 170, 171
Divine, D. 96
Dobelniece, S. 22
Dominelli, L. 95
Dominelli and McLeod 6, 8, 60
Donnison, D. 46
Double jeopardy 115
Doyal, L. 134
Drakeford and Morris 160
Duberman *et al.* 172
Durkheim, E. 63
Dwivedi and Varma 19, 96

Eastman, M. 107
Elder abuse 107
Elliot, F. R. 19, 70
Empowerment 68, 95, 103, 104, 109, 117, 118, 120, 130, 132, 135, 137, 138, 141, 146
Encyclopaedia Britannica 162
Engels, F. 65
Equal Opportunities Commission (EOC) 58, 71
Equal Pay Act 1970 5
Equality of opportunity 62, 85, 93
Ethnicity 64, 72–4, 77, 80, 82, 83, 87, 88, 93, 96, 97, 114, 115, 121, 142

Familial ideology 50, 59, 68, 69
family therapy 32
Farrell and Watt 97
Fawcett *et al.* 19
Featherstone 70
Featherstone and Hepworth 38, 70
Fennell *et al.* 25, 104, 111, 121
Fenton, S. 114
Fernando, S. 84, 85
Ferns, P. 88

Field, N. 152
Finch, J. 58
Finch and Groves 58
Fine and Asch 140, 141
Finkelstein, V. 128, 130, 131, 136, 143
Fisher, M. 58
Flower-power sixties 3
Fook, J. 20, 39, 47, 172
Foster-Carter, O. 91
Foucault, M. 39, 70
Francis, E. 80
Freire, P. 39
Friedan, B. 3
Froggatt, A. 102, 103
Fuss, D. 172

George, M. 130
Giddens, A. 22, 46
Ginn and Arber 113
Gittins, D. 8
Glendinning, C. 54
Graham, M. 97
Gramsci, A. 43
Green, J. 159
Gruber and Stefanov 70
Griffiths, R. 102
Grimwood and Popplestone 60, 70
Gurnah, A. 88

Hales, G. 147
Hallett, C. 71
Halmos, P. 14
Hanmer and Statham 8, 53, 59
Harris, V. 162
Hart, J. 153
Haselden, R. 153
Hearn, J. 7
Heather, N. 164
Hechter, M. 162
Hegemony 42, 43, 45, 48, 163
Heller *et al.* 172
Henley, A. 83
Heraud, B. 4
Heterosexism 6, 18, 151–6
Hierarchy of oppression 16, 43, 151
Higgs, P. 117
Hockey and James 100, 107
Hocquenghem, G. 153, 154
Homophobia 153
hooks, b. 91
Hornstein 121
housing 22, 69, 81, 86, 87, 103
Hudson, A. 56, 151
Hughes, B. 100, 101, 109, 111, 120
Hughes and Mtezuka 98
Hughes, G. 128, 135

Hugman, R. 38, 149, 172
Humphries, B. 20
Husband, C. 6, 88
Hutchinson-Reis, M. 80
Huws Williams *et al.* 172

Iley and Nazroo 80
Imperialism 8, 14, 34, 89
Individualism 8, 9, 12, 25, 38, 125,
  126, 128–30, 132, 135, 136, 143,
  144
Infantilisation 100, 107, 114, 119, 122,
  123, 135
Ingleby, D. 164
Interdependency 106, 117, 118, 170

Jack, R. 103, 120
Jackson and Jones 71
Jamieson *et al.* 121
Jansz, J. 66
Jones, C. 46, 177
Jones and Novak 9, 23, 46
Jong, G. de 138
Jordan, B. 19, 179

Kandola and Fullerton 46, 170
Katz, J. 31, 74, 88
King, D. 91
Kirton, D. 93, 96
Kubisa, T. 102
Kuhn, T. 138

Lago and Thompson 97
Laing, R. D. 3, 44, 164, 166
Laing and Cooper 44
Laing and Esterson 166
Lang, B. 97
Langan, M. 19
Langan and Day 54, 61, 70, 92
Langan and Lee 19
Laurance, J. 172
Lees, S. 57
Lentell, H. C. 50
Leonard, P. 3, 6, 14
Lešnik, B. 20
Lister, R. 50
Littlewood *et al.* 19, 80, 97, 166
Lived experience 15, 45, 171
Lonsdale, S. 71, 139–41, 147
Luthra, M. 19

MacLeod and Saraga 56
Macpherson, W. 76, 82
Malik, K. 97
Mama, A. 16, 52
Mandelbaum, D. G. 160

Marginalisation 25, 32, 60, 61, 72, 98, 100, 115, 118, 122–4, 136, 139, 146, 151, 153, 156, 167, 168, 178
Marks, D. 124, 147
Marlow and Loveday 93
Marshall, M. 107, 108
Marshall and Rowlings 115, 120
Marshall, V. W. 118
Marxism 6, 22, 29, 30, 34, 50, 51, 179, 180
Marxist-feminism 64
Maxime 93
Mays, N. 115
McLellan, D. 47
Mental health 19, 23, 54, 71, 80, 81, 97, 102, 148, 163, 166, 167, 172
Mental impairment 148, 167, 168, 172
Midwinter, E. 100
Miles, A. 166
Miles, R. 90
Miles and Solomos 86
Miller and Gwynne 131
Millett, K. 49
Milligan, D. 6
Mills, C. W. 4, 62, 70, 150
Milner and O'Byrne, P. 104
Mirza, K. 141
Morgan, K. O. 162
Morris and Williams 160
Morris, J. 16, 71, 128, 141, 143
Moss, B. 159, 172
Muldoon, J. 24
Mullaly, R. 19, 175
Mullender, A. 52, 70, 92
Multicultural 12, 86, 90
Muncie et al. 71
Munro and McCulloch 153

Nairn, T. 162
Nelson, A. 30, 66, 67
New Right 8, 179
Nolan et al. 120
Norman, A. 109, 115, 119

O'Brien, M. 66
Oliver, M. 22, 25, 122, 123, 128, 130, 131, 133–6, 140–3, 147, 167
Oliver and Sapey 34, 126, 129, 130, 147
Ong, B. N. 57

Pannick, D. 5
Partnership 106, 107, 128, 145
Parton and Parton 55
Parton and O'Byrne 46
Pascall 8, 50, 51, 71
Patel et al. 172

patriarchy 6, 8, 14, 33, 34, 49–53, 55, 58–64, 66, 67, 91, 140, 175
Payne, G. 46
PCS analysis 13, 26, 29, 30, 32, 33, 36, 46, 55, 62, 73, 74, 76, 79, 92, 99, 122–4, 153, 157, 174, 175, 179
Pearson, G. 14, 53
Penketh, L. 10, 82, 87, 97
Pennie P. 80
Personal level 26, 29, 30, 33, 36, 38, 41, 42, 49, 55, 62, 67, 157, 174
Phillipson, C. 99, 101, 105, 106, 110, 117, 121–3, 170, 177
Phillipson and Thompson 98
Pickering, M. 47
Pilkington, A. 97
Pizzey et al. 19
Polenberg, R. 3
Political economy 99, 110
Poverty 4, 22, 23, 42, 54, 69, 86, 87, 101, 103, 115, 134
Praxis 31
Prejudice 13, 27, 28, 30, 31, 41, 42, 123, 179
Preston-Shoot and Agass 106, 143
Preston-Shoot, M. 19
Pritchard and Taylor 9
Proud Old Lesbians 154
Psychodynamics 3, 26, 150

Race awareness training (RAT) 74, 88, 89, 92
Race Relations Acts 5, 12, 85
Racialism 30
Racism 6, 9, 13, 19, 24, 28, 30, 31, 33, 34, 37, 40, 45, 72–85, 87–95, 97, 103, 108, 113, 115, 116, 119, 126, 151, 153, 158, 177, 180
Radford, L. 52
Radical social work 5–9, 14, 19, 42, 69, 130, 179
Ramazanoglu, C. 91
Reductionism 10, 117, 151
Reform 9
Religion 8, 18, 27, 72, 148, 152, 156–9, 171
Reserve army of labour 65
Rex, J. 73
Richardson and Robinson 22, 71
Riches, G. 71
Roberts, K. 22, 46, 91
Robinson, L. 19, 82, 93
Rojek et al. 3, 39, 69, 150
Rooney, B. 31, 78
Rowbotham, S. 50
Roys, P. 89

Rush, F. 57
Ryan, W. 125

Sapey, B. 126, 147
Sapey and Hewitt 143, 144
Saraga, E. 56
Sartre, J-P. 45
Scarman (Report) 76
Sectarianism 151, 158, 159
Segal, L. 67, 71
Self-esteem 55, 69, 108, 109, 114, 119
Sex Discrimination Act 1975 5
Sexism 13, 24, 31, 32, 34, 40, 45, 48–54,
   58–60, 66, 68, 69, 92, 103, 108, 113,
   114, 119, 126, 140, 141, 151, 153,
   177, 180
Sexual harassment 69
Sexual orientation/identity 9, 12, 13, 15,
   18, 22, 148, 152, 154, 156, 171, 172
Shah, N. 77
Sibeon, R. 31, 151
Sidell, M. 100, 121
Simpkin, M. 7, 8
Sivanandan, A. 76, 88
Skellington, R. 22
Slee, R. 137
Smith, D. 79
Social Services Inspectorate (SSI) 60, 69
Social Trends 34, 83
Sociological imagination 4, 70
Sociopolitical (context) 6, 15
Solomos, J. 5, 19
Sone, A. 155
Sontag, S. 114
Soydan and Williams 74
Spicker, P. 50
Stanton, T. 172
Stereotypes 25, 35, 36, 41, 42, 60, 68,
   70, 74, 75, 77–9, 82, 90, 93, 96, 105,
   108, 117, 119, 120, 127, 130, 137,
   139, 145, 154, 158, 163, 165, 169
Storkey, E. 72
Structural level 27, 29, 33, 36, 41, 42,
   49, 55, 67, 75, 157, 166, 174
Stuart, O. 16, 142
Sullivan, M. 4
Swain *et al.* 147
Szasz, T. 164

Taken for grantedness 31
Taylor and White 46

Thompson, N. 2, 3, 10, 15, 17, 18, 20,
   21, 23, 25, 33–8, 41, 46, 47, 66, 69,
   71, 82, 96, 97, 100, 103, 104, 106–9,
   117, 149, 151, 156, 164, 171, 172,
   174, 177, 178, 181
Thompson, S. 22, 46, 98, 120
Thompson and Bates 105
Thompson and Thompson, 102, 121
Thompson *et al.* 2, 16
Thursz *et al.* 109, 120
Ticktin, S. 160
Tomlinson and Trew 20
Townsend, P. 111
Trade-unionism 8
Triple jeopardy 115

Ungerson, C. 8
United Nations 54
Union of Physically Impaired Against
   Segregation (UPIAS) 38, 39, 124,
   143

Victor 114
Vince, R. 60
Wadham and Mountfield 19
Walby, S. 64
Walker, A. 105, 110, 115
Warnes, A. 104
Watson and Woolf 19
Watters, C. 80
Waugh, P. 65
Webb, S. 154, 155
Weber, M. 22, 49, 157
Weeks, J. 51
Welfarism 104, 105
Welsh language 160, 161, 172
Westwood, S. 172
White, D. 166
White, J. 32
Whitehouse, P. 79
Whyte, A. 80
Williams. F. 16, 45, 61, 65, 91
Williams, J. E. 90
Wilson, E. 6, 70
Wise, S. 153
Wolfensberger, W. 169
Woodward, K. 150, 172
Woolfe and Malahleka 85
World Health Organisation (WHO) 38

Zacune, C. 93